# Research as Resistance

# Research as Resistance

Revisiting Critical, Indigenous,
and Anti-Oppressive Approaches

Second Edition

Edited by
Susan Strega and Leslie Brown

Canadian Scholars' Press
Women's Press
Toronto

**Research as Resistance: Revisiting Critical, Indigenous, and Anti-Oppressive Approaches, Second Edition**
edited by Susan Strega and Leslie Brown

First published in 2015 by
**Canadian Scholars' Press Inc.**
425 Adelaide Street West, Suite 200
Toronto, Ontario
M5V 3C1

**www.cspi.org**

**Library and Archives Canada Cataloguing in Publication**

Research as resistance: revisiting critical, indigenous, and anti-oppressive approaches / edited by Susan Strega and Leslie Brown. — Second edition.

Includes bibliographical references and index.
Issued in print and electronic formats.
ISBN 978-1-55130-882-1 (paperback).--ISBN 978-1-55130-883-8 (pdf).--ISBN 978-1-55130-884-5 (epub)

1. Native peoples—Research—Canada—Methodology. 2. Research--Methodology. 3. Oppression (Psychology—Research. I. Strega, Susan, author, editor II. Brown, Leslie Allison, 1954-, author, editor

H62.R42 2015      305.897'071072         C2015-904282-8         C2015-904283-6

Text design by Brad Horning
Cover design by Em Dash Design

Printed and bound in Canada by Webcom

MIX
Paper from
responsible sources
FSC® C004071

# Table of Contents

# From Resistance to Resurgence

## Susan Strega and Leslie Brown

Susan mused that when she first saw Gayle Cyr write "off the white board and onto the wall" that this was a sign we were at the beginning of a breaking apart of traditional ways of creating knowledge. We talked about how it hasn't happened quite as we thought, but that we were witnessing a resurgence of transgressive possibilities. Time to put together another book, perhaps.

## SOCIALLY JUST RESEARCH

Ten years ago, we were preparing the first edition of *Research as Resistance* in a time of hope and worry. While we could see neoliberalism entrenching itself around us, we were also aware that marginalized knowledges and ways of creating knowledge were once again emerging. Indigenous scholars, critical race theorists, and feminists have a long history of raising important questions about knowledge production, such as who is entitled to create meanings about the world; how some meanings and not others are accorded the status of knowledge; and how race, gender, and class factor into these entitlements.

Although marginalized knowledges are periodically circulated, they are also persistently pushed to the margins. The work to resist this comes in waves, and this second edition tries to capture that idea by taking account of the work done in the first edition when all seemed possible as we craft a second wave of transgressive possibilities.

In her discussion of racialized epistemologies, Gloria Ladson-Billings (2000) reminds us that early African-American scholars such as W. E. B. du Bois and Carter Woodson challenged Enlightenment epistemology. Second-wave feminists such as Mary Daly (1978) and Barbara Ehrenreich and Deirdre English (1973) recirculated women's historical ways of knowing, while feminist scholars such as Lorraine Code (1991), Wendy Hollway (1989), and Sandra Harding (1991) considered questions of who can know and how we come to know. Similarly, Linda Tuhiwai Smith (1999) charted the colonization of Indigenous knowledge and the re-emergence of Indigenous ways of knowing.

Over the past decade, resistance research has made further inroads into the academy and among researchers. Notably, information about Indigenous ways of knowing and Indigenous methodologies has been circulated through books, journal articles, and conferences. Recent Canadian books include Shawn Wilson's *Research Is Ceremony* (2008), Kathy Absolon's *Kaandosswin: How We Come to Know* (2011), and Margaret (Maggie) Kovach's *Indigenous Methodologies* (2010), the latter scholar also contributing to this book. Elsewhere, Linda Tuhiwai Smith (2012) published a second edition of *Decolonizing Methodologies*; Minde's (2008) edited collection included Sami perspectives on research; and Chilisa's (2011) *Indigenous Research Methodologies* brings African Indigenist perspectives to the table. Indigenous and non-Indigenous journals alike have published theoretical and practical pieces on Indigenous worldviews, knowledge, and research (see, for example, Chilisa & Ntseane, 2010; Dana-Sacco, 2010; Hart, 2010; Nicholls, 2009).

The array of publications now available confirms that cognitive justice is an essential requirement for social justice (Santos, 2007). The ability to think against dominant knowledge requires forms of knowledge creation that are grounded in diverse ontological and epistemological theories. In this book, Mehmoona Moosa-Mitha's chapter charts out how various theoretical positions affect the social justice orientation of research, while the chapters by Maggie Kovach and Susan Strega advocate two very different research approaches, each with the potential to disrupt dominant discourses. These ways of creating knowledge that continue to emerge, some of them resurgent and some of them new, bring with them different models of researcher engagement with communities. The need for marginalized communities to experience researchers as relationally accountable informs interest in community action research, participatory action research, and Indigenous forms of community engagement.

In the first edition, we were able to showcase the work of new scholars, many of them graduate students, who were exploring these possibilities. Their work embodied the idea that research must be socially just in its methods as well as its intentions. This second edition reflects a resurgence of the resistant ideas showcased in the first edition. Waves are powerful forces that carve deep channels in bedrock and create new routes. We want to reprise here two ideas that were central to the first edition and appear throughout the current volume: that the subjects of research must be meaningfully involved in research processes; and that critical reflexivity, especially about researcher positionality, is a necessary component of socially just research.

## "NOTHING ABOUT US WITHOUT US"

The phrase "Nothing about us without us" has multiple origins, but in recent times it is closely associated with the disability rights movement in the UK in the 1990s and James Charlton's (1998) book-length indictment of disability oppression, particularly the practice of developing disability policies and programs without the involvement of people with disabilities. It has since been taken up in a number of contexts, such as developing ethical research partnerships with Indigenous communities in Canada (Ball, 2005); the meaningful involvement of illegal drug users in HIV/AIDS research (Jürgens, 2005); and engaging young people in health research (McDonagh & Bateman, 2012).

The abuse and exploitation of marginalized people by researchers is well documented (Tuhiwai Smith, 1999, 2012), and human research ethics guidelines and protocols that attempt to safeguard the vulnerable from researcher malpractice are now in place everywhere, including protocols specific to certain populations. In Canada, for example, the most recent edition of the *Tri-Council Policy Statement on Ethical Conduct for Research involving Humans* has a chapter outlining specific researcher responsibilities related to First Nations, Inuit, and Métis peoples (Government of Canada, 2010). Although these sorts of documents emphasize the importance of engaging communities in research, they elide or ignore more fundamental social justice matters that infuse researcher-researched relationships.

Whatever safeguards might be in place for research participants, or the communities in which they live or with which they associate, a social justice orientation to research requires that we ask ourselves ethical questions about our research interests that have little to do with institutional standards. Most research about marginalized peoples has been done, and continues to be done, by those who are not marginalized. As Michelle Fine (Fine, 1998; Fine, Weiss, Weseen, & Wong, 2003) has noted, this research reinscribes the "Other" (the racialized, the disabled, women, sexual minorities, etc.) while preserving those dominantly located from scrutiny, all the while cloaking the researcher under a veil of neutrality or objectivity. As Jayati Lal (1996) discussed in analyzing her fieldwork experiences, even when researcher and researched are similarly positioned, these challenges remain. Fine's (1998) advice is that we "work the hyphen" (p. 135), meaning that we have to think through how and where we are in relation to the contexts, communities, and participants we study. Whose story will our research tell, why, to whom, and with what interpretations? Given the already widespread negative stereotypes of those on the margins, we should be concerned about whether our research will feed these stereotypes, or allow even more negative portrayals. Those of us who are dominantly located must contend with our sense of entitlement to not only solicit but also interpret stories told by those who are different from us. As Sholock (2012) notes, White people are socialized into an "epistemology of ignorance" about the racialized while at the same time being entitled and expected to behave as "authoritative agents of knowledge" (p. 8) about them and all others who are different from them. This belief in our right and entitlement to "know the Other," and to access marginalized populations for our research, is deeply held. From a social justice perspective, we must vigorously contest the notion that this is a natural or acceptable situation.

Ball's (2005) point that research in Indigenous communities occurs within a "historical context of exploitation and misrepresentation" (p. 33) can be extrapolated, albeit with some modifications, to other marginalized communities. As Absolon and Willett (2005, p. 120) point out, research that is centrally or even tangentially related to Indigenous peoples requires that we have, minimally, "a critical analysis of colonialism and an understanding of Western scientific research as a mechanism of colonization." Researchers who want to address issues pertaining to marginalized peoples and communities need to educate themselves not only about their socio-political history, but also about the history of relationships between marginalized and dominant groups. Memories and contemporary expressions of historically destructive relationships will influence research relationships.

Taking account of historical and present-day relations of domination and subordination in one's research may usefully problematize deficit findings, though from a social justice perspective, we suggest that investigating the strengths and strategies that allow communities and individuals to survive marginalization might make a better contribution. Ball (2005, p. 86) quotes a participant at an Aboriginal health conference who confirms the need for strengths-focused research:

> We are tired of researchers coming in and documenting all the things wrong with our communities: youth suicide, child neglect, alcohol abuse, family violence, poor nutrition, embezzlement. You would think people would want to figure out how we survived white people for so many hundreds of years. How we kept our children alive, kept our stories, kept our knowledge about how to live on the land, kept our ceremonies, kept our fires burning with hope for generations yet to come. How about some research on what's right with us? About what makes us resilient.

We align ourselves with researchers like Fine (Fine, 1998; Fine et al., 2003), Koster, Baccar, and Lemelin (2012), and Ball (2005) in calling for an end to research "on" the marginalized—research that lacks meaningful participation from those being investigated. When specific communities are the research sites, social justice might to some extent be ensured through community rather than researcher ownership of information shared with researchers; control over data and who has access to it; and physical possession of the data (Schnarch, 2004). Researchers should be prepared to negotiate values, conceptual frameworks, methods, and dissemination strategies with communities, matters that are discussed in this book by Adam Gaudry and Jenny Holder. But for affinity communities, such as LGBT people, or for geographically dispersed communities, such as the Métis, such processes and the agreements they might bring about are difficult, if not impossible, because such communities are not neatly organized for accessibility (Evans, 2012).

When we choose a research focus, we must ask not only whose story it has the potential to tell, but also whose story it will hide, why, for whom, and with what consequence. Whenever some lives are displayed through research, we must be cognizant that other lives are being protected. For example, the poor have been exhaustively researched, especially from a deficit orientation, and although we may now know more about how the rich live, we do not investigate wealth as an individual pathology in the same way that we explore poverty. Similarly, poverty has long been investigated as a social problem, while wealth has not. Researchers who are dominantly located are comfortable gazing down at the marginalized and may consider it their entitlement to do so, without any consideration of the possibilities of looking up at the elite, or even across at those who are like them. The consequences of this orientation to research are well documented.

Researchers played significant roles in the deliberate destruction and devaluation of intellectual, spiritual, and cultural resources in Indigenous communities, contributing to the complete eradication of ways of thinking and being. Interpretations circulated by researchers have also been allowed to stand as the realities of ways of thinking and being, contributing to the pathologization and demonization of affinity communities. For example, Gutterman (2012) documents how Caprio's interpretations of lesbian behaviour fed negative stereotypes for decades and supported the institutionalization and incarceration of lesbians. In her chapter in this book, Eli Manning describes how she is using a genderqueer methodology to investigate modern-day sex and gender stereotypes that have their own negative consequences. Her work, along with work in other chapters, leads us to a problematization of outsider research—that is, research conducted by those who are not members of the community being researched. While critical reflexivity, as we discuss below, may help researchers identify colonial or otherwise oppressive ways of thinking and acting, it cannot on its own ensure the protection of marginalized communities. Because the entitlement of the dominant to know the marginalized is so widely accepted, active resistance is required to denaturalize this practice (Matthews, 2013). We suggest that it is only when we reverse the gaze and investigate and problematize the other side of the equation—that is, the behaviours, discourses, and perceptions of the dominant—that we create possibilities for change that are transformative rather than incremental.

There are many reasons why looking up is difficult in ways that looking down is not. While the disadvantaged may be motivated to participate in research in the hopes that it will change their situation, or the circumstances of those who are like them, the advantaged not only lack this incentive, but may also be anxious that the ways in which they benefit from or enforce inequality could be exposed. Gaining access to elite informants is often problematic (Aguiar & Schneider, 2012; Gains, 2011). Financial and related incentives for participation in research are motivating for the marginalized but irrelevant to the privileged. Despite these challenges, there are methodologies that facilitate research about the actions and behaviours of the elite, as illustrated by Teresa Macias in chapter 9 of this book. Finally, it must be noted that research that challenges privilege, especially privilege accrued through unearned advantage, brings negative consequences in a way that looking down does not. For example, the French economist Thomas Piketty, who in 2014 published extensive documentation of capitalism's role in creating and increasing wealth inequality, has been widely attacked and vilified.

In essence, every decision a researcher makes, from choices about topic and research site to the minutiae of relationships with participants to the means by which findings are disseminated, has political significance and therefore affects the social justice potential of our work. Chapter 1 in this book, by Karen Potts and Leslie Brown, explores the myriad of choices that a researcher faces in every stage of the research, each of which can advance or impede one's pursuit of social justice. As Michelle Fine et al. (2003, p. 187) remind us, methods are not passive strategies but influence how we interpret our findings and how we construct representations, requiring that we reflect carefully on our social justice obligations and responsibilities. This means that critical reflexivity is foundational to socially just, anti-oppressive research.

## CRITICAL REFLEXIVITY

Historically in White Western research, researchers and their expertise, regardless of the methods they employ, have been portrayed as objective and disembodied and thus privileged over those they study (Tuhiwai Smith, 1999). As we have noted, this privileging can and does extend to being seen to have a "truer" knowledge of matters than the participants and communities that share their stories and lived experience. Introducing reflexivity into research does not preclude these pretensions to objectivity and neutrality.

Even in qualitative approaches, concepts like "bracketing" and "audit trail" contribute to the illusion that the researcher is separate from, rather than necessarily implicated in, every part of the research process.

Various forms of reflexivity and critical reflection have been developed and advocated in the research literature for several decades (Ryan & Golden, 2006). Some feminist scholars (e.g., Campbell & Wasco, 2000; Oakley, 1981; Reinharz, 1992) have proposed reflexivity as an essential methodological strategy because it enables us to examine the ways in which our own values, identities, and positionality affect our research and particularly our relationships with participants. Current discussion on reflexivity in feminist research emphasizes thinking through the power differentials that operate at various stages of the research process (Mauthner & Doucet, 2003). Fernandez (2009), writing from an anarchist perspective, positions reflexivity—a recognition that the researcher is not separate from but exists in relationship with what s/he is trying to understand—as a core component of ethical research practice. In other words, the researcher is a part of, rather than separate from, the research.

Socially just research requires critical reflexivity, an approach to reflection that focuses primarily on the politics and ideologies embedded within research processes and within the self of the researcher. It requires that we intentionally, consciously, and repeatedly bring our awareness to the question of what influences our perceptions, conceptions, and responses (internal and external) throughout the research process, from inception to dissemination. The intention is twofold: to uncover and challenge the power relations embedded in research, and to uncover and challenge hegemonic assumptions about the nature of the world, the self, and research. Hegemonic assumptions flow from the defining ideologies of our time: White supremacy (and its attendant processes of colonization and colonialism); capitalism; and patriarchy. Understanding these ideologies means learning how they are embedded in what we believe reality to be and who we believe ourselves to be. No part of our perceptions and responses, including our emotional responses, is free from embedded ideologies; they frame our ethical and moral reasoning, our ways of knowing, thinking, being, and experiencing (Matthews, 2013). As Stephen Brookfield (2009) points out, what we consider to be "natural" ways of understanding are actually conceptualized through internalized ideologies (p. 299). Here, it is important to keep in mind that marginality does not protect one from internalizing dominant ideologies, even when those assumptions operate against one's own best interests. As the anti-colonial writers Frantz Fanon (1967) and Steve Biko (1981) contend, colonialism inhabits the minds of colonizers and colonized alike. Similarly, the feminist scholar Monique Wittig (1992) makes clear that the minds of women are colonized by patriarchy, and the minds of lesbians by what we now call heteronormativity. In chapter 6, Heather Fraser and Michele Jarldorm demonstrate how critical reflexivity can contribute to uncovering deeply embedded ideologies, and therefore provide new readings of research data.

Taking a critical stance toward power, knowledge, and self can usefully begin with actively theorizing our social, cultural, and political positionality—factors such as race, class, ability, and gender, among others. Critical reflexivity requires consideration of how elements of power and privilege at play in the research process and in the self of the researcher shape decisions and interpretations. Because knowledge production is a politicized process, these are necessarily political and ideological matters. How and why do we choose one research problem or question over another? How and why do we choose a particular theoretical framework and research design through which to explore a topic? These processes are governed by our values and entwined with our positionality, and, reciprocally, these choices demonstrate our values (Reed, Miller, Nnawulezi, & Valenti, 2012).

Critical reflexivity is an ongoing process rather than an event. It is the active and ongoing analysis of how positionality and ideology are shaping decisions, relationships, and interpretations, rather than a static, formulaic declaration of who we are or what we believe. We can usefully analyze and report on, for example, the origin of our interest in the topic, and in investigating it in particular ways; the choices that were made in the course of the research, and how and why these were made; the nature of relationships with communities or participants, and how and why these evolved in certain ways; decisions as to what was included, and what was excluded, from the research findings; and dissemination strategies and how and why they were chosen. We advocate for visible engagement in these processes with the recognition that this sort of openness runs counter to the foundational rule of Enlightenment philosophy: knowledge comes only from a knowing subject separated and distant from the object of investigation. Along with many writers in this volume, we reject not only the possibility of objectivity, but also its usefulness for social justice researchers.

Critical reflexivity is unlikely to be a comfortable process, especially for those who are dominantly located and therefore unaccustomed to revealing themselves or analyzing their motivations (Reed et al., 2012). In her critique of reflexivity, Pillow (2003) suggests that explaining how our positionalities and values influence knowledge production is a strategy that many researchers engage in as rote rather than resistance. This critique is particularly salient for White researchers, for whom an atheoretical acknowledgment of Whiteness has too often become routine (Paredes, 2011). Pillow recommends an "uncomfortable reflexivity," in which we allow our explanations to be messy, confessional, and tentative. This means sharing not only the personal struggles experienced during the research, but also, more importantly, the political struggles that we have not necessarily resolved. This type of critical reflexivity explores the "ambivalent, guarded, conflictual, or even conflicted" ways in which we relate to communities and participants and to various aspects of the research process (Cosgrove & McHugh, 2000, p. 827)

Without attention to power and politics, the risk for White researchers, in particular, is that reflexivity becomes another process through which Whiteness (in this case, the researcher as person) is once again at the centre. Simply listing our biographical or personal information may even serve to establish and assert our authority. Matters of positionality (our own, and those of our participants) must be taken up in ways that recognize their inherent complexities. Paredes (2011), for example, contends that we can only traverse the spaces of White/Indigenous disconnect through recognition of colonial structures; active engagement in a practice of decolonizing; and anti-colonial actions and ways of thinking. Paredes posits that non-Indigenous researchers have two choices: learn to conduct research in ways that meet the needs of Indigenous communities and are non-exploitative, culturally appropriate, and culturally safe, or relinquish the role of researcher within Indigenous contexts and make way for Indigenous researchers.

Within many Indigenous cultures, locating yourself at the outset of a process is a cultural tradition that serves to identify who you are and your connections to the community. Absolon and Willett (2005) suggest that locating ourselves within our research is one way to ensure accountability, build trust, and decolonize research. The naming of one's location has epistemological value for Indigenous peoples and communities because it establishes relationships; something that is, according to Indigenous researcher Shawn Wilson (2008), "at the heart of what it means to be Indigenous" (p. 80). Many Indigenous theorists (Absolon & Willett, 2005; Martin, 2003; Nicholls, 2009; Tuhiwai Smith, 1999,

2012) point out that understanding who prospective researchers are is important to Indigenous communities, given the long history of misuse of research findings to disentitle, demonize, and stigmatize Indigenous peoples. These considerations are also salient when research involves any marginalized or stigmatized groups.

## THE NEXT WAVE

Ten years after the first edition of *Research as Resistance*, there is much to celebrate in research, including the continuing social justice work of many of our original contributors. For example, Maggie Kovach (2010) and Kathy Absolon (2011) explore Indigenous methodologies and knowledge creation in their books. Deborah Rutman continues to work with various colleagues conducting research work in support of marginalized communities, such as youth in care (Rutman, Hubberstey, & Hume 2014) and parents with Fetal Alcohol Spectrum Disorder (Rutman & Van Bibber, 2010). Mehmoona Moosa-Mitha interrogates inclusionary and exclusionary practices of citizenship around the world in her book *Reconfiguring Citizenship* (Dominelli & Moosa-Mitha, 2014). The resistant ideas of the first edition may have encouraged other researchers to pursue new methods and methodologies. Certainly we have seen the literature devoted to critical, anti-racist, and anti-oppressive research expand considerably over the past decade. While we are heartened by this work and influenced by it in our own projects, we also recognize that political events of the last decade imperil researcher commitments to social justice and have in some ways set back those efforts.

Neoliberalism has even more deeply entrenched itself throughout the world, in governance structures, popular culture, and media discourses. While there are challenges to the neoliberal hegemony, including from those who are dominantly located and therefore most stand to benefit from deepening inequalities (see, for example, the work of Thomas Piketty, 2014, and Richard Wilkinson and Kate Pickett, 2009), their voices are muted by the cacophony of scholars and pundits willing and often eager to naturalize inequality. Critical researchers face a difficult terrain, given that in many jurisdictions like Canada, research work has been affected by deep cuts to research funding, and by new requirements to make a "business case" for proposed research. Commitments to socially just methodologies are under attack on a theoretical level as well, with the retrenchment of positivism as the gold standard for research (Brekke, 2012) and the proliferation of evidence-based approaches and ideologies in practice professions such as education, nursing, and social work. Indeed, positivist approaches are coming to dominate social work research; Guo's (2014) recent survey found that a very significant majority (over 80 percent) of research articles in mainstream social work journals are positivist in orientation. Alternatively, researchers like Michelle Fine (2012) cast a critical eye on this movement:

> Surrounded by sprawling debris reflecting the gendered, raced, classed and sexualized collateral damage of economic and political crisis, I find it most peculiar that psychologists have eagerly answered calls for "evidence"—without a pause for asking: Why now? Whose evidence counts? What kinds of evidence are being privileged? What are we not seeing? (p. 3)

It is these sorts of questions that the mix of established and new scholars in this new edition of *Research as Resistance* seeks to answer, and to problematize. Because it is so clear that inequality continues to march apace around us and because racism, colonialism, and other forms of oppression are ongoing, understanding socially just ways to carry out research and construct knowledge are still essential contributions to resistance.

We hope this volume is part of the next wave, a resurgence of knowledges founded in a diversity of spiritualities, philosophies, cultures, languages, and experiences.

## REFERENCES

Absolon, K. E. (2011). *Kaandosswin: How we come to know*. Winnipeg, MB: Fernwood Publishing.

Absolon, K., & Willett, C. (2005). Putting ourselves forward: Location in Aboriginal research. In L. Brown & S. Strega (Eds.), *Research as resistance* (pp. 97–126). Toronto, ON: Canadian Scholars' Press.

Aguiar, L., & Schneider, C. (2012). *Researching amongst elites*. Aldershot, UK: Ashgate.

Ball, J. (2005). 'Nothing about us without us': Restorative research partnerships involving Indigenous children and communities in Canada. In A. Farrell (Ed.), *Ethical research with children* (pp. 81–96). Berkshire, UK: Open University Press/McGraw Hill Education.

Biko, S. (1981). Black Consciousness and the quest for a true humanity. *Ufahamu: A Journal of African Studies, 11*(1), 133–142.

Brekke, J. (2012). Shaping a science of social work. *Research on Social Work Practice, 22*(5), 455–464.

Brookfield, S. (2009). The concept of critical reflection: Promises and contradictions. *European Journal of Social Work, 12*(3), 293–304.

Government of Canada. (2010). *Canadian Institutes of Health Research, Natural Sciences and Engineering Research Council of Canada, and Social Sciences and Humanities Research Council of Canada, Tri-Council Policy Statement: Ethical conduct for research involving humans.* Retrieved from www.pre.ethics.gc.ca

Campbell, R., & Wasco, S. M. (2000). Feminist approaches to social science: Epistemological and methodological tenets. *American journal of community psychology, 28*(6), 773–791.

Charlton, J. I. (1998). *Nothing about us without us: Disability oppression and empowerment.* Oakland: University of California Press.

Chilisa, B. (2011). *Indigenous research methodologies.* New York, NY: SAGE Publications.

Chilisa, B., & Ntseane, G. (2010). Resisting dominant discourses: Implications of indigenous, African feminist theory and methods for gender and education research. *Gender and Education, 22*(6), 617–632.

Code, L. (1991). *What can she know? Feminist theory and the construction of knowledge.* Ithaca, NY: Cornell University Press.

Cosgrove, L., & McHugh, M. C. (2000). Speaking for ourselves: Feminist methods and community psychology. *American Journal of Community Psychology, 28*(6), 815–838.

Dana-Sacco, G. (2010). The indigenous researcher as individual and collective. *American Indian Quarterly, 34*(1), 61.

Daly, M. (1978). *Gyn/Ecology: The metaethics of radical feminism.* Boston, MA: Beacon Press.

Dominelli, L., & Moosa-Mitha, M. (2014). *Reconfiguring citizenship: Social exclusion and diversity within inclusive citizenship practices.* Aldershot, UK: Ashgate.

Ehrenreich, B., & English, D. (1973). *Witches, midwives and healers.* Old Westbury, NY: The Feminist Press.

Evans, M. (2012). Funding and ethics in Métis community based research: The complications of a contemporary context. *International Journal of Critical Indigenous Studies, 5*(1), 54–66.

Fanon, F. (1967). *Black skin white masks* (C. Markmann, Trans.). New York, NY: Grove Press.

Fernandez, L. A. (2009). Being there: Thoughts on anarchism and participatory observation. In R. Amster, A. Deleon, L. A. Fernandez, A. J. Nocella, & D. Shannon (Eds.), *Contemporary anarchist studies* (pp. 93–102). New York, NY: Routledge.

Fine, M. (1998). Working the hyphens: Reinventing self and Other in qualitative research. In N. Denzin & Y. Lincoln (Eds.), *Handbook of qualitative research* (pp. 130–155). Thousand Oaks, CA: Sage.

Fine, M. (2012). Troubling calls for evidence: A critical race, class and gender analysis of whose evidence counts. *Feminism & Psychology, 22*(1), 3–19.

Fine, M., Weiss, L., Weseen, S., & Wong, L. (2003). For whom? Qualitative research, representations and social responsibilities. In N. Denzin & Y. Lincoln (Eds.), *The landscape of qualitative research: Theories and issues* (pp. 167–207). Thousand Oaks, CA: Sage.

Gains, F. (2011). Elite ethnographies: Potential, pitfalls and prospects for getting "up close and personal." *Public Administration, 89*(1), 156–166.

Guo, S. (2014). Shaping social work science: What should quantitative researchers do? *Research on Social Work Practice,* 1–12. Retrieved from http://rsw.sagepub.com/content/early/2014/03/18/1049731514527517

Gutterman, L. J. (2012). Another enemy within: Lesbian wives, or the hidden threat to the nuclear family in post-war America. *Gender & History, 24*(2), 475–501.

Harding, S. G. (1991). *Whose science? Whose knowledge? Thinking from women's lives.* Ithaca, NY: Cornell University Press.

Hart, M. A. (2010). Indigenous worldviews, knowledge, and research: The development of an indigenous research paradigm. *Journal of Indigenous Voices in Social Work, 1*(1), 1–16.

Hollway, W. (1989). *Subjectivity and method in psychology: Gender, meaning and science.* New York, NY: Sage Publications.

Jürgens, R. (2005). *"Nothing about us without us"—greater, meaningful involvement of people who use illegal drugs: A public health, ethical, and human rights imperative.* Toronto, ON: Canadian HIV/AIDS Legal Network.

Koster, R., Baccar, K., & Lemelin, R. H. (2012). Moving from research ON, to research WITH and FOR Indigenous communities: A critical reflection on community-based participatory research. *The Canadian Geographer, 56*(2), 195–210.

Kovach, M. E. (2010). *Indigenous methodologies: Characteristics, conversations, and contexts.* Toronto, ON: University of Toronto Press.

Ladson-Billings, G. (2000). Racialized discourses and ethnic epistemologies. *Handbook of qualitative research, 2,* 257–277.

Lal, J. (1996). Situating locations: The politics of self, identity, and "other" in living and writing the text. In D. L. Wolf (Ed.), *Feminist dilemmas in fieldwork* (pp. 185–214). Boulder, CO: Westview.

Martin, K. (2003). Ways of knowing, being and doing: A theoretical framework and methods for Indigenous and Indigenist research. In K. McWilliam, P. Stephenson & G. Thompson (Eds.), *Voicing dissent, New talents 21C: Next generation Australian studies* (pp.203–214). St Lucia, QLD: University of Queensland Press.

Matthews, S. (2013). Reflections on the appropriate use of unjustly conferred privilege. *Theoria, 60*(135), 23–41.

Mauthner, N. S., & Doucet, A. (2003). Reflexive accounts and accounts of reflexivity in qualitative data analysis. *Sociology, 37*(3), 413–431.

McDonagh, J. E., & Bateman, B. (2012). "Nothing about us without us": Considerations for research involving young people. *Archives of Disease in Childhood—Education & Practice Edition, 97*(2), 55–60.

Minde, H. (Ed.). (2008). *Indigenous peoples: Self-determination, knowledge, indigeneity.* Delft, Netherlands: Eburon Uitgeverij BV.

Nicholls, R. (2009). Research and indigenous participation: Critical reflexive methods. *International Journal of Social Research Methodology, 12*(2), 117–126.

Paredes, J. (2011). *Decolonising spaces and the exemplary life of Tess Brill's activism.* (Unpublished honour's thesis). Southern Cross University, Australia. Available at http://works.bepress.com.ezproxy.library.uvic.ca/julie-ann_paredes/1

Piketty, T. (2014). *Capital in the twenty-first century.* Boston, MA: Harvard University Press.

Pillow, W. (2003). Confession, catharsis, or cure? Rethinking the uses of reflexivity as methodological power in qualitative research. *International Studies in Education, 16*(2), 175–196.

Reed, S., Miller, R., Nnawulezi, N., & Valenti, M. (2012). Erecting closets and outing ourselves: Uncomfortable reflexivity and community-based research. *Journal of Community Psychology, 40*(1), 11–26.

Reinharz, S. (1992). *Feminist methods in social research.* London, UK: Oxford University Press.

Rutman, D., & Van Bibber, M. (2010). Parenting with fetal alcohol spectrum disorder. *International Journal of Mental Health and Addiction, 8*(2), 351–361.

Rutman, D., Hubberstey, C. & Hume, S. (2014). *Avoiding the precipice: An evaluation of Aunt Leah's Link Program in supporting youth from foster care.* Victoria, BC: University of Victoria.

Ryan, L., & Golden, A. (2006). "Tick the box please": A reflexive approach to doing quantitative social research. *Sociology, 40,* 1191–1200.

Santos, B. S. (2007) *Cognitive justice in a global world: Prudent knowledges for a decent life*. Lanham, MD: Lexington Books.

Schnarch, B. (2004). Ownership, control, access, and possession (OCAP) or self-determination applied to research. *Journal of Aboriginal Health*, *1*(1), 80–95.

Sholock, A. (2012). Methodology of the privileged: White anti-racist feminism, systematic ignorance, and epistemic uncertainty. *Hypatia*, *27*(4), 701–714.

Tuhiwai Smith, L. (1999). *Decolonizing methodologies: Research and Indigenous peoples*. Dunedin, NZ: University of Otago Press.

Tuhiwai Smith, L. (2012). *Decolonizing methodologies: Research and Indigenous peoples* (2nd ed.). London, UK: Zed Books.

Wilkinson, R., & Pickett, K. (2009). *The spirit level: Why greater equality makes societies stronger*. New York, NY: Bloomsbury.

Wilson, S. (2008). *Research is ceremony: Indigenous research methods*. Winnipeg, MB: Fernwood Publishing.

Wittig, M. (1992). *The straight mind and other essays*. Boston, MA: Beacon Press.

# Chapter One

# Becoming an Anti-Oppressive Researcher

## Karen L. Potts and Leslie Brown[1]

## BEGINNING WITH CHOICES, ASSUMPTIONS, AND TENETS

Given the choice between being an oppressive or anti-oppressive researcher, hopefully we would all choose the latter. However, the choice is not really that simple or straightforward. A commitment to anti-oppressive research means committing to social justice and taking an active role in that change. It means that there is political purpose and action to our research work, whether that purpose is change on a societal level or within our own lives. Anti-oppressive research involves making explicit the political practices involved in creating knowledge. It requires making a commitment to the people you are working with, personally and professionally, in order to mutually foster conditions for social justice through research. It starts with paying attention to, and shifting, how power relations work in and through the processes of doing research.

Our own journeys to anti-oppressive research were fuelled by running into the same problem that perplexed another researcher committed to social justice, Patti Lather (1991): how is it that "our very efforts to liberate (through our research) perpetuate the relations of dominance" (p. 16)? Like Lather, we realized that the answer to that question required an examination of our own complicity in creating and sustaining oppression. This is not any easy task!

Most of us recognize oppression when it occurs "out there" or when we are being oppressed ourselves, but can we also recognize how we are implicated in sustaining systems of inequality? This is often harder, especially if we are well-meaning people who espouse social justice ideals. But if we are committed to anti-oppression, we have to be prepared to critically analyze how oppression occurs through the various activities and social practices we engage in with others, including research activities. For example, as White women academics, we recognize that our ability to implement an anti-oppressive research approach rests (to some extent) on tapping into our privilege, and we acknowledge that researchers from the margins face different challenges in attempting to enable anti-oppressive research.

We want you to consider that anti-oppressive work, including research, is not contingent upon location. Social justice work can happen anywhere, including in dominant institutions such as governments, schools, and hospitals. The political nature of our environment is important to recognize and work with, but we do not have to have a job description that says "anti-oppressive researcher" (good luck waiting for that one!) before we can do anti-oppressive research. Anti-oppressive research is a commitment to a set of principles, values, and ways of working, and can be carried out anywhere—it's a matter of choice amid various constraints. We ask that you believe in your capacity for agency: you can act in ways that alter the relations of oppression in your own world. There are conversations among academics and activists that specifically interrogate the term *anti-oppressive* (McLaughlin, 2005). This chapter does not participate in these conversations. For us, we were attracted to and are using the term because we still feel challenged by it (in all our paradoxical and simultaneous, marginalized and dominant social locations) to "do" our research work in ways that move us closer toward social justice.

The purpose of this chapter is to explain our ideas about anti-oppressive research in ways that we hope will be helpful to all researchers, and to research students in particular. We start by outlining three key principles or tenets of anti-oppressive research. These are not discreet; rather, they are interrelated, and our articulation of them reflects how they inform one another. When we want to critically assess whether the research work we are doing is actually anti-oppressive research, it is these principles that we use to reflect on our topic, our methods, our relationships, our analysis, and our action. We then discuss what anti-oppressive research processes may look like. Finally, we illustrate our ideas through one student researcher's experience of applied anti-oppressive research.

## Anti-Oppressive Research Is Social Justice[2] in Processes and Outcomes

Research can be a powerful tool for social change—and for maintaining the status quo. Research can be used to suppress ideas, people, and social justice—and it can be used to respect, empower, and liberate. Good intentions are never enough to ensure anti-oppressive processes or outcomes. Many research endeavours contribute to social justice outcomes, but are not necessarily anti-oppressive in their processes and procedures. The Canadian Centre for Policy Alternatives, for example, publishes important statistical research on poverty, taxation systems, and environmental degradation (www.policyalternatives.ca). While we applaud this work, there is an important difference between research that contributes to social justice and what we describe here as anti-oppressive research.

Choosing to be an anti-oppressive researcher means choosing to do research that challenges dominant ideas about research *processes* as well as research outcomes. This means that each step of the research work is carried out in a socially just way. For example, anti-oppressive research questions why we so easily think of researching those who are marginalized by reason of race, class, ability, gender, and so on while it is so difficult to think about researching dominance. "Reversing the gaze" on whom and what gets studied can be an important first step in anti-oppressive research. Similarly, we can ask how research participants can also be the researchers, and we can ensure equitable distribution of any money, credit, and direct benefits generated by the research work.

## Anti-Oppressive Research Contends That All Knowledge Is Socially Constructed, All Knowledge Is Political, and, Currently, Shaped by the Neoliberal Context

How do we know what we know? The answer to this epistemological question is key to understanding an anti-oppressive approach to research. From an anti-oppressive perspective, knowledge does not exist "out there" to be discovered. Rather, knowledge is produced through the interactions of people, and as all people are socially and politically located (in their race, gender, ability, class identities, and so on), with biases, privileges, and differing entitlements, so too is the knowledge that is produced socially located and political. Knowledge is neither neutral nor benign, as it is created within and through power relations between people. Knowledge can be oppressive in how it is constructed and utilized, or it can be a means of resistance and emancipation. Often, it is a complex combination of both.

Recognizing that knowledge is socially constructed means understanding that truth is created, rather than pre-existing and available to be measured and observed. Therefore, in anti-oppressive research, we do not look to prove or disprove a singular "truth" about the social or political world. We look for meaning, for understanding, for insights that can enable resistance and change. However, anti-oppressive researchers recognize that we live in a culture biased toward positivist research—that is, using natural science principles of counting, quantifying, and measuring to claim to understand social issues. As anti-oppressive researchers, we argue that we must trouble the dominance of positivism, because while counting, measuring, and quantifying can measure inequalities, the complex causes of injustice and inequity remain unexamined.

We contend that, in the present moment, positivism is part of the infrastructure that allows neoliberalism to flourish and the transformation to a knowledge economy to occur. Recognizing knowledge as socially constructed means being politically astute about this context. Knowledge has been turned into a commodity in the new knowledge economy (David & Foray, 2002), and an increasing emphasis on patents, copyrights, and other regulations is restricting the free sharing of knowledge. Knowledge becomes a profitable commodity, and knowledge creation a profit-making endeavour, when knowledge can be made scarce or where access to knowledge can be limited and controlled (AUCC, 2001). Anti-oppressive research resists the commodification of knowledge and instead advocates "democratizing knowledge" by ensuring knowledge is accessible for the common good (Hall, 2011). As anti-oppressive researchers, we set out to construct emancipatory and liberatory knowledge that can be acted on, by, and in the interests of the marginalized and oppressed.

## Anti-Oppressive Research Foregrounds Relationships

Consider the relationship in positivist research between the researcher and those who are being researched. In positivism, the researcher is the expert and is seen as being the primary, and often only, person with power and the ability to create knowledge, to act on that knowledge, and to profit from its creation. Those who are being studied, although they are not necessarily treated badly, are nevertheless objects; they are acted upon, without any input or real involvement or control in the process, and positivist research principles constrain researchers from having any interpersonal relationships with research participants. From a positivist perspective, there is usually no need to recognize these hierarchical and distant power relations, nor any attempt to change them. Researchers and participants are not equals: money paid to participants may be called an "inducement" or "honorarium," while money paid to researchers is usually called "wages" or "salary."

The problematic nature of researcher-researched relationships is not confined to positivism. Even in "empowerment"[3] approaches to research, the relationship between researchers and the researched may be hierarchical and paternalistic: members of the group being researched might conduct interviews or surveys, but otherwise have no control or involvement in research processes. Providing people with an opportunity to have their voices heard and hearing their stories can be exploitative or empowering, or a confusing mix of both.

In anti-oppressive research, key relationships and their attendant power relations are foregrounded, including relationships between the knower and known; groups of knowers; knowers and any outside researchers; and researchers and institutions. Constant attention is given to these relations, and care is taken to try and shift the balance of knowledge-creating power from outside researchers to those with lived experience of the issue under study (Ceglowski, 2000). As anti-oppressive researchers, we say that "we do not begin to collect data in a community until all the dogs know us." This is our way of saying, "No research without authentic relationships." Research relationships are not time specific or disposable (Huisman, 2008). Rather, we approach them as if we may be in relationship with people for life.

## RE-THINKING THE RE-SEARCHING PROCESS: ANTI-OPPRESSIVE PRACTICE IN THE PROCESS OF INQUIRY

There are some basic tasks that are common to most social science research processes. People come together with an issue. A question is articulated. A research design is drafted. An agreement about who will be involved and how people will work together is developed. Information to answer the question is captured. There is a meaning-making process to learn from the data. Some type of product, such as a write-up, is produced. These elements are present in anti-oppressive research, though they usually appear in particular ways. Anti-oppressive research is rarely a linear process, and few elements are determined at the outset. Anti-oppressive research is emergent, in that the issue under study, the people doing the studying, and the environments we are working within are constantly changing. The "tasks" of the research need to respond accordingly. For example, during the analysis we may realize we need to go back for more data. And sometimes, it is only after the analysis that we realize what the real question was that we answered.

Aside from the emergent nature of these research tasks, there are other activities that are a bit unique to anti-oppressive research. First is the time and attention given to relationship building. Second is the doing—the tasks that will come from making a commitment to acting and creating change from the research. This is much more than the authoring of a report to make action someone else's responsibility. We now turn our attention to these research tasks.

## IT STARTS WITH NEGOTIATING WHO'S WHO

As a central tenet of anti-oppressive research, attending to relationships is foregrounded in all research tasks, and it is also the place we start. We spend time getting to know the people involved and the history and context of wherever the research will take place, and becoming savvy to the politics we will be immersed in. Before we can enter into authentic relationships with others, we need to be vigilant about our own biases and motivations, and attend to the gap between how we see ourselves (well meaning, caring, grounded in our own experiences of marginalization) and how others may see us (privileged, representing dominant institutions, not having as much at stake).

Anti-oppressive researchers are constantly negotiating their position along a continuum of insider/outsider relations. Insiders have epistemic privilege—that is, the intimate knowledge from lived experience of the issue under study. The outsider end of the continuum is the traditional academic researcher, positioned outside the situation, removed and in a position of studying "Others." Most of us on the journey toward becoming anti-oppressive researchers find ourselves somewhere in the middle of the continuum. Often we have a personal connection to the issue or topic, but we are also usually connected to government, human service, or academic institutions. In practice, negotiating and positioning ourselves as researchers is seldom as simple as declaring which position we hold. In some instances, we may think we are insiders only to find that others involved in the project (especially those providing data) see us as set apart, an outsider. Linda Tuhiwai Smith (2012) illustrates this when she talks about her experience doing research in her own Maori community:

> I was an insider as a Maori mother and an advocate of the language revitalization movement, and I shared in the activities of fund raising and organizing. Through my different tribal relationships I had close links to some of the mothers and to the woman who was the main organizer.... When I began the discussions and negotiations over my research, however, I became much more aware of the things which made me an outsider. I was attending university as a graduate student; I had worked for several years as a teacher and had a professional income; I had a husband; and we owned a car, which was second-hand but actually registered. As I became more involved in the project, interviewing the women about their own education stories, and as I visited them in their own homes, these differences became much more marked.... An interview with a researcher is formal. (Tuhiwai Smith, 2012, p. 139)

As Smith illustrates, outsider relations are established in the very declaration that a question is "research," with all its formal connotations.

## QUESTIONING

Questioning is the "mess-finding" stage in the research process, as well as the one that opens us up to possibilities and directs our gaze. What are the issues? What do we know already? What is our relationship to the issues and questions? What do other people know about it? What do we want to really understand?

There is enormous power in distilling the research question from a general research focus. The research question articulates what is and isn't explored and who is and isn't under scrutiny. Once a question has been put on the table, anti-oppressive researchers step back to critically consider: "Who says this is a question that needs to be studied, anyway?" And, "Whose interests are served by this research question being asked, and in this way?" Too frequently as researchers, we are influenced by funding, interest, curiosity, and previous research. Often, we have been trained to think of marginalized people as the "proper" objects of study and have given little consideration to studying those who are dominantly located. For example, if we are curious about racism, we are inclined to study visible minorities rather than White people. If we are concerned about accessibility for people with disabilities, we tend to study disabled people rather than the able-bodied. From an anti-oppressive perspective most research is organized with a gaze facing the wrong way, toward those who suffer from inequities rather than those who benefit from them or those who are indifferent. Our ability to shift the research gaze is often complicated by our connections to dominance. As well-intentioned, professional social justice workers, it is challenging to look at ourselves and our own positions as being complicit in creating and perpetuating oppression. But in anti-oppressive research, our complicity is an important focus for study. For example, instead of studying how the poor cope with poverty or homelessness, we might ask, "How do we (yes, you and I) contribute to the conditions creating poverty in our own community?" Reversing the gaze requires us to put dominance and power under scrutiny. We research "up." While it is also important to know the scope of inequality (for example, the number of homeless people), from a social justice perspective, perhaps it is more important to know how many buildings are left empty by land speculators waiting for prices to go up. Poverty is about a gap between the rich and the poor. But one side of the gap is more likely to be studied by the other side. Anti-oppressive research seeks to balance this.

To distill an issue into a guiding research question, anti-oppressive researchers do their homework. This involves finding out what knowledge is already available about the topic. Traditionally, this means checking the academic literature. As anti-oppressive researchers, we still do this, but we examine this existing knowledge critically to understand how, by whom, and for whose benefit it was constructed. And we do not stop there. We recognize knowledge from sources other than academic books and articles or reports published by governments and institutions. For instance, our lived experiences and those of others can provide valuable insights. Oral histories, blogs, and community conversations may also flesh out our starting point. Anti-oppressive research values diversity in knowledge. Critical assessment of many existing sources of knowledge on a topic and the credibility assigned to each source is part of the initial "questioning."

As important as it is to have a clear starting place, finding the question is seldom simple. Research questions are always political. Often, questions have to be extracted from our positivist and preconceived ideas about what a good research question "should" be. Sometimes questions are more like hunches, experienced tensions or disjunctures sensed in our own lives. But even when we get some initial clarity around the research question, this seldom lasts long. Questions usually change as the inquiry moves. Sometimes we never do find the question; instead, it finds us—at the end of the day, when the new knowledge from the analysis tells us what question we just answered. Keeping ourselves open to an emergent research process allows us to deepen our understanding about what it was we really wanted to know in the first place. But we have to be open to the art of the question through re-searching—the willingness to look again.

## DESIGNING, AND RE-DESIGNING, A PLAN TO STUDY THE QUESTIONS

More often than not, social justice research strives to be anti-oppressive in terms of purpose—that is, the desired outcomes are consistent with goals of social change. But this focus alone can replicate traditional research power relations, in which the dominant study the marginalized, with little shared control, relationships, or mutual benefits of participating in the research work. Because of this, we argue that we need the research process itself to be consistent with socially just and anti-oppressive values. Significant thought and strong relationships are integral to the designing and planning of an anti-oppressive research process. Given that most of us have been entrenched in Western scientific notions of research, doing research differently requires constant vigilance and support. A good plan always helps.

There are many questions that an anti-oppressive researcher asks in the ongoing process of articulating a research plan or design. Who has an interest, or stake, in the research? Who are we going to involve, and how? What are the ethical considerations? How are we going to collect data, and once collected, how are we going to interpret it? Who owns the data? What constraints and limitations do we face? What criteria will we use to judge the quality of our research? What do we do when things change or come up along the way?

The first question posed asks us to consider the various interests, power relations, and stakeholders in our research. We do not want the research work to be oriented toward external interests, but we do not want to be naïve about them, either. The interests of funders, target audiences, and hosting organizations should be considered. For example, if we are doing a research project as part of a university course, then we have to be aware of how the requirements of the assignment construct the research and constrain the possibilities. Or, if our purpose is to secure future funding for an addictions support program and we know that the funders want to know the extent of the problem, who needs to be served, and what alternative programs cost, we would not likely design a research project that interviewed one client in great depth about her experience as a drug user. Going back to our relationship work, it is useful to develop relationships with our potential audience and with those we are targeting for change. Politically, we have to consider when is the best time to get this stakeholder group engaged. There may be some merit to engaging this group throughout the research process in order to build rapport and possible support. There are a variety of ways to do this, including developing an advisory group or connecting the marginalized with the dominant through the research processes. Touraine, for example, achieved change in an organization through the process of putting labour and management representatives together in the same focus group in order to "reproduce social relationships in a research context, bringing together dominant and contesting actors in the same research groups" (McDonald, 2003, p. 248). Whatever the approach, the intention is that the actual process of the research becomes an intervention for change, rather than relying on changes coming through the research outcome or product.

At some point, decisions will need to be made to respond to the question of whom to involve in some or all of the research processes. This is what positivist researchers may call developing a sampling strategy. However, the goals for anti-oppressive research are very different, as involving people is done for purposes like community building, empowerment, and more nuanced understandings, rather than solely to achieve representativeness or validity. Sampling in anti-oppressive research is seldom random. Sampling is a power-laden decision, and is seen as one of many political acts in research. Ideally, an outsider researcher is never the sole source of invitations to participate; instead, it is a community of participants and insider researchers who do the inviting and including.

Ethical questions affect every research design. The ethics of anti-oppressive research reflect a commitment to and respect for people and relationships, as well as a commitment to action and social justice. The use of informed consent is one example. Constant renegotiation around a process of informed consent is important, as this highlights our commitments to the community, and our relationship to it, the data, and the process. Although most informed consent processes have become institutionalized for purposes of avoiding liability (Martin, 2007), we have reclaimed the concept of consent agreements to be a formal contract of our obligations to research participants, and a declaration of their ownership of the data, their right to a transparent research process, and their right to as much involvement or control as they choose. Certainly this way of working has led to some interesting situations for us (such as a community deciding to withdraw its data toward the end of a study), and as logistically difficult as these situations have been and can be, it does show that these processes work to shift power and ownership to the people living with the issues.

Respecting people and relationships also guides our responses to questions of ownership of data. The term *data* in its origins means "gift." From an anti-oppressive perspective, we see data as a gift that participants bestow, and we work to respect those gifts and treat them ethically. This means we must ask: Who owns the data, and what does ownership mean? If we (researchers) agree that participants own the data, and if after the research is completed the participants decide they don't like what we, the researchers, have said, what happens then?[4] Or if we hear the story of a participant that is compelling but filled with tangential comments and expressions we feel are distracting to what the research is saying, do we have the right to edit their story? Once edited, whose story is it? There are at least three voices in interpreting data: the participant who gave the story, the writer or researcher who records and retells it, and the reader who interprets it (Marcotte, 1995). We ask ourselves: "How are all these voices attended to?" Developing and attending to relationships, including those to data and data sources, is critical in anti-oppressive research.

Identifying the constraints to any design is important so that an anti-oppressive researcher can then identify the spaces within those constraints that can make the research less oppressive in its process, and ultimately in its outcome. The types of constraints you will encounter will be different and changing in every inquiry. However, there are some constraints that you can commonly anticipate, such as time, resources, and institutional and organizational structures. For example, if your research is connected with a university, you will be expected to submit your proposed study for approval to an ethics review committee and mould your research design to fit institutional regulations. Or, suppose the government has asked you to do some research. You will likely have a limited time frame and budget, and may face the constraints of having the research questions and possibly the design predetermined. But it is possible to engage in anti-oppressive processes even within constraints. For example, if we are confined to using a standardized survey questionnaire, we can still think about how to involve participants in the research, its process, and its outcome. Rather than designing the questionnaire yourself, in isolation, it is possible to share control of question design and questionnaire administration with those being researched, or give control to them entirely. Similarly, rather than administer a questionnaire *to* participants, we could complete it *with* participants. This is more than just semantics; this shift in language produces a different relationship among the people involved in the research. It is also important that we never ask questions of others that we are not willing to answer and share ourselves.

Within the design, it is important to be clear about the criteria by which we want the quality of our research work to be evaluated, so that we can ensure there are methods in place to achieve them. It is the operationalization of "quality" that will make your research credible, publishable, actionable, and worth listening to. Without quality-assurance strategies, research can be dismissed as an opinion essay with no relevance for possible action. So what criteria are appropriate to judge the quality of anti-oppressive research, and who gets to decide this? Figuring this out requires attention to the perspectives of those who have an interest in the research, all within the framework of the tenets and ethics of anti-oppressive research.

And finally, there is the reality of implementing the research plan. When you are on a planned road trip, you often find you run across opportunities and obstacles that didn't exist on your map. Modifications to the plan are made, within the context of your purpose, the participants on the trip, how much time and money you have, and so on. Similarly, a research design is a dynamic plan that gets tweaked and altered along the way.

# COLLECTING DATA: SEEKING, LISTENING, LEARNING

As anti-oppressive researchers, we strive to be perceptive, to pay attention to what we are in the midst of. However, this is hard work. We have to try to make what is usually invisible to us, visible. We have to find ways to see what we take for granted—the water we swim in. By paying attention, being creative, and being open, we can be responsive to seeing data, however it presents itself, in whatever forms are most meaningful to the people involved in the research. Data can be pictures, visuals, films, poems, music, numbers, or words. In our research classes we often encourage students to collect data on their own lives through mapping (Amsden & VanWynsberghe, 2005) and photovoice, a participatory research methodology first articulated by Caroline Wang and Mary Anne Burris (1997), in which research participants create, analyze, and discuss photos that represent their community (see also Castleden, Garvin, & Huu-ay-aht First Nation, 2008); these strategies are often meaningful for participants more comfortable with pictures than words. Sharing meaning between participants who speak different languages can help capture the materiality or embodiment of social issues, and it can help shake up those of us battling old biases about numbers and statistics being a superior form of data.

Regardless of the form our data takes, as all anti-oppressive research is relationship work, we still have to develop our political listening and critical reflecting skills. Mindfulness, being present, and being prepared to have the responsibility of witnessing are key skills. A good audio recorder, camera, or other technology can help to capture the details of the data, but it is the act of truly listening that propels the research forward. By articulating their experiences and thoughts, participants make meaning of their lives. By paying attention and listening, we become increasingly aware of contexts, histories, and social dynamics. Solidarity is nurtured. We can discover new opportunities for acting collectively that we had not foreseen or planned. Through paying attention and listening, research is reconceptualized and becomes an emergent, unfolding process, rather than a trip to a predetermined destination.

# MAKING MEANING

Making meaning is often thought of as analyzing data. When doing anti-oppressive research, we assume that meaning-making is not restricted to any one part of the research process, but rather happens throughout the research process. As such, we pay attention to our processes of interpretation, reflection, and constructing meaning as the research journey unfolds.

While meaning-making is ongoing, we do have data to compile and make sense of, and this is the focus of this next part of the discussion. In practice, we have found that it is useful, as we begin to review our data, to revisit our research questions and design and consider how they have evolved and shifted from the original plan. By rearticulating our research design, we can open ourselves to understanding more specifically what we want to know and thus ask of the data. We can also become more aware of the kinds of data and data sources we have and our positioning in relation to the data. This clarity serves to ground our interpretations and analysis of the data. Our ways of gathering and working with data have probably been modified as the research process has unfolded. All these shifts and changes influence and determine what data we actually have and how we make sense of it.

There are a number of questions that we reflect upon as we plan for and engage in making meaning. These include issues of power and who does the analysis, as well as what concepts frame the analysis, who benefits from the meaning-making, and what analytic tools are appropriate.

Power lurks in all our reflections and decisions. Just figuring out who gets the privilege of making meaning is laden with issues of power. For us, research is a social process, and therefore the more positivist notion of one or two designated researchers who are responsible for analyzing the data is not our reality. Yet, even though we work collaboratively with participant-researchers, potential users of the research, and others in making meaning of our data, underlying hierarchies inherent in our relationships often challenge us. The analysis stage presents an opportunity for the social construction of knowledge to be facilitated in an intentionally liberatory way. Some people in the process are seen as experts in the topic of study, while others are seen as experts in particular data analysis techniques or in the lived experience of the data. Our collaborative meaning-making processes are influenced by the perceived and exercised power that we each bring to the process. These differences often become visible when there are disagreements about meanings or the importance of meanings. Further, while it may be ideal to have everyone possible involved in the meaning-making, the reality often is that not everyone has the time or interest to participate. Figuring out how to enable individuals to participate, as they would wish, is challenging.

Another point of reflection in planning and engaging in meaning-making concerns the conceptual framework that informs the research. Kirby and McKenna (1989, p. 32) challenge us to articulate our "conceptual baggage"—that is, the concepts, beliefs, metaphors, and frameworks that inform our perspective on and relationship to the research topic. The term "baggage" has a somewhat negative connotation, so we prefer to think about our "luggage." We carry our framework, which is not inherently good or bad, around with us, and it is through this framework that we view the data. Making the luggage visible is an individual and a collective process. Ensuring that everyone has had the opportunity to discuss the concepts that inform our perspectives helps to alleviate conflicts that can arise during the analysis around different perceptions of meaning and can expose contradictions in helpful ways. The conceptual framework that informed the project at the outset evolves during the project, and new or additional concepts, metaphors, and frameworks emerge. Winnowing through minutes of meetings about the topic or trying to explain to your friends what the research is about are often fruitful ways to discern the emergent frameworks. Discussing these frameworks with research participants can illuminate contradictions in concepts that may be held. Different concepts, metaphors, and frameworks produce different meanings and knowledge, and such discussions often bring up questions around which interpretation(s) is (are) seen as more valuable or believable than others, and why.

As researchers, we have found it particularly helpful to revisit the topic and questions in order to think through the fit between our approaches to analysis and what we really want to know. This revisiting is vital and informs the ability to make meaning and to extend the findings into conclusions and action.

The other point of reflection in the meaning-making process is thinking about who benefits from the chosen research process. What (and whose) purpose does the research serve? There is an old saying that "figures don't lie, but liars can figure." The techniques of analysis, of making meaning of data, contribute to the meaning made. What is the intended outcome, and how is the data analysis, whether statistical or not, being constructed? What data is being included in the analysis and what is being left out? Why? If using interview data, who decides which quotations from participants to include, and by their inclusion, who is excluded? Again, knowledge is constructed, and paying attention to why and how it is constructed in certain ways is an ongoing challenge for anti-oppressive researchers.

One of the strategies that Kirby and McKenna (1989) suggest as part of analyzing data is living with the data, meaning getting some distance from the analysis in order to reflect on it. While we have found that being connected with and reflecting upon the data is critical in every stage of a research project, and that this process needs to be shared with co-researchers/ participants, it is a particularly useful task to incorporate in the meaning-making process. This means that the participant-researcher(s) have to step back from the analysis for a while in order to reflect upon the data, the analysis, and the destination of the research. Once again, this illustrates that research is about relationships. Researchers develop an intimate relationship with data. Understanding that relationship (as articulated by the questions posed earlier in this section), and reflecting on the data in light of that relationship, is what analysis is about.

What kind of approach is to be taken? Some options include involving participants in analyzing the data or having those ultimately affected by the research (who may not be the participants) involved. What about having an advisory group to our research and having them conduct the analysis? Or finding a way to involve the people who will be responsible for making change as a result of the research? Whatever approach is used, consider how it will affect the results of the research and how those results could be used.

## POSING CONCLUSIONS AND NEW QUESTIONS, TAKING MORE ACTION

> Knowing is not enough, we must apply. Willing is not enough, we must do.
>
> —Goethe

> Knowing without doing, isn't really knowing.
>
> —Fortune cookie

We continuously think about new questions, new realizations, and new applications of ideas as we travel the research journey. Yet at some point along the journey, there will be times when we are asked for conclusions and summary thoughts. Conclusions have a particular power in that they are the construction of knowledge that leads to recommendations and actions. As well, conclusions are often the sound bites in the research that an audience listens for. Sometimes, these consumers of our research are interested in our trip, the story of our process, but more often they are interested in what we have "found." How conclusions are constructed, therefore, has particular impact on how the audience will take up the research in their own lives.

Common practice is for research to be "written up" in a formal report, or perhaps turned into a journal article. This practice is inherently classist, exclusionary, and appropriative in that it requires translating marginal knowledges into the language of the elite. Written reports and journal articles are read by some audiences, but are they the audiences that will help mobilize our new knowledge into social justice? Other options are worthy of consideration. Brainstorming with co-researchers for options that could facilitate the goals of empowerment and social justice then becomes a key part of the work. For instance, would it be better to hold a community workshop to discuss the research, or write a letter to the editor, or put the findings into a popular theatre presentation, or convene a session of strategic planning, or produce a video or a website?

As we have noted throughout this paper, research happens in relationships between people. It is a site for practicing democracy. Recognizing our agency, our ability to make a choice in how something will be done, enables us to be purposeful in our anti-oppressive actions. As researchers, reframing research as part of our practice of knowledge democracy has helped us to move beyond the trap of oppositional thinking within anti-oppressive research. How we pose conclusions and devise actions is yet another opportunity to practice democracy and thereby make real our beliefs about power relations and social justice. Posing conclusions brings us to ask the critical question, "So what?" How will the research be used, and by whom? Who else could make use of it, and how? What uses could it have that were not intended? Remember that producing a product that sits on a shelf does not mean that the research, or the research report, does not fill a purpose. Too often, research is used to delay decision-making or distract attention from an issue. What is the professional obligation of the researcher in ensuring that the research is used for social change, not only throughout the process of conducting the research, but also after the research is concluded? We have found that by returning to our original discussions about the issues and what we wanted to know, we discover a nest of possibilities about what to do with the findings, who will use them, and how they will or could be used. Anti-oppressive action in the research process means taking up the processes and tools of research in ways that are congruent with the principles and values of empowerment and social justice wherever and whenever possible.

## PUTTING THE TENETS TO WORK: ONE STUDENT'S EXPERIENCE

Christine, a student in an undergraduate research class, and Charles, an interviewer in Christine's class project, agreed to let us share their experience of anti-oppressive research with you.

Initially, Christine really struggled with grasping the anti-oppressive research principles talked about in the course; she did not do very well on her research proposal assignment for the class, but she had good intentions. She worked with mentally challenged people and was concerned about how they were treated by professionals in the community (police, health workers, etc.). But in her initial research design, she proposed to have other professionals talking on behalf of people with mental disabilities. In her next attempt, she switched and proposed surveying the clients herself, so that the clients at least got to tell their own stories. But she, as the researcher, was still in control. Both of her initial designs were loaded with "power over" relations, where she was going to get direct benefit (getting course credit, learning how to do research, developing relationships) from using marginalized people and their stories.

Then one day, as Christine describes it, it came to her what anti-oppressive research was all about. She asked the people labelled as "clients" in the day home where she worked if any of them would like to be researchers into why professionals sometimes treat them so badly. Several said yes. She helped them learn about research and design their own interview questions, and they got to pick the professionals they would interview ("researching up"). It was an amazing process; they interviewed professionals about their training and attitudes toward people with mental illnesses and cognitive disabilities, and at the end of the interview they revealed that they were people living with mental illness or disability. The professionals were shocked, and change happened through the *process* of the research interviews. These participants (now called "interviewers," not "clients") have gone on with Christine to present at research conferences and write articles for newsletters, and have been truly empowered to become advocates in their own lives. This is what anti-oppressive research can look like for marginalized people with the support of an "outsider" who believes in anti-oppressive research.

In Christine's words:

> The fact that I have simply provided these people with the environment to share their stories with the goal of educating people about mental illness has resulted in individual change with the interviewers and with (myself), the facilitator.... They were involved in who was going to be interviewed, how the interviews were going to take place, where the interview was going to be, what type of questions were going to be asked, who they wanted to interview, how the information was going to be documented and if they wanted to disclose their mental illness. (Christine, electronic communication, October 2, 2001)

Christine also went on to support the co-researchers in presenting their research at a conference. One researcher was Charles, and this is how he described the experience:

> It all started when Christine asked me if I was interested in participating in a school project she was doing.... Intrigued, I immediately asked to interview a police officer. I thought to myself that this could be quite exciting; the shoe on the other foot type thing.... We sat down together and discussed the interview. She (Christine) let me help in the formulation of the questions for the interview. This boosted my self-confidence quite a bit, having someone show interest in my ideas and suggestions. This way, I did not feel like a mindless test subject, and I was determined to do the interview to the best of my ability.

Charles goes on to describe his interview with the police officer regarding police attitudes and training about mental illness:

> In our discourse, I was informed that there was no real training provided about the mentally ill in the RCMP infrastructure. She (the officer) said her department left days open for various training seminars. Upon learning that their training was on the

streets, I understood why when I was ill, various officers treated me so differently. This opened my eyes to the humanness of the police in general. As we were talking, the officer asked me if I was a student, like Christine. When I told her I suffered from mental illness, she was quite surprised. When I told her my diagnosis, she found it hard to believe. I felt surprised and delighted, for here was a police officer, a ten-year veteran on the force, dead wrong about my illness. I thought to myself that these people are heavily trained in psychology and human nature. Her surprised reaction broke the stereotype I felt about myself.

We conversed further, and then the ice broke. She relaxed suddenly, leaning forward and sideways [and] at the same time easing her arms up a little. Instead of her steely gaze of authority, her eyes were much warmer and friendly. In return I lowered my guard a little more and, in my perspective, we developed what could be defined as a good rapport. I think we both learned something. Her, the experience of talking with someone who is mentally ill, in a rational state of mind, and me, I learned that a police officer could casually chit-chat, in a friendly manner, with the public, while on duty. It was a nice experience—I will always remember it. (Charles, personal writing, March 10, 2001)

The three tenets of anti-oppressive research that we outlined at the beginning of this chapter are very much present in the above story. The research project turned power on its head; it was all about relationships; and it recognized that socially constructed knowledge as could be clearly focused toward social justice.

## IDENTIFYING AND MEETING THE CHALLENGES TO ANTI-OPPRESSIVE RESEARCH

Anti-oppressive research is exciting, engaging, and critical. Why wouldn't we do anti-oppressive research all the time? In our efforts to become anti-oppressive researchers, we will come across a number of barriers and challenges—some of our own making, some external to us, and some that are a combination of both. Here we explain three significant challenges.

Dominant discourses: We live in a world with shared dominant myths that we encounter every day, and we need to make these visible in order to address them. Beliefs that continued economic growth is possible, desirable, and good for everyone, or that technology and science will save us from our current economic and environmental crises, have an unconscious influence on our lives and research work, shaping the research questions we pose, the methods we see as credible, and the value we place on the wisdom of the "oppressed" versus the "experts." Likewise, we need to acknowledge the current discourses that dominate human service research discussions. Outcome-based measurements and evaluation and evidence-based decision-making continue to be popular (Campbell & Ng, 1988). As a social justice worker, you will encounter these discourses, and it will be up to you to understand the deep positivist and neoliberal epistemological roots they extend from. You will need to see how these discourses will try to construct and constrain your work. And most importantly, you will need to know how to engage anti-oppressive practices to try and produce social justice outcomes despite the constraints. For example, in program evaluation, empowerment or participatory evaluation approaches are a good place to start (Secret, Jordan, & Ford, 1999).

The project paradigm: Those of us trained to do research have been conditioned to think in terms of research "projects." This project paradigm sees research as a linear, time-limited, beginning-middle-end, textually based (proposal to report) process. Anti-oppressive research moves research into being part of a community-building, social change process. Anti-oppressive research needs to be entwined in the complex context, part of something larger, not an end in itself. The goal of anti-oppressive research is not a finished report, but an ongoing community-building enterprise helping us to develop complex understandings about our lives. Relationships and action are the prioritized components, not surveys and reports.

Funding: One factor that gets in the way of switching from the project paradigm is applying for and receiving money. A lot of good anti-oppressive research work can happen without money, but realistically, there are often costs to getting people together. Participants' time and work should be compensated. Money for meeting spaces and "getting the word out" can be a good thing. But most funding processes are geared to projects. Funders like time-limited, outcome-focused projects and rely on traditional proxies of proposals and reports as indicators of research work. To respond to funder guidelines, researchers are often transformed from community participants into research managers. However, it is possible to be accountable to community and run a fiscally responsible project! Strategies like negotiating time concessions or exploring non-traditional funding sources, such as credit unions or those interested in community-based work, can be explored. And, once money is obtained, sharing is an important principle for anti-oppressive research. Researchers taking the lion's share of the money out of the community as salaries or contracts are acting in ways that are counterproductive to community-building processes and social justice values.

Our own epistemology: Doing research differently requires a different acceptance of what counts as knowledge. While we all "know" there are different types of knowledges, most of us have been schooled in Western knowledge paradigms, and when it comes right down to it, most of us do not truly accept non-Western knowledges as equal. Most of us are still caught in valuing objectivity over subjectivity. We tend to believe that scientific, experimental knowledge is more valid than experiential knowledge. We tend to be biased toward large sample sizes versus seeing the value of learning from one person's "outlier" experience. We get caught up in looking for one truth instead of continually digging to find multiple perspectives. We still hope for one simple answer to questions when we have to learn to live with knowledge being ambiguous, temporal, and partial at best. These are tough challenges for us as researchers. But the good news is that we have the capacity within ourselves to meet these challenges.

## A FEW CONCLUDING THOUGHTS ... FOR NOW

By now you may be wondering: Is there a distinctive anti-oppressive method of inquiry? In a word, no. There is no fixed or bona fide set of methods or methodologies that is inherently anti-oppressive. Various emancipatory and critical social science research methodologies, such as feminist and Indigenous research and Freirian emancipatory or participatory research, are potential "allies" in doing anti-oppressive research. Many methodologies touch on some, but not necessarily all, of the tenets we are trying to foreground in anti-oppressive research. If anything, we are arguing that anti-oppressive research is not methodologically distinctive, but is epistemologically distinctive. We have come to believe that if we are to transform research into an anti-oppressive practice, then it is the epistemological underpinnings (e.g., relationships of the knower, the known, and those who want to know) that are key.

Part of the concept of agency that we have talked about is the ability to change one's self. This requires constant reflection and critique. In proposing the idea of anti-oppressive research, we do not want to create another dogma. In later life, Horkheimer critiqued the arrogance of any revolutionary tradition that can turn around and be itself oppressive (Ray, 2003, p. 164). Always being reflective about yourself and your work is not easy. Just when we think we're getting it right, we realize we're only getting it better. Becoming anti-oppressive is not a comfortable place to be. It means constantly reflecting on how one is being constructed and how one is constructing one's world. This chapter is part of our becoming. We hope it helps you in your research journey as well.

## NOTES

1. The authors acknowledge the University of Victoria social work students who have been with us on this journey toward anti-oppressive research, with special thanks to Christine and Andrea for their unique contributions.
2. For us, social justice work means transforming the way resources and relationships are produced and distributed so that all people can live dignified lives in a way that is ecologically sustainable. Our critical view of social justice includes economic justice, intergenerational equity, global justice, and eco-centric justice (Ife & Tesoriero, 2006). It takes direct aim at the sources of structural disadvantage, whether those are through institutions, like income security, or through human relations, such as racism. It is also about creating new ways of thinking and being, not only criticizing the status quo. Social justice means acting from the standpoint of those who have the least power and influence, and valuing the wisdom of the oppressed.
3. Empowerment is a problematic term because its meaning can be so variable. In this chapter, when "empowerment" appears in quotations, it is being contested as a term that often implies a feeling without real power, upward mobility, or individual self-confidence, or an illusion of real power. When we as authors truly speak of empowerment, we are using the term as Lather (1991) does, "drawing on Gramsci's (1971) ideas of counter-hegemony ... empowerment to mean analyzing ideas about the causes of powerlessness, recognizing systemic oppressive forces, and acting both individually and collectively to change the conditions of our lives" (pp. 3–4).
4. Cultivating co-researchers is one way that many who try to be more anti-oppressive in their research engage the tenets of anti-oppressive work. As

knowledge is socially constructed, and what is created through coming together as knowers is more than what each knew before, co-researching can become a way of producing knowledge and producing knowers. Yet such an approach is not without its own power issues. Too often, we have seen projects where insiders are co-researchers but are only given a token position within the research design. It posits the question: To what extent can research truly be anti-oppressive unless the people experiencing the issue under study *are* the researchers and are in control of the research decisions?

# REFERENCES

Amsden, J., & VanWynsberghe, R. (2005). Community mapping as a research tool with youth. *Action Research*, *3*, 357–381.

AUCC. (2001). *The commercialization of university research*. Ottawa, ON: Association of Universities and Colleges of Canada.

Campbell, M., & Ng, R. (1988). Program evaluation and the standpoint of women. *Canadian Review of Social Policy*, *22*, 41–50.

Castleden, H., Garvin, T., & Huu-ay-aht First Nation. (2008). Modifying photovoice for community-based participatory Indigenous research. *Social Science & Medicine*, *66*(6), 1393–1405.

Ceglowski, D. (2000). Research as relationship. *Qualitative Inquiry*, *6*(1), 88–103.

David, P. A., & Foray, D. (2002). An introduction to the economy of the knowledge society. *International Social Science Journal*, (171), 9–23.

Hall, B. (2011). Towards a knowledge cemocracy movement: Contemporary trends in community-university research partnerships. *Rhizome freirean*, *9*.

Huisman, K. (2008). "Does this mean you're not going to come visit me anymore?": An inquiry into an ethics of reciprocity and positionality in feminist ethnographic research. *Sociological Inquiry*, *78*(3), 372–396.

Ife, J., & Tesoriero, F. (2006). *Community development: Community-based alternatives in an age of globalisation*. Toronto, ON: Pearson Education Canada.

Kirby, S. L., & McKenna, K. (1989). *Experience research social change: Methods from the margins*. Toronto, ON: Garamond Press.

Lather, P. (1991). *Getting smart: Feminist research and pedagogy with/in the postmodern*. New York, ON: Routledge.

Marcotte, G. (1995). *"Metis c'est may nation. 'Your own people', Comme on dit": Life histories from Eva, Evelyn, Priscilla, and Jennifer Richard*. Paper prepared for the Royal Commission on Aboriginal Peoples.

Martin, D. G. (2007). Bureacratizing ethics: Institutional review boards and participatory research. *ACME: An International E-Journal for Critical Geographies*, 6(3), 319–328.

McDonald, K. (2003). Alain Touraine. In A. Elliott & L. Ray (Eds.), *Key contemporary social theorists* (pp. 246–251). Oxford, UK: Blackwell Publishing.

McLaughlin, K. (2005). From ridicule to institutionalization: Anti-oppression, the state and social work. *Critical Social Policy*, 25(3), 283–305.

Ray, L. (2003). Max Horkheimer. In A. Elliott & L. Ray (Eds.), *Key contemporary social theorists* (pp. 162–168). Oxford, UK: Blackwell Publishing.

Secret, M., Jordan, A., & Ford, J. (1999). Empowerment evaluation as a social work strategy. *Health & Social Work*, 24(2), 120–127.

Tuhiwai Smith, L. (2012). *Decolonizing methodologies: Research and Indigenous peoples* (2nd ed.). London, UK: Zed Books.

Wang, C. & Burris, M. (1997). Photovoice: Concept, methodology, and use for participatory needs assessment. *Health Education and Behavior* 24(3), 369-387.

# Chapter Two

# Emerging from the Margins: Indigenous Methodologies

## Margaret Kovach

## INTRODUCTION

For this second edition of *Research as Resistance: Revisiting Critical, Indigenous, and Anti-Oppressive Approaches*, the editors invited an updated chapter. I willingly accepted, given that since its first publication in 2005, Indigenous methodologies have increasingly become an option alongside myriad qualitative approaches seeking to give voice to marginalized peoples. Thus, I was eager to review the chapter, with particular attention toward reflecting upon developments within Indigenous methodologies in the last several years.

In addition, I, too, had seen shifts in my academic life. When I wrote the 2005 chapter I was a PhD graduate student studying at the University of Victoria. I have since completed my PhD, written a book on Indigenous methodologies resulting from my doctoral research, and accepted an academic position in my home province of Saskatchewan (at the University of Saskatchewan), and I was granted tenure in 2012. I moved from being on the margins of academia to finding myself as part of the firm. While there are limitations bound with concessions that accompany work within as large a bureaucratic institution as the academe, there remain freedoms and possibilities. Of the latter, I have been exceptionally fortunate to write, publish, and (most rewarding) teach to the passion that propelled my doctoral work. Over the last six years I have had opportunity to first develop and then instruct a yearly elective research course on Indigenous methodologies. Initially, the course began with a small enrolment of Indigenous graduate students, but it has since increased threefold, with students from a range of heritages and disciplines attending. That graduate students have such an option suggests that the academy is becoming increasingly open to Indigenous research processes. This change is indeed hopeful.

It is from the above vantage point that I revisit the 2005 chapter, "Emerging from the Margins: Indigenous Methodologies." This chapter integrates recent literature not available in 2005, along with minor revisions and editing. It is less a revision than an update, given that many of my core understandings about Indigenous methodologies shared in 2005 remain consistent. However, there are aspects that are useful to consider anew. In dialoguing with graduate students, colleagues, and community about Indigenous methodologies, it is these aspects of Indigenous methodologies that often arise. Thus, in a closing section of the chapter I have included an "if you asked me now" reflective commentary. It has been interesting to revisit this chapter, as I find it impossible to rediscover the blessed angst of doctoral study, which I was amid when first writing this piece, in an authentic manner, other than to say it was a place I once visited.

*And so to begin, a return to a former time and a memory resurfaces....
Venturing into a graduate course, I was anxious because I was presenting on my graduate research.[1] I was the second presenter of the day, with the instructor leading with a seminar on Indigenous knowledge. Given the topic, I would normally prepare for a range of reactions, but on this day I did not, as I was preoccupied with my own presentation. The seminar and the atmosphere it provoked were not uncommon. A tension entered the room, with the usual remarks prefaced with qualifying apologies (e.g., "I am sorry, but I think Natives...") from some students, while other students were quietly uneasy, with eyes downcast, and still others were attempting bridging comments so as to lessen the anxiety in the room. I was silently listening to the conversation unfold and sensed that people were wondering about my reaction. Would she be upset? In similar instances I have offered comments, arguably emotionally charged, leading to a range of responses with my words having impact because I, an Indigenous woman, uttered them. However, on this day I was less occupied with such questions and was mostly saving my energy for my presentation. All I could think was, "Oh*

*great, the class is already stressing about Indigenous issues and I have to talk about Indigenous research—wonderful timing."*

*I did not speak during the class discussion, but was likely grimacing. The seminar was winding down and I was presenting in five minutes. I slipped out of the classroom for a quick restroom break. As I re-entered the room, I noticed a hush among the students, and the instructor was talking. I slid quietly into my chair, feeling eyes on me. I noticed a familiar gnawing sensation in the pit of my stomach that this break had been interpreted as a political act—a walking out, as it were. I was up next and did not have time to process what had happened. Rather, I picked up my overheads, walked to the front of the room, and pushed forward with my seminar.*

*The goal was to introduce my research and its purpose. Excited about generating dialogue on my research, I planned to use liberatory language stressing the social justice possibilities for Indigenous peoples inherent in this project. I did not. I rushed quickly through the topic of my research question, then pulled out my methodology overheads. I moved quickly through three common methodological paradigms (critical, interpretative, and positivist), identified each, and explained that I was drawing from both critical and interpretative. I did not even mention Indigenous methodologies or conflicts arising from using mainstream methodologies in Indigenous research. Using the vernacular of academic research language, I skirted around social change, dodged upsetting the status quo, and was as apolitical as possible. People started to relax. As I spoke the language of theory, of definitional criteria, of epistemologies fitting with methodology, the tension dissipated and the classroom space became considerably less edgy. At this point some may wonder: Didn't the methodology discussion delve into the political? It could have, but I made a choice to use language to deflect rather than engage. My only defence is that I didn't have the energy to go to contentious places, and I offer this writing as a make-up assignment.*

There were two significant teachings that arose from this experience. What I learned, through the acuteness of personal choice and action, is that critical research can be emancipatory—*or not*—depending on where you want to take it (either way, it's political). What was the second insight? For many Indigenous people in contemporary academic classrooms in this country, going to the restroom can be interpreted as taking a stance. By merely walking through (or out of) mainstream doors, we tend to make spaces alive with a politicality that creates both tension and possibility. Indigenous researchers make research political simply by being who we are.

Value-neutral research methodologies are not likely to be a part of the Indigenous researcher's experience, or any researcher's, for that matter, and as such there is a natural allegiance with emancipatory research approaches. In recognizing this relationship, there needs to be equal recognition that emancipatory methodologies have largely been defined within an epistemological framework of Whiteness, arising predominately from western European culture and thought. This includes allied White emancipatory scholarship active on behalf of decolonizing efforts. As a result, Western-defined methodologies, such as community-based designs, that can effectively integrate anti-colonial theory to deconstruct the Indigenous-settler power dynamic have, at times, been taken up as Indigenous approaches to research. Certainly emancipatory theories and approaches are critical and necessary as Indigenous people continue to face racism born of colonial relations; however, such approaches are Western, not Indigenous.

As Indigenous methodologies have emerged within the mainstream research discourse, awareness of its epistemological distinctiveness, alongside what this means for research design and interpretation, has been challenging for both friend and foe. It is with an awareness of the assimilating force of dominant discourse that exists within sites of formal education that this chapter speaks to the nature and promise of Indigenous methodologies. This chapter is written knowing that a challenge for Indigenous methodologies is to stay true to their theoretical roots of what counts as emancipatory. Given the intersection between emancipatory and Indigenous methodologies, it is useful to consider the research landscape that has led to the emergence of Indigenous methodologies within post-secondary knowledge production sites.

## EMANCIPATORY METHODOLOGIES

Humphries, Mertens, and Truman (2000) identify transformative research approaches arising from epistemologies in feminism, critical hermeneutics, postmodernism, and critical theory. The attention to power dynamics suggests that such approaches are anti-oppressive, given Potts and Brown's (2005) assertion that "anti-oppressive research involves making explicit the political practices of creating knowledge" (p. 255). The epistemological assumptions of these varied methodologies contend that those who live their life in the margins of society experience silencing and injustice.

Anti-oppressive methodologies offer a counter-approach to positivist approaches, which consistently reproduce the epistemic privilege of the scientific paradigm. It is no small task, given that positivism has a lengthy history beginning in the Enlightenment era, a period marked by the celebration of science and a perception that through scientific reasoning *man* could understand, control, and shape the natural, social, political, and economic world. From this perspective emerged a belief in a universal truth applicable to all people and cultures (Dockery, 2000).

The emergence of modernity in the early 1920s, with its mantra of "knowledge for progress," entrenched the scientific model in both physical and social sciences. In North America, positivism became the answer for an individualist, industrial-centric society that was feverishly focused on production outcomes and the profit factor. Universities became think tanks for knowledge production culminating in research methodologies, extractive in nature, which served industry and business. Arguably, the scientific method was producing knowledge benefiting society; however, the difficulty was the privilege it was acquiring. As positivism took increasingly more space to serve an economy-driven approach to science, it inexorably dominated other forms of knowledge (Tandon, 1988, p. 9).

As positivism held primacy status, quantitative methodologies were equally advantaged. Qualitative research, as we are currently familiar with it, does not have a privileged history. Qualitative studies were introduced in North America in the early 1900s with the well-known ethnography *The Polish Peasant in Europe and America (1918-1920)*, conducted by Thomas and Znaniecki through the Chicago School of Sociology (Abott & Egloff, 2008). However, it was not until the post-war period that qualitative research began to gain traction. The 1960s saw qualitative methodologies fermenting and surfacing in North America. Glaser and Strauss's 1967 publication of *The Discovery of Grounded Theory* was formative in this period, falling within qualitative inquiry's second period or "modernist phase" of the 1950s to 1970s, as described by Denzin and Lincoln (2005, p. 17). Though qualitative research during this period was positivist in orientation, there was a reintroduction of story into research.

In the third phase of qualitative inquiry, during the 1970s to 1980s, there were an increasing number of researchers "exploring new methods" (Denzin & Lincoln, 2005; Hall, 1982, p. 14). This period saw an expansion of research paradigms from empiricism (positivism) to include interpretative and critical approaches (Kemmis, 2001; Denzin & Lincoln, 2005). Participatory research methodology was an example of a critical approach that sought voice and involvement in the research process from those being researched. Over this period, participatory research projects with Indigenous communities included the 1977 MacKenzie Valley pipeline inquiry; the Big Trout Lake project (1971–1982); the Dene Mapping Project that took place between 1972 and 1989; Abele's 1986 study of Northern Native employment programs; and so forth (Hoare, Levy, & Robinson, 1993; Jackson & McKay, 1982).

Amid this shifting landscape, the 1990s can be described as the period in which Indigenous knowledge systems emerged as part of the qualitative research discourse. As a result of decolonizing efforts exposing extractive research practices involving Indigenous peoples, there was a focus on the recognition and protection of Indigenous knowledges. In 1996, the Royal Commission on Aboriginal Peoples (RCAP) identified guidelines for research undertaken by the commission. Outlined in Appendix E of the commission's report were guidelines for ethical considerations in research involving Aboriginal knowledges, the significance of collaborative research, access to research results, and community benefit (1996). It is important to note that since RCAP, ethics involving research with Aboriginal peoples has seen progress. For example, within Canada, the Canadian Institutes of Health Research, the Natural Sciences and Engineering Research Council of Canada, and the Social Sciences and Humanities Research Council of Canada (2010), known as the Tri-Council, have adopted ethical guidelines for research involving Aboriginal peoples. This is outlined in chapter 9 of *Ethical Conduct for Research Involving Humans*. However, prior to this movement, RCAP, specifically Appendix E, offered foundational guidelines for ethical protocols involving research with Aboriginal peoples. During the 1990s, there came a series of scholarly publications by Indigenous peoples relating specifically to knowledge creation and research. In 1998, Maori scholar Russell Bishop published a thought-provoking article on knowledge creation from a Maori perspective entitled "Freeing Ourselves from Neo-colonial Domination in Research: A Maori Approach to Creating Knowledge." In 1999, Linda Tuhiwai Smith's book *Decolonizing Methodologies: Research and Indigenous Peoples*, now in its second edition, was released. In that same year, Lester-Irabinna Rigney (1999) published his article on Indigenist research methodology. Such work was influential in its discourse on the need to "take back" research from an anti-colonial perspective, and all contributed to breakthrough discourse on the significance of Indigenous knowledge systems in knowledge production within contemporary research practice.

*A memory emerges as I reflect upon the above.... In returning to university in 2003 to complete my PhD coursework, I knew I needed a "brush-up" research course to sharpen my skills and to reorient myself to new thinking in research. When I was a master's student, several years previous, the heated debate centred on qualitative versus quantitative methodological approaches. Feminism and participatory research were the new methodologies from the margins within the academy. They broadened epistemological choices, allowing for experience and action to enter into research discourse and practice. At that time, research objectivity versus subjectivity was a hot debate, and the radical research approaches were branded as "soft," with these new methods raising eyebrows about scientific rigour and validity. There were few qualitative research books on the market, and mostly one had to scan the recent left-of-centre journals to seek out this research approach.*

*When I went back to school, the first place I went to was the campus bookstore. As I approached the general research section, I was truly in awe of what I saw before me. There were at least 30 books on the shelf relating to qualitative research approaches. Mixed in with the selection was Linda Tuhiwai Smith's book* Decolonizing Methodologies. *Seeing the words Decolonizing Methodologies on a book jacket was a rush, an external validation that Indigenous research counted. I swiftly put the book into my shopping cart, thinking smugly, "This is excellent—there's going to be a choice of books with chapters on Indigenous methodologies." Eagerly, I started to browse through the selection, searching the tables of contents of various books for the Indigenous methodologies chapter I knew must be there. After a thorough scan, I left the bookstore with one book and considerably less enthusiasm. Though I knew I was guilty of high expectations, I really wanted to see my experience, as an Indigenous researcher, reflected in that row of glossy books. I left the bookstore and went to the library, where my spirit was slightly lifted. Indigenous research publications may have been a rare find on general reference shelves in campus bookstores, but publications on Indigenous knowledge systems were increasingly evident (Deloria, 1991; Wilson, 2001; Battiste, 2002).*

When I first wrote this chapter, and as I write now, I am acutely aware of the power politics of knowledge and the research practices that produce it. Indigenous scholars are increasingly speaking of the centrality of Indigenous cultural paradigms in decolonizing work (Wilson, 2008; Innes, 2009; Debassige, 2010). This body of work suggests that to serve Indigenous knowledge systems there must be ethical, epistemological, and methodological inclusion of Indigenous voice, understandings, and practices. Further, there is a need for Indigenous presence within the academy that places value upon Indigenous knowledges, to provide a stewardship role for those knowledges. Stewardship assumes self-determining control, without which assimilative practices thrive. As Hoare, Levy, and Robinson (1993) state, "If knowledge is fundamental to understanding, interpreting and establishing values within a society, then control over its production becomes an integral component of cultural survival" (p. 46). Culture and knowledge in any social grouping are intrinsically linked, for it is these processes that are implicated in a group conveying its identity. To lose control of knowledge (and knowledge production efforts as research) is akin to having another tell one's own story. For too long, Indigenous peoples have had outsider research tell their story.

As a result, the Indigenous community has made an effort to take control of research and move toward the recognition of Indigenous knowledge systems within the research process itself. Since the 1990s there has been an increasing body of work that moves from creating space for Indigenous research approaches to focusing on Indigenous methodologies themselves (Steinhauer, 2002; Thomas, 2005; Wilson, 2008; Hart, 2009; Kovach, 2009; Absolon, 2011; Wilson & Restoule, 2010).

While there has been progress, one could argue that there has also been a relapse toward conservatism within post-secondary institutions today, as they increasingly mirror a corporate model (Polster, 2005; Woodhouse, 2009). Denzin and Lincoln (2005) argue that we are currently in a precarious eighth stage of qualitative inquiry as critical researchers confront a re-emergence of positivism and "the evidence-based social movement" (p. 21). As conservatism is recharging itself in the academy, it is an arduous (though not unfamiliar) struggle for intellectuals engaged in critical discourse to procure a slice of the epistemic pie. Carving space for emancipatory research in the academy, particularly for "new" methodologies like Indigenous research, remains taxing, as questioning established views about what counts as meaning, knowledge, and truth often provokes backlash.

For Indigenous methodologies, this has always meant going against a strong current, given that it is an approach that does "talk back" to oppressive mentalities and structures within existing Western knowledge production systems. Further, and perhaps more challenging, Indigenous methodologies introduce a knowledge system distinctive from Western thought in a formal educational system that continues to view Indigenous peoples as less than. In finding a place in academic research, emancipatory and Indigenous approaches require a special vigilance within the politicality of the academic environment. This is of particular relevance for Indigenous methodologies coming into their own in the academy.

## INDIGENOUS METHODOLOGIES

Indigenous conceptual framing has emerged as a research process with its own methodology (Battiste, Bell, & Findlay, 2002). It encompasses Indigenous ways of knowing (i.e., Indigenous epistemology); it incorporates what Tuhiwai Smith (1999) refers to as "researching back," indicating a decolonization objective (p. 7); it has an ethical basis that is respectful of the natural world; and finally, it values relational techniques in data collection.

Given the significance of conceptual framing vocabulary in research, it is helpful to reflect upon such language within the context of Indigenous methodologies. The language that we use shapes the way we think. Postmodern deconstructivists have illuminated the link between the dominant society's use of language to the silencing of voices belonging to those who are marginally located. It is the tool by which a metanarrative of "truth" and "normalcy" is perpetually reproduced. In centres of knowledge production like universities, the language of research becomes powerful and pervasive. Through stretching the parameters of what counts as legitimate research, anti-oppressive methodologies have either absorbed some of the traditional research vernacular or experienced the academy's cold shoulder. It is no surprise that in reviewing textbooks of research from the margins, readers are still likely to find the standard vocabulary (epistemology, methodology, methods, qualitative, quantitative, and so on). For Indigenous research, there are two difficulties here. One difficulty arises from Indigenizing a Western concept, such as research, that is rigid with definitional categories, evaluative criteria, outcomes, and goals. The second relates to language and epistemology—how language influences how we think, feel, and act.

The first issue is not new to research. Does putting the word *Indigenous* in front of a non-Indigenous concept like research, child welfare, or education make a difference? Indigenizing a Western model of research without critical reflection can result in the individualistic approach of a researcher determining the question, methodology, and methods and asking an Indigenous person to act as the "front" or "face" of the research. Tuhiwai Smith shares her experience of this type of research: "I was a researcher in those types of projects and that is why I don't want to go back to those types of projects ever again because, to put it crudely, you get set up as an Indigenous researcher" (Battiste, Bell, & Findlay, 2002, p. 183). Yet, many Indigenous researchers may still be approached for involvement in such projects. It is their task then to use their own personal and cultural knowledge to assess this type of "Indigenous research" and ask critical, difficult questions. Is the research goal manipulative or helpful for my community? Is the methodology respectful to culture and community? Do the methods meet cultural protocols? What are the research's collectivist ethical considerations? Who is driving the research and what is the purpose? The usual yes-or-no binaries are not helpful here. For those who are non-Indigenous, the questions are perhaps more challenging: "Am I creating space *or* taking space?"

An equally important language issue relates to epistemology itself. Manu Aluli Meyer (2001) identifies epistemology as "the philosophy of knowledge," with language as the means for interpreting and communicating ideas. She underscores the difficulty of using a language not one's own to construct knowledge. In relating her own experience with the vernacular of knowledge-making, she says, "I understand the tenuous line I walk between 10-dollar words and my Hawaiian people who say in exasperation 'Don't throw that word at us'" (p. 101). Further, the stronghold of language, writing, and worldview in generating "truth" creates difficulties for Indigenous people, whose traditional philosophies are held deep within constructs that are neither written, nor consistent with the patterns of dominant language. Most Indigenous languages are verb-based and tell of the world in motion, interacting with humans and nature (Cajete, 1999). This is in contrast to the noun-based nature of the English language, which accentuates an outcome orientation to the world. Language is a central system for how cultures code, create, and transmit meaning. Cultural values remain alive and are reflective of a worldview found in their native language. Values that honour relationships are important for cultures that value the journey as much as the destination.

Written language adds additional complexity in transmitting Indigenous ways of knowing, given that most Indigenous cultures are oral. Even storytelling (Thomas, 2005), an important method used in Indigenous research, loses a level of meaning in the translation into written script. Russell Means (1989) puts the dilemma squarely on the table: "I detest writing. The process itself epitomizes the European concept of 'legitimate' thinking; what is written has an importance that is denied the spoken" (p. 19). Indigenous epistemology is fluid, nonlinear, and relational. Knowledge is transmitted through stories that shape-shift in relation to the wisdom of the storyteller at the time of the telling. The additional task of delivering knowledge in 12-point-font, Cerlox-bound written research reports is a little difficult, not least because of the frequent pauses from literature reviews, coding, and analysis to ask, "What am I thinking and feeling? What exactly am I doing? Am I helping?" For the Indigenous researcher, incorporating an Indigenous worldview into a non-Indigenous language, with all that implies, is complex. It is a troublesome task of crisscrossing cultural epistemologies. We must pay attention to our discomfort; it may be an indication that we experiencing the tension that accompanies going against the grain. Within writing, for example, I am conscious of the pressure to conform to academic prose but recognize that the discomfort of masking a more authentic voice reveals a concession of the academic life.

## ASPECTS OF INDIGENOUS METHODOLOGIES

While there are numerous aspects of Indigenous methodologies, I have found the following four to hold a central focus:

- Holistic Indigenous knowledge systems are a legitimate way of knowing.
- Receptivity and relationship between researcher and participants is (or ought to be) a natural part of the research methodology.
- Collectivity, as a way of knowing, assumes reciprocity to the community.
- Indigenous methods, including story, are a legitimate way of sharing knowledge.

The following offers a brief commentary on these four aspects: Indigenous knowledge foundation, the relational, the collective, and the methods.

**Indigenous knowledge foundations.** At the core of Indigenous methodologies lie Indigenous knowledge foundations and cosmology. An Indigenous cosmology values inclusivity of ways of knowing. It is a relational Indigenous way of knowing that encompasses the spirit of collectivity, reciprocity, and respect (Wilson, 2008; Hart, 2009). Indigenous ways of knowing are organic, with emphasis on reciprocity and humour. These knowledge systems are born of the land and locality of the tribal group, and are thus particular to place (Battiste & Henderson, 2000). Shared characteristics of Indigenous knowledge systems include a way of knowing that is fluid (Little Bear, 2000; Hart, 2009) and experiential. They emerge from traditional languages emphasizing verbs, not nouns (Cajete, 1999). Valuing inclusivity, they are systems that hold valid insights arising from dreams and vision quests (Castellano, 2000; Atleo, 2004). In teaching and knowledge, Indigenous knowledge systems recognize stillness and quietness (Sandford, Williams, Hopper, & McCregor, 2012). Derived from oral teachings passed from one generation to the next through the relationality of storytelling (Thomas, 2005; Archibald, 2008), each story is alive with the nuances and wisdom of the storyteller (King, 2003). Indigenous knowledge systems are interpreted through personal story and self-location (Absolon & Willett, 2005). These ways of knowing are both cerebral and heartfelt. As the elders say, "If you have important things to say, speak from the heart." The practices of Indigenous knowledge are as purposeful in the practicalities of the need to feed and clothe as they are in transmitting values. As Kirkness and Barnhardt (1991) succinctly state, Indigenous knowledges and methods are about respect, relevance, reciprocity, and responsibility.

**The relational.** The philosophical premise of take what you need (and only what you need), give back, and offer thanks suggests a deep respect for other living beings and is integral to Indigenous methodologies. A relationship-based model for research with Indigenous communities is critical on several levels. Philosophically, it honours the cultural value of relationship, it emphasizes people's ability to shape and change their own destiny, and it is respectful. In a relationship-based model, research is a sincere, authentic investment in the community. This requires the ability to take time to visit with people from the community (whether or not they are research participants); the ability to be humble about the goals; and the ability to have conversations at the start about who owns the research, its use, and its purpose (particularly if it is academic research). While the emphasis on relationship can frustrate timelines and well-charted research designs, the journey is truly amazing. Eber Hampton's (1995) words hold wisdom: "I had found that the cut-and-dried, rigid, cold, hard, precise facts are dead. What is alive is messy, and growing, and flexible, and soft, and warm, and often fuzzy" (p. 49). Research, like life, is about relationships.

**The collective.** Woven with the philosophical premise of relationship is the collective underpinning of Indigenous research. The collective nature of Indigenous culture is evident in traditional economic, political, and cultural systems. It is almost instinctive—Indigenous people know that you take care of your sister or brother (the big family, not just the nuclear one), and that's just the way it is. Inherent in this understanding of life is reciprocity and account-ability to each other, the community, clans, and nations. It does not serve anonymity or rugged individualism well. It is a way of life that creates a sense of belonging, place, and home. Western research tends to be individualistic, with the principal researcher defining the question, determining the participants, designing the methodologies, documenting the findings, and publishing the report. In the university context, pre-tenure faculty researchers are put in the situation of "publish or perish," and graduate students who wish to pursue an academic appointment are often encouraged to show evidence of publication ability. Indigenous researchers are equally susceptible to this system, but we can only get so far before we see a face—our elder cleaning fish, our sister living on the edge in East Vancouver, our brother hunting elk for the feast, our little ones in foster care—and hear a voice whispering, "Are you helping us?" This is where Indigenous methodology must meet the criteria of collective responsibil-ity and accountability. In the protocols surrounding Indigenous research, this is a central theme. And as Indigenous research enters the academy, this principle needs to stay up close and personal.

**The methods.** Research methods have expanded to fit a more expansive range of methodological choices. My sense is that Indigenous research will further broaden the range of methods in research. While traditional approaches, such as surveys, in-depth interviews, and focus groups, are integral to method choices, other options that capture alternate ways of knowing will emerge as legitimate. For example, dreams have long been a source of knowledge for Indigenous cultures. Solitude with nature and the gift of insight we receive from those experiences are another source of knowledge. Methods, such as dream journalling, that capture subjective data are destined to be a part of the discourse on Indigenous research methods. It will be an exciting new dialogue about what counts as legitimate knowledge and how that knowledge is garnered. Currently, such methods are still considered by many mainstream researchers to be in the realm of soft philosophy and soulful words; yet given time ...

Inherent in Indigenous research is a plethora of conflicts. It is a maze of ethical issues compounded by the real need to sleep at night because there is so much work to do. The issues arising from a relational research approach rooted in a collectivist epistemology bring into light distinct dilemmas for researchers. A fundamental question about epistemology is, "How much do we share?" We need to ask how much knowledge we should share for the common good, and what knowledge needs to be kept sacred. Questions about purpose, benefit, and the protection of research subjects may arise across a range of methodologies; however, it is the answers to these questions and the standards around community accountability in a collectivist, relational research model that will be different. Protocols for research with Indigenous communities in the last 10 years are defining the standards. For the past 20 years, non-Indigenous research approaches, like participatory research, have been debating what it means to be authentically participatory, and the dialogue continues. Indigenous methodology is an argument for a different way of research based on intellectual, philosophical, ideological, and cultural premises. It is likely that our culture will be our greatest resource in clearing a path.

## "IF YOU ASKED ME NOW"

In the past several years, Indigenous methodologies are gaining a presence in research methodology discourse and instruction and as a viable methodology in research projects. I have been fortunate to talk with a range of individuals about various aspects of Indigenous methodologies. In the final section of this chapter, I offer responses to several questions that I have had opportunity to reflect upon since first writing this chapter in 2005.

### What is one of the most critical aspects of Indigenous methodologies?

In the earlier publication of this chapter, I wrote, "The challenge for Indigenous research will be to stay true to its own respective theoretical roots of what counts as emancipatory as it ventures into mainstream academia." This point is critical in understanding Indigenous methodologies. In the above sentence I used the term *theoretical roots*. Much like *epistemology*, *paradigm*, or *worldview*, it is a term within Indigenous research discourse that references Indigenous philosophical foundations. Indigenous knowledge systems are the heartbeat of Indigenous methodologies. If only one understanding is to be garnered about Indigenous methodologies, it must be this. It is not possible to engage in Indigenous methodologies without a foundational understanding of Indigenous knowledge systems. Indigenous knowledges are not Western knowledges; Indigenous methodologies are not built upon Western thought. A working understanding of Indigenous knowledges moves beyond identity alone. Certainly, this statement raises the question of whether Indigenous identity itself is a prerequisite for taking up Indigenous methodologies. The following question is one I have been often asked, and I offer a response to the above statement.

### Who can apply an Indigenous methodological approach in their research?

As a research instructor, my initial response is to first determine whether an Indigenous methodology is the desired approach in responding to the research question. This is the initial, arguably easy first response. The subsequent conversation then moves from matters of research approach to identity. Here there are no definitive answers, and there are many factors that move swiftly into the realm of the personal. Much depends upon one's preparedness to go this route and the individual's ability to be knowledgeable about, conversant in, and comfortable with speaking to Indigenous knowledge systems and sharing their personal relationship to Indigenous thought. It is pertinent to have knowledge of the politicality surrounding Indigenous knowledge systems, given the history of assimilation. In applying Indigenous methodologies, researchers are putting forth an identity standpoint (whether they desire this or not) and there is an expectation for them to engage in anti-colonial work. The long and short of it is that Indigenous methodologies, like any other, ought to be a choice; however, there must be a deep, abiding respect for Indigenous knowledge systems and Indigenous experience. This often requires unpacking one's understanding of what respect means in this context.

Often, the above conversation takes place with those newly exploring their Indigenous identity or those without Indigenous ancestry. For others, having Indigenous methodologies recognized in the academy has allowed for a growing number of researchers to assert Indigenous conceptual frameworks (Thompson, 2008; Lavallee, 2009; Wilson & Restoule, 2010; Hart, 2010; Debassige, 2010; Absolon, 2011). As Indigenous peoples are moving into research, the most protected realm of the Western academe, we are *not* forgetting where we have come from! We thank our ancestors, our families, and our kin for the strength of spirit that is our birthright.

## What resources are needed to support Indigenous methodologies?

As mentioned above, Kirkness and Barnhardt wrote an article entitled "First Nations and Higher Education: The Four Rs—Respect, Relevance, Reciprocity, Responsibility" in 1991. While this article was written over 20 years ago, the four *r*'s apply now, as they always did. However, it cannot be assumed that there is a mutual understanding of what these terms mean within the research relationship. We cannot assume that relationship itself is a respected entity. We need ethical regulatory processes that can monitor the research relationships. There currently exist a number of ethical guidelines and processes. As mentioned in Appendix E of RCAP (1996), outlining ethical process remains relevant. *Ownership, Control, Access, and Possession* (OCAP) (Schnarch, 2004) principles continue to apply. Canadian funding body guidelines on ethics involving Aboriginal peoples are currently in place, such as the Tri-Council (CIHR, NSERC, SSHRC) policy on research ethics, which now includes a chapter 9 that focuses on research involving Aboriginal peoples. At the community level, Inuit Tapiriit Kanatami put out an ethical statement in 2005; the Mi'kmaq Ethics Watch has been in place since 1999; and the Nuu chah nulth Tribal Council (2008) has an ethics protocol and committee for monitoring research with member communities. As Indigenous methodologies flourish, so too must operational structures that support them.

Human resources are necessary to support Indigenous methodologies. In particular, Indigenous faculty have a key role in ensuring that Indigenous knowledges and methodologies flourish. This requires attention and action. In their yearly *Almanac of Post-secondary Education*, the Canadian Association of University Teachers (2012) reported that, according to 2006 statistics, Aboriginal faculty comprised a mere 1 percent of faculty in Canada. Given that Indigenous identity is significant in the representation of Indigenous knowledges within the academy, these numbers are problematic. Without Indigenous knowledges, Indigenous methodologies and research will stall. There is a unity between Indigenous knowledges, methodologies, and pedagogies. For all to survive within post-secondary sites, there must be focused, funded, programmatic efforts. Without this, action is ad hoc and vulnerable to remaining on the margins as universities prioritize goals. In pursuing a more systemic and systematic effort, non-Indigenous allies have a responsibility and role in creating space for Indigenous methodologies.

## CONCLUDING THOUGHTS

That Indigenous communities have been researched to death is not news. Researchers extracting data from Indigenous communities and then publishing "their" research, with little benefit to the people studied, has been well documented in literature and has become a part of the oral history of many Indigenous groups. The purpose of this chapter was not to spend time reviewing the history of research and Indigenous people, but rather to ask, "Given our uneasy relationship with Western research, why do we endure?" Research is a tool that has become so entangled with haughty theories of what is "truth" that it's easy to forget that research is simply "about learning and so is a way of finding out things" (Hampton, 1995, p. 48).

The overrepresentation of Indigenous people in poverty, in prison, and involved in child welfare persists. Those of us who have pursued academic study and dipped our toes into the murky pool of research have obligations to use our skills to improve the socio-economic conditions of Indigenous people. In his article *Research, Redskins and Reality*, Vine Deloria (1991) suggests that apart from documenting narratives of traditional culture for future generations, "there is a great and pressing need for research on contemporary affairs and conditions of Indians" (p. 461). We need to take back control of research so that it is relevant and useful to us. By defining the research inquiry based on actual, not presumed, need and by designing a research process that is respectful and effective, we can use research as a practical tool. In the larger struggle for self-determination, we need to engage in what Tuhiwai Smith (2001) terms "researching back." Like "talking back," it implies resistance, recovery, and renewal (p. 7).

Academic settings will likely continue as centres for research activity, with all the difficulties of conducting Indigenous research in such places. The tensions range from epistemological predicaments resulting from parallel ways of knowing to methodologies that place different value on process and product. Additionally, tensions arise from divergent opinions on who should define, control, and own research, and the extent to which social justice is pursued as a goal of research. The greatest ally of Indigenous research will be those non-Indigenous methodologies from the margins that do not hide from but rather embrace the political nature of research. The sustained autonomy but continued alliance between such approaches is critical. Mutually beneficial and open, spirited dialogue that is critically reflective, and respectful, of each other's practice will be necessary for growth. As positivism holds fast to its turf inside the academy, the methodologies from the margins will need each other.

A narrow definition of Indigenous methodologies is antithetical, because, as Tuhiwai Smith suggests, it is as much a conceptual framing as a recipe (Battiste et al., 2002). Indigenous methodologies developed by Indigenous scholars, researchers, and community members have an authenticity, even if they are carried out within the parameters of research language. Though we may have to strategically use the '10-dollar words" of the academy, there will be breaks in the conversation for humility and respect to surface. As I reflect on all the history, negative associations, and complexities of carving out space for such an Indigenous approach, I continue to marvel at how we persist. I smile and think of a quote from Indigenous senior scholar Eber Hampton (1995): "A friend of mine said, 'I know a good word for Indians.' I said, 'What?' He said, 'Relentless.' We laughed, but there is a strong element of truth in this statement" (p. 48). Hmm, yes … relentless, strong, and still here.

## NOTE

1. This is a composite accounting of several personal experiences.

## REFERENCES

Abott, A., & Egloff, R. (2008). *The Polish peasant in Oberlin and Chicago: The intellectual trajectory of W. I. Thomas. American Sociologist, 39*(4), 217–258.

Absolon, K. (Minogiizhigokwe). (2011). *Kaandossiwin: How we come to know.* Black Point, NS: Fernwood Publishing.

Absolon, K., & Willett, C. (2005). Putting ourselves forward: Location in Aboriginal research. In L. Brown & S. Strega (Eds.), *Research as Resistance* (pp. 97–126). Toronto, ON: Canadian Scholars' Press.

Archibald, J. (2008). *Indigenous storywork: Educating the heart, mind, body, and spirit*. Vancouver, BC: University of British Columbia Press.

Atleo, E. R. (2004). *Tsawalk: A Nuu-chah-nulth worldview*. Vancouver: University of British Columbia Press.

Battiste, M. (2002). *Indigenous knowledge and pedagogy in First Nations education: A literature review with recommendations*. Ottawa, ON: Apamuwek Institute.

Battiste, M., Bell, L., & Findlay, L. M. (2002). An interview with Linda Tuhiwai Te Rina Smith. *Canadian Journal of Native Education, 20*(2), 169–186.

Battiste, M., & Henderson, Y. (2000). *Protecting Indigenous knowledge and heritage*. Saskatoon, SK: Purich Publishing.

Bishop, R. (1998). Freeing ourselves from neo-colonial domination in research: A Maori approach to creating knowledge. *International Journal of Qualitative Research, 11*(2), 199–219.

Canadian Association of University Teachers. (2012). *Almanac of post-secondary education, 2012–13*. Ottawa, ON. Retrieved from http://www.caut.ca/pages. asp?page=442

Canadian Institutes of Health Research, Natural Sciences and Engineering Council of Canada, Social Sciences, and Humanities Research Council of Canada. (2010). Research involving the First Nations, Inuit and Métis Peoples of Canada. In *Tri-Council policy statement: Ethical conduct for research involving humans*. Ottawa, ON: Canadian Institutes of Health Research, Natural Sciences and Engineering Council of Canada, Social Sciences and Humanities Research Council of Canada.

Cajete, G. (1999). *Native science: Natural laws of interdependence*. Santa Fe, NM: Clear Light Publishers.

Castellano, M. (2000). Updating Aboriginal traditions of knowledge. In G. Sefa Dei, B. Hall, & D. Rosenberg (Eds.), *Indigeneous knowledges in global contexts: Multiple readings of our world* (pp. 21 –36). Toronto, ON: University of Toronto Press.

Debassige, B. (2010). Re-conceptualizing Anshinaabe mino-bimaadiziwin (the good life) as research methodology: A spirit centred way in Anishinaabe research. *Canadian Journal of Native Education, 33*(1), 11–28.

Deloria, V. J. (1991). Commentary: Research, redskins, and reality. In R. A. Black & T. P. Wilson (Eds.), *The American Indian quarterly* (Vol. XV, pp. 457–467). Berkeley: The Native American Studies Program, University of California at Berkeley.

Denzin, N., & Lincoln, Y. S. (2005). Introduction: The discipline and practice of qualitative research. In N. Denzin & Y. S. Lincoln (Eds.), *The SAGE handbook of qualitative research* (3rd ed) (pp. 1–33). Thousand Oaks, CA: SAGE Publications.

Dockery, G. (2000). Participatory research: Whose roles, whose responsibilities? In C. Truman, D. Mertens, & B. Humphries (Eds.), *Research and inequality* (pp. 95 –110). London, UK: UCL Press.

Hall, B. (1982). Breaking the monopoly of knowledge: Research methods, participation and development. In B. Hall, A. Gillette, & R. Tandon (Eds.), *Participatory research network series* (pp. 13–26). Toronto, ON: International Council for Adult Education.

Glaser, B. & Strauss, A. (1967). *The discovery of grounded theory*. Hawthorne, NY: Aldine Publishing Company.

Hampton, E. (1995). Memory comes before knowledge: Research may improve if researchers remember their motives. Paper presented at the First Biannual Indigenous Scholars' Conference, University of Alberta, Edmonton, AB.

Hart, M. A. (2009). For Indigenous people, by Indigenous people, with Indigenous people: Toward an Indigenist research paradigm. In R. Sinclair, M. A. Hart, & G. Bruyere (Eds.), *Wicihitowin: Aboriginal social work in Canada* (pp. 153 –168). Winnipeg, MB: Fernwood Publishing.

Hart, M. A. (2010). Indigenous worldviews, knowledge, and research: The development of an Indigenous research paradigm. *Journal of Indigenous Voices in Social Work, 1*(1), 1–16.

Hoare, T., Levy, C., & Robinson, M. (1993). Participatory action research in Native communities: Cultural opportunities and legal implications. *Canadian Journal of Native Studies, XIII*(1), 43–68.

Humphries, B., Mertens, D., & Truman, C. (2000). Arguments for an "emancipatory" research paradigm. In C. Truman, D. Mertens, & B. Humphries (Eds.), *Research and inequality* (pp. 3–23). London, UK: UCL Press.

Innes, R. (2009). "Wait a second. Who are you anyways?" The insider/outsider debate and American Indian studies. *American Indian Quarterly, 33*(40), 440–461.

Inuit Tapiriit Kanatami. (2005). Checklist: Inuit involvement in research projects. *ITK Environment Bulletin, 3*, 25–26.

Jackson, T., & McKay, G. (1982). Sanitation and water supply in Big Trout Lake: Participatory research for democratic technical solutions. *The Canadian Journal of Native Studies, II*(1), 129–145.

Kemmis, S. (2001). Exploring the relevance of critical theory for action research: Emancipatory action research in the footsteps of Jurgen Habermas. In P. Reason & H. Bradbury (Eds.), *Handbook of action research: Participative inquiry and practice* (pp. 91–102). London, UK: SAGE Publications.

King, T. (2003). *The truth about stories: A Native narrative.* Toronto, ON: Dead Dog Cafe Productions & CBC Corporation.

Kirkness, V., & Barnhardt, R. (1991). First Nations and higher education: The fours Rs—respect, relevance, reciprocity, responsibility. *Journal of American Indian Education, 30*(3). Retrieved from http://jaie.asu.edu/v30/V30S3fir.htm

Kovach, M. (2009). *Indigenous methodologies: Characteristics, conversations, and contexts.* Toronto, ON: University of Toronto Press.

Lavallee, L. (2009). Practical application of an Indigenous research framework and two qualitative Indigenous research methods: Sharing circles and Ansishnaabe symbol-based reflection. *International Journal of Qualitative Methods, 8*(1), 21–40.

Little Bear, L. (2000). Jagged worldviews colliding. In M. Battiste (Ed.), *Reclaiming Indigenous voice and vision.* Vancouver: University of British Columbia Press.

Means, R. (1989). The same old song. In W. Churchill (Ed.), *Marxism and Native Americans* (pp. 19–33). Boston, MA: South End Press.

Meyer, A. M. (2001). Acultural assumptions of empiricism: A Native Hawaiian critique. *Canadian Journal of Native Education, 25*(2), 188–198.

Mi'kmaw Ethics Watch. (1999). *Mi'kmaw research principles and protocols: Conducting research with and/or among Mi'kmaq People.* Mi'kmaw Ethics Watch (Mi'kmaw Eskinuapimk), Mi'kmaq College Institute, Cape Breton University.

Nuu chah nulth Tribal Council Research Ethics Committee (2008). Protocols and principles for conducting research in a Nuu chah nulth context.

Potts, K., & Brown, L. (2005). Becoming an anti-oppressive researcher. In L. Brown & S. Strega (Eds.), *Research as resistance: Critical, Indigenous, and anti-oppressive approaches* (pp. 255–286). Toronto, ON: Canadian Scholars' Press.

Polster, C. (2005, August 25). Privatizing Canada's public universities. *Canadian Dimensions.* Retrieved from http://canadiandimension.com/articles/1909

Royal Commission on Aboriginal Peoples. (1996). *Ethical guidelines for research.* Ottawa, ON: Ministry of Supply and Services Canada.

Rigney, L. (1999). Internationalization of an Indigenous anticolonial cultural critique of research methodologies: A guide to Indigenist research methodology and its principles. *Wicazo Sa Review*, fall, 109–121.

Sandford, J., Williams, L., Hopper, T., & McGregor, C. (2012). Indigenous principles informing teacher education: What we have learned. *In Education, 18*(2). Retrieved from http://www.ineducation.ca/article/indigenous-principles-informing-teacher-education-what-we-have-learned

Schnarch, B. (2004). Ownership, control, access, and possession (OCAP) or self-determination applied to research: A critical analysis of contemporary First Nations research and some options for First Nations communities. *Journal of Aboriginal Health*, *1*(1): 80–94.

Steinhauer, E. (2002). Thoughts on an Indigenous research methodology. *Canadian Journal of Native Education*, *26*(2), 69–81.

Tandon, R. (1988). Social transformation and participatory research. *Convergence*, *XXI*(2/3).

Thomas, R. (2005). Honoring the oral traditions of my ancestors through storytelling. In L. Brown & S. Strega (Eds.), *Research as Resistance* (pp. 237 –254). Toronto, ON: Canadian Scholars' Press.

Thompson, J. (2008). Hede kehe' hotzi'kahidi': My journey to a Tahltan research paradigm. *Canadian Journal of Native Education*, *31*(1), 24–40.

Tuhiwai Smith, L. (1999). *Decolonizing methodologies—Research and Indigenous peoples*. London, UK: Zed Books.

Wilson, D., & Restoule, J. P. (2010). Tobacco ties: The relationship of the sacred to research. *Canadian Journal of Native Education*, *33*(1), 29–45.

Wilson, S. (2001). What is an Indigenous research methodology? *The Canadian Journal of Native Education*, *25*(2), 175–179.

Wilson, S. (2008). *Research is ceremony: Indigenous research methods*. Winnipeg, MB: Fernwood Publishing.

Woodhouse, H. (2009). *Selling out: Academic freedom and the corporate market*. Montreal, QC: McGill-Queen's University Press.

# Chapter Three

# Situating Anti-Oppressive Theories within Critical and Difference-Centred Perspectives

## Mehmoona Moosa-Mitha

## INTRODUCTION

Anti-oppressive theoretical approaches to research and practice consist of a set of theories that hold common epistemological and ontological assumptions. But they can differ significantly on the basis of their understanding and interpretation of particular experiences of marginalization and oppression that result from holding shifting and multiple social identity positions. In this chapter I provide a conceptual framework for understanding anti-oppressive theories through a discussion and comparison of their epistemological and ontological claims with those of other social theories. I argue that anti-oppressive theories are distinguished by embracing both difference-centred as well as critical claims of social justice as a result of their ontological and epistemological assumptions. This differs from other social theories, which are positioned on the axis of either difference-centredness or critical theoretical perspective, but not on both.

Implicit throughout my discussion is a critique of the view that anti-oppressive theories are discrete and separate from other social theories. Anti-oppressive theories represent sets of ideas that are the result of a deep and dialectical engagement with a spectrum of social theories that they engage in by contesting, influencing, and in turn being influenced by their ontological and epistemological assumptions. These conversations affect social theories, including anti-oppressive theories, through a process that is both creative and unpredictable, so that over time it is not always easy or possible to distinguish the manner in which various strands come together in any one theoretical framework.

## DIAGRAMMATIC MODEL OF ANTI-OPPRESSIVE THEORIES

Over the course of this chapter, I examine the epistemological and onto-logical claims of all social theories along two axes (please refer to Figure 3.1). The horizontal axis represents the normative- or difference-centred orientation of social theory, where theories that are invested in making sin-gular truth claims are located closer to the left or normative end of the spectrum. Those that centre their analysis in ways that challenge normative truth claims and embrace a diversity and multitude of truths are closer to the right end of the spectrum. The vertical axis represents the critical versus mainstream divide and locates those theories that engage in oppositional knowledge claims on the basis of material injustices as being at the north end of the axis. Theorists that seek to conform to normative assumptions of social reality through a tinkering with the dominant liberal ideology and the structures it produces, I locate in the south end of the axis.

While a diagrammatic depiction of this spectrum of theories is necessar-ily rigid, I argue for an understanding of anti-oppressive theories as those sets of concepts that challenge paradigmatic claims of any social theory through a centring of difference, as a politico-cultural reality, resulting in a shift in their epistemological and ontological assumptions. Individual theorists may therefore choose to position themselves differently within the broad parameters of their theoretical orientation as depicted in the diagram below. For example, individual liberal thinkers may choose to be more criti-cal in their analysis than others. The diagram is not meant to provide a rigid classification; rather, it explicates the wider parameters within which differ-ing theories make contesting claims.

The distinctive contribution of anti-oppressive theories becomes clear when situating various social theories along these two axes. The ontological and epistemological claims of other social theories are not as inclusive in their analysis, and when they are inclusive, they are not necessarily critical in their perspective. The ontological and epistemological claims of liberalism,

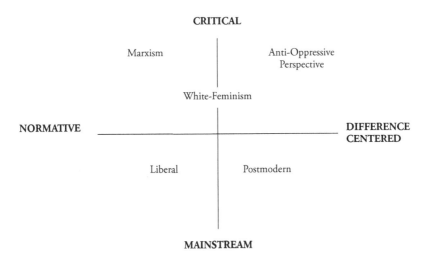

Figure 3.1: Spectrum of Anti-Oppressive Theories

for example, couched as they are within a universal and transcendental language, seek to maintain the status quo, thus positioning liberalism within a normative and mainstream orientation. White feminism, on the other hand, I position as edging more toward a difference-centerd position, although this perspective is limited because it privileges gender as a difference over any other, while taking a critical perspective. Marxism, which provides the foundation for critical thought, I position at the high end of the critical edge on the vertical axis but at the normative end on the horizontal line because of its Eurocentric orientation and its acknowledgement of only one kind of oppression, which has its basis in the class-based structures of society. I would argue that postmodern perspectives, although the theorists themselves contest any form of categorization, are theoretically situated as difference-centred, but not necessarily critical in their theorization. I situate anti-oppressive theories as being both critical and difference-centred.

## LIBERAL THEORY

### Liberal Visions of Social Justice
There are various interpretations of liberalism, from highly individualistic (neoliberal) interpretations at one end of the spectrum to communitarian

at the other. Yet all of these locate themselves in the 17th- and 18th-century Enlightenment theories of Hobbes and Locke (Taylor, 2004). In my discussion, I focus largely on Rawlsian analysis due to the influential position it holds for contemporary liberal thought. I also touch on the writings of communitarian liberals such as Kymlicka (2001, 2012) and Taylor (2004).

According to Rawls (1971), social reality is characterized by social relationships that are individualist and consensual by nature. In his writings, he envisages social justice as principled and redistributive at the level of rights and privileges (although he does allow for a modicum of redistribution of goods and services). Consistent with Hobbes and Locke, Rawls argues that socially just democratic societies are governed and measure themselves against the two principles of liberty and equality. Rawls suggests that when asked to rationally identify principles by which a socially just society should be governed, people would conclude that citizens should have the right to enjoy the greatest individual freedom possible to pursue social and economic advantage, while redistributing goods and services in such a way that the least equal among them is the least worse off. According to Rawls, in common with other liberal theorists, the twin principles of autonomy (freedom) and equality universally represent all people's envisioning of a socially just society.

Communitarian liberals such as Kymlicka (2001, 2012) and Taylor (2004) are less individualist in their vision of social justice. They argue for the freedom rights of individual members within communities and the communal rights of equality by being treated with the same respect as all other communities or groups in society. This vision of liberalism deviates from Rawls's view solely in terms of its conception of the basic unit that makes up societies. Rawls considers the individual to be the basic unit of society, and communitarians believe communities to be foundational to any society. Both define their vision of social justice as being rights-based, formal, and principled in nature.

## LIBERAL APPROACHES TO RESEARCH

### Ontological Claims: Universal, Individualist, Transcendental, and Singular
The ontological assumptions of liberal theories are defined in universalist terms on the basis of the fact that liberal theories claim that all members

of society value individual freedom and the pursuit of self-interest. Social reality is conceived not only in universal terms but also in individualist ones. This individualist bent in liberal ontology disregards alternative views such as feminism, that conceive reality in interdependent and interconnected terms (Dietz, 1987; Mookherjee, 2011). Feminists have contested the individualist interpretation of autonomy in male-stream liberal thought by pointing out that mothers do not necessarily wish to pursue individual freedom when looking after very young children (Young, 1997; Lister, 2003). Anti-racist struggles for social justice are also based on communal or group experiences of exclusion that challenge the individualist interpretation of mainstream notions of autonomy in liberal theory (Young, 1997). By universalizing a singular vision of social justice, liberal ontology ignores differing views of social reality that are grounded in the everyday experiences of oppression.

Feminist and anti-racist theorists also critique liberal interpretations of equality for their legalistic and formal character (Dietz, 1987; Williams, 1998; Lister, 2003). This formal view of equality is critiqued for not being substantive and for ignoring equality in terms of redistribution. Dominant narratives of equality also interpret sameness through an individualist focus that overlooks the collective nature of oppression such as racism.

The ontological assumptions of liberalism are principled in nature, seeking to identify the ethical standards by which social justice can be achieved. Principles are normative; they assume sameness of people's experiences of social (in)justice by making transcendental claims that overlook or ignore differences of social locations. For example, Rawls arrives at his articulation of social justice by creating a scenario whereby a few people are put behind a veil so that they are not aware of others' social identity locations and asked to envision social justice. The resulting principles of equality and autonomy that they arrive at transcend any social identity attributes (Stasiulus, 2002). Equality is translated as the respectful treatment of all people as possessing dignity, regardless of their race, gender, or other social identity indicators (Staeheli, 2013). Humanist language is used to evoke the view that underneath all our social differences, we are all the same due to our common humanity.

Communitarian liberals' ontological claims acknowledge difference that is communal. According to communitarians, citizens are not just rights-bearing individuals but also members of society and participants in the culture of that society (Kymlicka, 2001, 2012; Taylor, 2004). Thus, communitarian liberals are closer to a difference-centred axis, but, like other liberals, not critical on the redistributive plane. For example, communitarian liberals define racial differences in terms of culture and cultural pluralism. The racialized nature of economic stratification that is a feature of all liberal welfare states is ignored. Arguably, the ontological claims of communitarian liberals are more difference-centred than those of individualist-minded liberals. Yet its approach to difference is limited and uncritical of its structural implications (Roberts & Mahtani, 2010).

## Epistemological Claims: Positivist and "Objective"

A universal vision of social justice relies on rational and deductive analysis as a way of perceiving social reality and envisioning social justice. Knowledge is understood in positivist terms, which can be deduced by abstracting principles or laws assumed to govern social relationships. Transcendental and universal notions of social justice exist independently of one's subjective views. For example, Rawls (1971) arrives at his vision of social justice through a process of deductive thinking and by employing the language of "objective" reasoning on the "universal laws of nature."

Epistemological approaches to knowledge rooted in "objective" reasoning result in the construction of true-or-false dichotomies, through the treatment of "truth" as certain and knowable. Liberal epistemologies assume that the role of theories is to capture, uncover, and explain social truths (Battiste & Youngblood, 2000). In cases where liberal philosophical assumptions can be proven to be false in practice, the attempt is to adjust these so as to more accurately represent "universal truths." For example, Kymlicka (2001) critiques the role that liberal welfare states have played in relation to marginalized communities in the past. However, rather than rejecting the notion that states are neutral entities—a fundamental assumption of liberal theory—Kymlicka calls these past practices "mistakes" that need correcting. The epistemological and ontological assumptions of liberal theories therefore don't change; they are only fine-tuned.

Liberal epistemological assumptions are also normative in nature, perceiving knowledge as a tool to uncover universal laws or "norms" by which nature and social relationships are assumed to function. Knowledge is used to regulate and control nature through acts of categorization and generalization (Battiste & Youngblood, 2000). Such epistemological assumptions are consistent within an ontology that constructs its vision of social justice in universal terms. Anti-oppressive theorists have argued that normative epistemological assumptions valorize sameness in their efforts to uncover universal laws of predictability. This, they argue, is the reason why "difference" is considered a problem and a deviance in liberal theories (Yuval-Davis, 1999).

The role of the researcher using liberal theoretical frameworks to undertake research is that of an expert who regards the participant as an "object" of inquiry, a receptacle of knowledge whose significance is revealed only through the efforts of the researcher (Lather, 1991; Creswell, 2014). Social reality is knowable, and through the research effort the researcher is poised as a "knower." Mainstream approaches to research are dominated by liberal theoretical frameworks, which guide all aspects of research.

Certain research methodologies and methods fit well with liberal epistemological and ontological assumptions. Quantitative methodologies that assume knowledge to be objective and attainable through deductive processes are particularly suitable to liberal ontological and epistemological assumptions (Creswell, 2014). Similarly, qualitative methodologies that are positivist in nature find an easy alliance with liberal frameworks. Within a positivist tradition of inquiry, research findings are defined as valid on the basis of their applicability to a universal norm that is generalizable from a sample population. Research findings are also considered reliable if one can show that they were arrived at "objectively," are replicable, and use deductive thinking. The subjective inclinations of the researcher and the participants are treated as irrelevant at best and problematic at worst, and they have to be controlled so that their influence on the research process can be eradicated. In the same way, specific and context-bound findings are considered less valid unless they can be generalized on a more universal level.

## CRITICAL THEORY: MARXIST, STRUCTURALIST, AND BEYOND

Marxist, structuralist, and, later, "the Frankfurt School" mark the starting point for theories that root themselves in critical perspectives. Critical theory, which is an amalgamation of theories, has emancipatory aims, targeting both knowledge and the social structures that oppress people. Mullaly (2007) defines critical theories as having a twofold characteristic: they engage in critiques of traditional mainstream theories and are motivated by emancipatory claims. For critical theorists, it is knowledge as much as the market economy that forms an integral part of the structure of society, producing hierarchical power relations. Research endeavours reflect a political commitment that includes the conscious goal of producing emancipatory social change.

Critical theory, particularly in the works of Karl Marx, challenges the transcendentalist assumptions of liberal theorists by positing a materialist vision of social justice. This is achieved through an interrogation of the systems of production and the attendant processes by which material goods are produced in society. The mode or processes of production are analyzed as being historically situated, transforming themselves in different historical times as reflected in different types of societies (Corrigan & Leonard, 1978; Fook, 2002). Marxists argue that throughout history, the mode of production is based on the oppression of the working class for the benefit of the privileged class, who own the technologies of production, such as factories. Hence, class definitively marks social relationships in society and is characterized by the proletariat (the working class) and the bourgeois (the privileged class).

Marxists envision social justice as consisting of the overthrow of unequal class relationships in the name of collective experiences of equality and liberty (Mullaly, 2007). Not unlike liberals, critical theorists also define their vision of social justice in terms of liberty and equality. However, for Marxists, freedom exists through the presence of social conditions that enable people to live freely. Social justice aims are therefore achieved through the collective ownership of technology, or means of production (Corrigan & Leonard, 1978; Mullaly, 2007).

Marx also utilized a stronger sense of the concept of liberty. Liberty lies in the idea that human beings are by nature productive and that labour, or work, represents a form of self-fulfillment for people (Taylor, 2004). Labour itself is not seen as oppressive, but the social relationship within which it is situated is oppressive for the working class. Equality is similarly translated in materialist terms, by which it is defined as having all people's needs, however different, being met equally (Mullaly, 2007).

Structural theorists have applied and translated classical Marxist theory to post-industrial societies and have defined the dominant classes to include those who have access to and control of technology, media, political power, and other social structures that are integral to the functioning of society (Mullaly, 2007). Rather than focusing solely on economic production, Althusser (1969) extends Marx's analysis by paying close attention to all concrete material practices, which produce culture, ideology, and people's sense of subjectivity. Like the cultural materialist scholar Gramsci (1971), Althusser believed that not only the economic system but also the culture of society was political. Institutional and structural practices that define the culture of societies serve the interests of the dominant in society over others.

# MARXIST AND STRUCTURALIST APPROACHES TO RESEARCH

## Ontological Claims: Universal, Objectivist, Materialist, and Collectivist

The ontological vision of Marxism is contradictory in relation to the difference-centred or normative axis. Marxist and structuralist theories refute the atemporal claims of universalism present in liberal theories. Marxist and structuralist visions of social justice are historically situated and contextualized within specific eras as characterized by the particular system of economic production, as well as grounded in the specific nature of oppression that the working class experiences. Yet, Marxist analysis is predicated on Enlightenment thinking by aiming to uncover fundamental laws that govern society and social relationships. Marxist theorization is based on efforts to abstract the "true" laws of nature that can be used to predict social events and relationships within the lived specificities of social reality. Marx was an Enlightenment thinker who used deductive powers of reasoning to arrive at an understanding of society on the basis of economic scientific theory. One of Marx's fundamental claims was that understanding the laws of nature could liberate people from being controlled by them (Taylor, 2004). Therefore, the oppressions experienced by research participants are considered significant to the degree that they conform and correspond to the "laws" of oppression already made explicit in the theories. Critiques of Marx note that he is solely interested in the difference that class location makes in people's lives. Differences based in gender, race, age, and so on are not discussed. For example, Marx assumed that all people universally find self-fulfillment in being economically productive members of society (Lather, 1991). Similarly, Marx assumed that there was a universal expression of the oppression of the labour class (Hill-Collins, 2000). Feminists have also argued that Marx does not take into account gendered differences (Pateman, 1992), and Aboriginal writers have pointed out that Marx's analysis of the economic system is entirely Eurocentric (Chrisjohn & Young, 1997).

Latter-day Marxist feminists have incorporated gender into class analysis. However, the ontological assumptions of Marxism, based on a universal idea of oppression, overlook the intersectional, multiple, and shifting nature of oppression. Hence, critical theories that are influenced by structural and Marxist analysis are very well situated on the critical axis, having played a foundational role in undertaking critical materialist analysis, but score rather low on the difference-centred axis.

Mullaly (2002, 2007), a structuralist social work theorist, claims that structuralism has an advantage over Marxism because it is more inclusive of difference. According to Mullaly, structuralism critiques institutional and structural practices in terms of not only class but also other identity locations, such as gender, race, and sexuality. However, an examination of structuralist theorization, including Mullaly's writings, shows that difference is treated as fixed, prescribed along lines of singular social identity locations. The concept of "difference" is not analyzed in all its subtleties, nor is it a focus of analysis as it is in social identity, anti-oppressive, and postmodern theories, as discussed later. This results in an analysis where the ontological assumptions of structuralist theories continue to be centred on material and structural inequalities.

Critical theorists, particularly Marxists, use the term *praxis*, defined as social institutional practices that reflect the values and assumptions of society, to signal the inseparability of knowledge claims from value claims. However, for the sake of clarity, in the present discussion I have deliberately analyzed Marxist ontological claims separately from their epistemological ones.

## Epistemological Claims: Knowledge as Constructed and Ideological

The critical perspective initiated by Marxism, and also reflected in other critical theories, rests on the epistemological assumption that knowledge is socially constructed by and in the interest of the dominant in society (Kincheloe & McLaren, 2002). The assumption that knowledge is historically situated is an important insight of Marxism and also informs anti-oppressive theories that are social constructionist in their epistemological assumptions (Burke & Harrison, 2002). Knowledge is understood as having an ideological function, used to create a "hegemonic" or dominant view of reality that produces hierarchical social relations under the guise of authoritative "Truth" claims. Marx takes the example of monarchs, who are able to assume their authority over others by appealing to not only temporal power but also divinely inspired power (Corrigan & Leonard, 1978; Kincheloe & McLaren, 2002). The construction of royalty as being divinely appointed provides sanction for one class of people to rule over another.

Knowledge is not assumed to be neutral, as it is in classical liberalism. Knowledge production and transference constitutes an important site in the fight for social justice, as it does in anti-oppressive and postmodern theories. Researchers undertake research in order to deconstruct dominant views of reality and expose the interests that these serve, both historically and contemporaneously within specific socio-cultural contexts. Paradoxically, while Marxists and structuralists assume knowledge to be constructed, they seem unaware of their own complicity in using knowledge to gain a position of power through their insistence on alternative metanarratives (truth claims) by which to explain how things "really" are (Lather, 1991). Like all metanarratives that preach singular visions of truth, Marxism and structuralism set up true-or-false binaries. They are interested in pursuing the *certainty* of truth claims.

While knowledge is recognized as having an ideological function, paradoxically, there also exists the view that one can arrive at real knowledge as a result of scientific and deductive thinking. Hence, even in epistemological terms, Marxism and structuralism retain a critical edge on the critical/mainstream axis while continuing to maintain a normative position on the normative/difference-centred axis.

Like all critical theorists, Marxist and structuralist thinkers are not only interested in arriving at explanations through their epistemological efforts. They theorize in order to make emancipatory claims and create social change (Kincheloe & McLaren, 2002). Marx's term for this dialectical tension between theorizing and practice, *praxis*, suggests that knowing something differently liberates people to do things differently.

Research methods using Marxist analysis are grounded in creating oppositional knowledge and critiquing the status quo, as well as creating social change (Lather, 1991; Kincheloe & McLaren, 2002). Methods such as participatory action research have consonance with the ontological and epistemological visions of structuralism and Marxism. The outcome of the research is expected to change both the material realities of the participants and the ways in which the participants understand that reality.

Unlike liberalism, Marxism and structuralism do not view the research process or the researcher to be neutral, due to the researcher's investment in creating social change (Lather, 1991; Kincheloe & McLaren, 2002). Validity is understood and measured by emancipatory social change resulting from particular research efforts. Research activity is considered reliable if it is replicable by another researcher, as research findings are based in tangible material changes. For example, research that uncovers the relationship between immigration policies and low-paid wage earners is valued to the degree to which this understanding results in changing the material realities of immigrant communities. Reality is always knowable, and the researcher works in ways that allow her to be a "knower" as a result of participating in the research activity.

## FEMINIST THEORIES

Feminist theories are grounded in oppositional knowledge claims from their inception. Through their theoretical analysis, they explicitly aim to contest hegemonic and dominant constructions of gender, particularly womanhood. This critical stance adopted by feminists was also reflected in the rise of feminist social movements that it engendered. Feminists, like Marxists and other critical theorists, clearly intend their theorizations to serve emancipatory ends, specifically using theory as another site of struggle for the liberation of women from gendered oppression (Tronto, 2010). Unlike liberalism and latter-day Marxism, feminist theories challenge reliance on a canonical theoretical tradition in formulating its analysis (Huyssen, 1990; Hankivisky, 2004). Feminists have used multiple theoretical lenses to conduct their analyses. In fact, I would argue that a significant contribution of feminist theories is their insight that knowledge is not based on singular truth claims. Feminists position themselves within a spectrum of theories, such as liberalism, postmodernism, Marxism and structuralism, and so on, using gender as the focus of their analysis in combination with other theoretical insights. For example, liberal feminist Susan Okin (1989) argues against the patriarchal assumptions embedded in liberalism, positing an alternative that is more inclusive of women. Meanwhile, Marxist feminists focus on labour laws and the production of labour, including women's reproductive labour, using a more inclusive definition of work (Weedon, 1997, 2004).

Gendered injustices are theorized as occurring as a result of patriarchal conventions and assumptions that exist at ideological, institutional, and societal levels (Dominelli, 2002b). There are basically three waves of feminist theorization and envisioning of social justice.

First-wave feminists are individualist in their orientation, emphasizing women's sameness to men (Offen, 1992). Feminists such as Pateman (1992), MacKinnon (1990), and to some extent Okin (1989) challenge mainstream theories of social justice as inherently patriarchal. These are critiqued for being gendered, wherein "maleness" is constructed as rational, individuated, and capable of making decisions for the common good, while "femaleness" is constructed as emotional, interdependent or dependent, and incapable of forming disinterested judgments about public good. Individualist feminists argue against the privileging of a male norm that treats women as inferior. Central to their analysis is the claim that women are in fact the same as men, and both are capable of being rational and exercising judgment. Women's freedom is analyzed as limited due to gendered societal norms. This is reflected in the dichotomous ways that society treats men and women within a private/public binary that assumes women's place to be in the private realm, which carries none of the rights and privileges that exist in the public space, properly considered the domain of men. Individualist feminists argue that both men and women should participate equally in the public realm. They contest normative constructions of a private/public divide by pointing out that the "private realm," such as the home and the family, are in fact public institutions that reflect societal norms and values. First-wave feminism is firmly on the normative axis of the model, while retaining a place on the critical axis.

Second-wave feminists, also known as relational feminists, emphasize women's differences from men. They valorize "feminine" differences as virtues and contest the patriarchal construction of women as inferior. Feminists such as Carol Gilligan (1982) and Olena Hankivisky (2004) argue that women, as mothers and caretakers, live more interconnected lives than men and are better at maintaining social relationships. This they consider to be an important contribution of women that complements men's role in society. Women's differences from men are understood as fixed and mutually exclusive. Relational feminists would argue that women should have the freedom to pursue their different interests and to be acknowledged as equal and complementary participants in society. Hence, while second-wave feminists are difference-centred, they really only take into account one type of difference.

Third-wave feminists have challenged feminist theorization that is confined within a "same" versus "different" binary. These feminist theorists occupy multiple social identity locations, such as lesbian, queer, racialized, postcolonial, and so on, and analyze oppression as it exists in multiple and intersecting ways as a result of having divergent identities. They challenge the assumed universality of first- and second-wave White feminists' analysis of gendered oppression. Hill-Collins (2000, 2005), for example, points out that while White feminists were engaged in debating whether women's role in the home was "natural" or "constructed," they overlooked the plight of Black women in Western societies, who did not have the relative privilege of having the choice to stay at home. Similarly, women writing from postcolonial societies, such as India, rejected the universality with which White feminists assumed that their own experiences of oppression were the same for women everywhere (Mohanty, 1991). Lesbian writers contested the heterosexist assumptions in the writings of first-wave feminists, as did queer theorists who extended feminist analysis of gender by questioning if "gender" was even a useful or necessary concept (Butler, 2004). Freedom is understood in collectivist, relational terms, and equality is interpreted as the right to be differently equal. Third-wave feminists are therefore both difference-centred and critical of mainstream theories; however, they are still not the dominant version of feminism. Therefore, I discuss their view of social justice in greater detail when analyzing anti-oppressive and social identity theorists.

## FEMINIST APPROACHES TO RESEARCH

### Ontological Claims: Multiple, Collectivist, Women-Centred, Grounded in Lived Experience

Feminism, like Marxism, claims to privilege the specific and contextual over the transcendental and universal in its theorizations. However, a fundamental break between feminist theories and the two theories previously discussed is its contestation of singular truth claims. Feminists challenge the dichotomous rendering of knowledge about social reality into true-or-false categories as it exists in metatheories such as Marxism and liberalism. Truth is regarded as being multiple and contextualized within subjective and specific lived experiences of gendered oppression.

However, feminists do not always confront the possibilities of their own theoretical assumptions. While theorizing about the multiplicity of truth claims and allying itself with multiple theoretical frameworks, White feminism in particular is at tension with acknowledging other social differences, particularly if these are viewed as inimical to their understanding of what it means to be a feminist. For example, White feminists have generally had a hard time with accommodating the presence of Muslim women who claim that wearing a hijab (head scarf) can be a sign of protest against patriarchy (Moosa-Mitha, 2009). They continue to privilege and single out gender as the exclusive focus of analysis, to the detriment of intersectional analysis. The result is that White women's experiences of injustice are privileged over those of women of colour.

The privileging of White women's experiences of oppression over multiple and intersecting oppressions results in envisioning social justice in singular and universal terms. Therefore, although I position mainstream feminism as being more on the difference-centred than the normative edge of the difference/normative axis, I find that the focus of its theorization is gender and not difference, and the many ways in which it intersects in the lives of women to produce oppression.

In terms of critical analysis, feminists, like other critical theorists, base their theorization within lived experiences and oppositional social movements (Weedon, 1997). Feminist theorization, like all critical theories, is emancipatory in intent, and is a contiguous site in the struggle for social justice. Feminism therefore occupies a position at the critical end of the critical/mainstream axis.

### Epistemological Claims: Knowledge as Subjective and Inductive

Feminist theories challenge the assumptions found in Enlightenment thinking as articulated in metatheories (Stanley & Wise, 1983). They therefore contest the assumptions of knowledge as being positivist and deductive, emphasizing instead inductive thinking that has its basis in the subjective and lived experiences of women (Haraway, 2003). The specific rather than the general provides the definitive background within which feminist theorizing takes place.

Like Marxists, feminists are social constructionists and regard mainstream knowledge to be the purview of privileged men who construct particular views about women that are then accepted as natural (Lather, 1991). Like other critical theories, feminism assumes knowledge production to be an important site in the struggle for social justice. There is also an acknowledgement within feminist theory of multiple ways of knowing. Rather than validating only literate, academic, and positivist ways of knowing, feminists accept that knowledge is derived from everyday experience as it is reflected in song, art, personal narratives, and so on (Trinder, 2000). Hence, feminist researchers consider knowledge to be value-laden and partial in nature, supporting the interests of maintaining patriarchy. Consistent with their epistemological assumptions, feminists do not define reliability by the degree to which their statements are seen to be objective or neutral; rather, they seek to make their own biases and values transparent (Stanley, 2013).

Research participants are considered to be subjects of the research endeavour, which is viewed as being emancipatory in nature (Smith, 1990; Stanley, 2013). The participant is not viewed as a repository of knowledge, an object of the research to "collect data" (Lather, 1991). Researchers and participants are engaged in self-reflexive activities, in which their collaborative efforts at making meaning reveal to both the different possibilities of understanding social realities (Stanley & Wise, 1983; Stanley, 2013). Like other critical theorists, feminists are also concerned with linking their research to social justice claims and not with "merely justify[ing] and rationalis[ing] the power relationships that oppress women. They also provide the concepts, models and methods by which experience can be translated and transformed" (Stanley & Wise, 1983, p. 163).

Due to its epistemological and ontological assumptions, feminist research is largely undertaken using qualitative research methodologies that include focus group discussions, narrative research methodologies, semi-directed interviews, and so on. These approaches to research use inductive reasoning and are more conducive to feminists' attempts at theorizing in order to understand rather than predict the multiple meanings and patterns that emerge from the narrative of people's lives (Creswell, 2014).

## POSTMODERN THEORIES

Postmodernism, a term first used in architectural criticism, has become a philosophical movement that is embraced by a growing number of social scientists (Lather, 1991). The fundamental theoretical claim of postmodern theories is that social reality cannot be explained with certainty or authoritative terms (Huyssen, 1990). According to postmodern theorists, reality is too complex, multiple, and fluid to be captured by the singular, universal explanations found in Enlightenment-based theories, with their attendant true-or-false dualisms (Huyssen, 1990).

Not only is knowledge understood as constructed, but reality itself is viewed as existing solely in representational terms (Weedon, 1997; Pease & Fook, 1999). There is no fundamental truth that knowledge can allude to, and truth claims are therefore produced and constructed as a result of a complex interplay of interests by various actors engaged in the production of knowledge (Butler, 2004). Postmodern theorists' response to the question of how social reality is constituted is that such a query cannot be answered in generalities. Reality is both multiple and fluid as well as historically specific in character. Hence, nothing can be said for certain about social reality; one can only interpret it based on one's own culture, values, and biases and within specific instances (Lather, 1991). Postmodern theorists therefore do not make normative statements when analyzing social reality or envisioning social justice claims.

Postmodern theorists and those they ally with are engaged in difference-centred theorizing. For example, Edward Said (1986; Said & Hitchens, 1988) "deconstructed" the images and representations that were used by White or European scholars to depict the "Other," in this case Muslim societies, as inferior. Similarly, Michel Foucault (1980), who is influential in postmodern analysis, undertook genealogical analysis to examine the language by which the "Other," such as gay men and those who were treated as criminals in society across various historical epochs, are represented within mainstream society. Foucault analyzed how different discourses, such as religious, medical, and scientific discourse, are used as bases by which to make particular constructions of the "Other" in society. Medical discourse, for example, to construct homosexuality as a "disease" was used to make truth claims that were in fact grounded in the desire to control or regulate sexual behaviour. For postmodern thinkers, therefore, there is no one Truth; however, there are "regimes of truth" that occupy a dominant space in representing and creating truths about the "Other" on the basis of their "difference" (Foucault, 1980).

Knowledge is therefore clearly linked to relations of power, but unlike Marxism, where it is understood in binary terms between the oppressor and the oppressed, power is analyzed as existing in multiple relationships (Lather, 1991; Pease & Fook, 1999). Taking their cue from Foucault, postmodern theorists consider everyone to be a participant in maintaining particular representations or discourses of themselves and others in society. Hence, postmodern thinkers are concerned with analyzing how "we are constituted as subjects of our own knowledge" (Lather, 1991). For example, postmodernists would argue that people who occupy the lower echelons of power internalize the need for hierarchy in societies and their place in it. Thus, like in feminist and anti-oppressive theories, the subject within postmodern theories is treated as having agency and capable of self-reflexivity.

Postmodern theorists' envisioning of social justice lies in the multiple self-reflexive possibilities that exist for people to engage in transforming their selves in a way that contests their participation in practices of dominance. It is their capacity to speak "truth to power" (Foucault, 1980) that allows for emancipatory justice. Therefore, rather than making social justice claims that are singular in nature, postmodern theorists deconstruct mainstream representations by maintaining a stance of criticality toward the normative practices of society, thereby contributing to furthering social justice.

## POSTMODERN APPROACHES TO RESEARCH

### Ontological Assumptions: Multiple, Representational, Individuated, and Fluid

Postmodern theorizing does not necessarily aim to explain, predict, or emancipate, but simply to deconstruct. As postmodern theorizing does not make any normative assumptions, it aims to map out, usually through the use of genealogical analysis, how certain phenomena take on specific meanings (Spivak, 1987). Fishkin (1996) has argued that postmodern theorizing does in fact make a foundational ontological assumption when it assumes that different voices and a diversity of multiple meanings are important facets of social reality that have to be acknowledged. There is some validity to this argument, although one could argue that as postmodern theories do not commit themselves to notions of "good" in certain terms, it is difficult to assert that postmodern theorizations affirm anything fundamentally. Postmodern theorists have been critiqued for not treating difference as political by not making a distinction between difference that perpetuates dominance and difference that marks marginalization, thus inhibiting them from contesting oppression more directly in their theorization (Spivak, 1987).

On the difference-centred/normative axis, postmodern theories very much position themselves on the lines of difference-centred analysis. Their critical stance toward normativity clearly marks them as situated in difference-centred analysis.

However, in terms of the critical/mainstream axis, I would argue that postmodern theories are more individualist in orientation. Their emphasis on the particular constrains their ability to speak in terms of solidarity and collectivities (Dominelli, 2002a). On the axis of critical/mainstream, postmodern theorists pose a quandary, as they are not clearly positioned in critiquing oppression, even if their attempts at deconstructing mainstream assumptions are aimed at emancipatory ends. However, their lack of a specific political agenda can lead to the treatment of all claims of difference as being equal, and they are therefore less likely to be represented at the critical end of the mainstream/critical spectrum.

Like Marxism, feminism, and other social identity theories, there is an abiding assumption within postmodern theories that "in the knowing is the doing," suggesting that ontological and epistemological separation does not exist in reality. This is consistent with the postmodern notion that we are socially produced by performing our truths in the many ways that we engage and participate in society.

### Epistemological Assumptions: Fluid, Subjective, and Subject Making; Representational

In postmodernism, knowledge is understood as being fluid and cannot be cast into rigid categories, as reality is multiple and always changing. Hence, postmodern theorists align themselves to varying and multiple theoretical frameworks in their analysis. For example, Weedon (1997) describes herself as a postmodern, Marxist, feminist theorist. Like feminist theory, one cannot speak of postmodern theory in singular terms.

Knowledge is assumed to exist in the formal structures and institutions of society, and also as it constitutes the subjectivity of individuals. Foucault (1980) defines this theorizing as "thinking more about how we think." Thus, epistemology, or knowledge itself, is the object of study through an analysis of how we come to know the things we know as given (Baines, 2011). Postmodern theorists assume self-reflexivity on the part of individuals and researchers as subjects of their own knowledge, able to examine their own knowledge base and the assumptions they hold (Lather, 1991).

Postmodern theorists' view of the multiple nature of social reality, which is unknowable and largely interpretive, results in a fundamental assumption that all individuals possess only partial knowledge and are never in a position to "know" anything completely (Lather, 1991). Anti-oppressive theorists also emphasize the "not-knowing" stance of the researcher over that of "expert"; however, for postmodern theorists, it is the universal metanarratives and their authoritative voice that they position themselves against. The researcher is therefore always positioned as the "learner" when undertaking research (Lather, 1991; Sheurich, 2001). Rather than theorizing, postmodern theorists construct a narrative about their observations and efforts at deconstructing social reality as the outcome for their research process (Rorty, 1998).

Research undertaken using this stance is likely to be qualitative in nature. It is also likely to include narrative methodology, using genealogical research that deconstructs mainstream narratives, either textual or verbal, as revealed by the participants. Generally, postmodern thinkers prefer research methodologies that use interpretative methods, such as hermeneutics, that de-emphasize the certainty of truth claims and only acknowledge interpretations of truths (Creswell, 2014). Attention is likely to be paid to participants' experiences and the meanings that they make of their experiences, so as to deconstruct dominant representations of participants' realities as well as to understand participants' subjectivity through their meaning-making processes.

The researcher is self-reflexive when undertaking research, and open to shifting from her assumptions upon understanding the meanings and definitions that others place on social phenomena (Lather, 1991; Sheurich, 2001). One of the hallmarks of postmodern approaches to research is that they are participant-centred, ensuring that the voice of the participant is central to the analysis or deconstruction effort of the research project.

## SOCIAL IDENTITY AND ANTI-OPPRESSIVE THEORIES

I use the term *social identity theories* to refer to those theories that are grounded within oppositional social movements, often referred to as the new social movements, organized around social identity locations such as race, ability/disability, queerness, homosexuality, and so on. Also known as recognition theorists, social identity theorists adopt a critical stance toward mainstream characterizations of "difference" as problematic, inferior, or invisible (Dominelli, 2002a). As with feminist theories, no one ontological tradition defines social identity theories. Anti-oppressive theories represent a second movement of social identity theories that go beyond the confines of analyzing oppression on the basis of a singular social identity to an analysis of the multiplicity and intersectionality of oppression itself, a result of multiple marginalized identity locations (Dominelli, 2011).

The two central features of the social justice visions of anti-oppressive theories are an examination of how differential social identities mark people's lives, and a conceptual and empirical analysis of oppression (Dustin & Montgomery, 2010). Injustice is understood in terms of limits to collective and personal freedom that arise as a result of one's perceived difference from the norm, expressed through the unequal power that characterizes social relationships in society. Oppression exists at the structural, relational, and cultural levels of society. However, unlike Marxists, who focus only on the structural nature of oppression, anti-oppressive theorists recognize cultural oppressions as constituting the other side of structural oppression. Struggle for social justice is therefore as much about recognition rights as it is about redistributive rights. Anti-racist theorists such as Stuart Hall (1996) were forerunners in positing that structural injustices, such as homelessness and poverty, among marginalized communities existed within a contiguous site of cultural signifiers that were used to rationalize structural oppression. For example, the term *welfare queen*, used by US president Ronald Reagan to describe the overrepresentation of Black women in receipt of social services, resulted in racialized imagery of Black women as living off the welfare state. This allowed for an attitudinal change in the public, facilitating a retrenchment in access to social welfare.

Equality is understood in more substantial terms as a struggle for equality on the basis of, rather than in spite of, difference from the norm (Yuval-Davis, 1999). This takes into account structural inequalities located both in the political, economic, and social systems of society as well as in the distribution of unequal recognition rights that treat the other as subaltern (Spivak, 1987). Historical, collective, and individual inequalities experienced on the basis of shifting and multiple identity locations are acknowledged.

The shifting nature of social identities is reflected in anti-oppressive theories, resulting in a recognition of social reality as fluid and changing. This is particularly evident in anti-oppressive theorists' contribution to theorizing difference and oppression. Anti-oppressive theorists resist an essentializing concept of difference that views social identities as static, singular, and rigid (Baines, 2011; Hines, 2012). They point out that the normative attributes assumed of the ideal citizen, such as the autonomous individual participating in society as an equal, are a myth, largely because of the unchanging nature of the individual assumed in this metanarrative. Thus, decentring the norm is an important aspect of anti-oppressive theorizing (Hill-Collins, 2000; Baines, 2011). It follows, then, that oppression is also not understood in static or singular terms. Anti-oppressive theorists critiqued earlier contributions by theorists who analyzed oppression using a singular social identity as their main platform for assuming a hierarchy of oppression in their theorizing. Multiple relationships, where one could be oppressed and oppressor at the same time, were acknowledged (Razack, 1998). Concepts that treat the margin as being in a dichotomous relationship with the centre are also disrupted in anti-oppressive writings, as the "margin" is also recognized as being a space of power (hooks, 1989, 1990).

An important theoretical contribution of anti-oppressive writing is intersectionality. Intersectionality is defined as the interweaving of oppressions on the basis of multiple social identities, as well as marginalization that is both relational and structural (Phoenix, 2004). Dhamoon (2011) defines the intersectionality of social identity locations in this way: "More than one category should be analyzed ... categories matter equally and the relationship between categories is an open empirical question" (p. 231). Intersectionality, therefore, is a dynamic concept that seeks to uncover oppression as it exists within, between, and in relation to social identity categories in their multiple interactions with the changing structural, polit-ical, and cultural levels of society. No one oppression is deemed as having a priority over another, nor are the interrelationships between various forms of oppression comprehensible in advance.

Anti-oppressive theorists resist mainstream assumptions of a transparent and universal truth that transcends social difference, emphasizing instead experiential truth as contextualized and given voice by those experiencing specific forms of marginalization (Burke & Harrison, 2002). One can see examples of this "theorising as a matter of survival," as hooks has termed it, in the writings of anti-racist, queer, and disability theorists (hooks, 1990, p. 195; see also Hill-Collins, 2000; Wendell, 1996). As with all critical theory, theorization becomes yet another site of struggle against oppres-sion. As Hill-Collins (2000) suggests, "Social injustice is the maintenance of intersectionality of oppression that has to be eliminated both in practice and ideas" (p. 27).

Difference is complicated within this analysis as being multiple, chal-lenging earlier critical theorists who assumed what Mouffe (1992) has called "false universals," such as the idea that all women or people of colour are universally the same or different (Pateman, 1992; Mouffe, 1992). Moreover, difference, which is seen to have its basis in people's social identities, is viewed as fluid and changing (Yuval-Davis, 1999). Not all claims based on difference are considered equally legitimate. As Mouffe (1992) suggests, only those claims of difference that are liberatory and address themselves to emancipating people's lives from oppression are acknowledged. Anti-oppressive theorists also envision the transformations that would occur if difference was acknowledged. Yuval-Davis (1999), for example, discusses an inversion of the liberal notions of equality, from the right to be equally different to being differently equal. Similarly, Hall and Held (1989) recast individualist definitions of autonomy as participatory and relational ones.

While postmodern theories are difference-centred, they are not necessarily critical or emancipatory in their claims. On the other hand, critical theorists, such as Marxists, are critical in their theoretical orientation, but not difference-centred. Anti-oppressive theories both reflect a normative stance against oppression and are difference-centred by seeking to interrogate normative assumptions, acknowledge the multiplicity of social positions and disrupt essentialist thinking. It is the juxtaposing of these two axes—critical thought and difference-centred analysis—that characterizes and distinguishes anti-oppressive theories from the other theories discussed in this chapter.

## ANTI-OPPRESSIVE APPROACHES TO RESEARCH

### Ontological Assumptions: Specific, Dialogical, Fluid, and Anti-Oppressive

Anti-oppressive theorists contest the ontological assumptions of Enlightenment-based theories that are rooted in universal, transcendental, and singular truth claims. The ontological assumptions of anti-oppressive theories are rooted in the subjective, as well as particular socio-historical experiences that simultaneously occupy multiple positions. Yet, unlike postmodern theories, anti-oppressive theorists acknowledge collective and structural social justice claims as being sites of oppression (Crenshaw, 1991; Baines 2011). The specific and differential nature of oppression is acknowledged without losing the sense of collective experiences of oppression. For example, Hill-Collins (2000) acknowledges differences in individual people's experiences of racism while harkening to Black communities' collective experiences of oppression. Similarly, within queer theory there is an acknowledgement of differential experiences of oppression that are gendered and intersect in complex ways with other forms of oppression. However, this is grounded in the experiences of oppression that the queer community faces as a result of transgressing gender lines (Vaid, 1995; Phelan, 2001).

The ontological vision of anti-oppressive theorists is also multidisciplinary in nature. Anti-oppressive theorists create strategies of resistance that target formal, structural, and cultural analysis in resisting oppression and moving toward a vision of a difference-centred society.

Dichotomous and binary constructions of social reality are contested, and ontological assumptions emphasize the multiple, fluid, and interweaving or intersectionality of social phenomena (Brah, 1996; Dhamoon, 2011). As anti-oppressive practices are both critical and difference-centred, research using this paradigm targets both discursive and social practices that reinforce power relationships that enable oppression (Rogers, 2012). Power relationships become the focus of interrogation and analysis in research projects using this theoretical framework.

Research participants are treated as active and owning agency (Dominelli, 2002a). Analyses of injustice are not predicated on a priori categories, nor are they normative, enabling free expression of differences in self-identity and identifying resistance outside of prescribed expectations. The participant subject is seen not only to have agency but also as being deeply dialogical and relational, a subject who affects and is also affected by a multitude of relationships and experiences of oppression.

Given its liberatory intent, anti-oppressive research projects tend to be action oriented as well as participatory in their approach. The experiential expertise of the participant is acknowledged, and the researcher is not viewed as an expert.

## Epistemological Assumptions: Knowledge as Partial, Multiple, Situated, and Subjugated

Positivist epistemological assumptions are contested, and multiple ways of knowing are acknowledged. Knowledge is not only understood as subjective, grounded as it is in one's lived experiences; it is also conceived of as being situated and subjugated. Situated knowledge contests the notion of an omniscient viewpoint, where everything is considered knowable (Haraway, 2003; Harding, 1987). Knowledge is understood as being situated on the basis of one's social location and as a result of privileges and oppressions experienced. Embodied knowledge is an important site of knowing. For example, it is acknowledged that it is not possible for someone to know what it feels like to be racialized unless one has had the experience of being racialized, and even then differences within those experiences are acknowledged.

Knowledge is also subaltern, where subjugated people are recognized as possessing knowledge that is the result of their lived circumstances; this knowledge requires translation in order to be understood by the mainstream. There are many examples of "translated" knowledge, such as in the case of immigrant communities who are aware of their own traditions and value systems as well as those of the country in which they have settled, and have to translate one to the other because they live in multiple worlds. Aboriginal communities interact with White settler societies through an intimate knowledge of those cultures, but through a prism of their own knowledge and understandings about the world they live in (Battiste & Youngblood, 2000).

An important insight of anti-oppressive theorists is their articulation of knowledge as partial, where not everything is knowable. For example, subaltern knowledge is owned, belongs to particular communities, and is not accessible to the mainstream (Burke & Harrison, 2002; Dominelli, 2002a). The researcher therefore holds the attitude of a learner, one who does not know but through the act of empathetic imagination and by possessing critical self-consciousness comes to garner a sense of what the other knows. The researcher is reflexive in her practice, and the knowledge of the subaltern is used to reflect on dominant practices in which the researcher herself is complicit (Lather, 1991).

As with all critical theories, anti-oppressive theorists make a connection between knowing and doing, and research as "praxis" (hooks, 1994). Knowledge is therefore not conceived of as being "neutral," nor is it abstract in nature. It is for this reason that knowledge holds the potential for "liberatory" practice, because knowing things differently results in acting differently (Friere, 1970).

Anti-oppressive theorists' understanding of difference as fluid is reflected in their view of knowledge as intersubjective and dialogical. For example, knowledge about an entity is gained through interaction of the subject with the observer, where both are understood as having agency and being involved in defining it (Hall, 1996).

Anti-oppressive theorists employ a variety of research methods. Qualitative, inductive methods of research are most suited to the ontological and epistemological assumptions of these researchers. Research methods such as narrative, ethnography, and phenomenology can be used in a way that facilitates the centring of the participants' voices and critiques dominant representations of the "Other."

## CONCLUSION

The purpose of this chapter was to define and clarify the ontological and epistemological assumptions of anti-oppressive theories. I have undertaken to do so by situating anti-oppressive analysis in relation to a spectrum of other theories. I have analyzed the ontological and epistemological assumptions of these theories with reference to their orientation on two axes: critical/mainstream and difference-centred/normative.

I have argued that anti-oppressive theories are distinguishable from other theories by their juxtaposition of difference-centred and critical orientations. I situate liberal theories as being normative and mainstream, Marxism as being critical but normative, White feminism as being critical but gender normative, and postmodernism as being difference-centred but not necessarily critical.

In an attempt to retain a sense of the fluidity of theoretical analysis, I have cast my analysis in the form of a "conversation" between theories that allows for a continual reshifting of the boundary lines that characterize particular theories. It includes the possibility for individual theorists to align themselves on the two axes that structure my analysis differently from dominant characterizations of the theoretical orientation to which they are allied. Theories are much more about movement than they are about rigid classification.

## REFERENCES

Althusser, L. (1969). *For Marx*. London, UK: Allen Lane.

Baines, D. (2011). An overview of anti-oppressive social work: Neoliberalism, inequality, and change. In D. Baines (Ed.), *Doing anti-oppressive practice: Social justice social work* (2nd ed., pp. 25–48). Winnipeg, MB: Fernwood Publishing.

Battiste, M., & Youngblood, H. (2000). *Protecting Indigenous knowledge and heritage: A global challenge*. Saskatoon, SK: Purich Publishing.

Brah, A. (1996). *Cartographies of diaspora: Contesting identities*. London: Routledge.

Burke, B., & Harrison, P. (2002). Anti-oppressive practice. In R. Adams, L. Dominelli, & M. Payne (Eds.), *Critical practice in social work* (pp. 227–236). New York, NY: Palgrave.

Butler, J. (2004). *Undoing gender.* New York, NY: Routledge Press.

Chrisjohn, R. D., & Young, S. L. (1997). *The circle game: Shadows and substance in the Indian Residential School experience in Canada.* Penticton, BC: Theytus Books.

Corrigan, P., & Leonard, P. (1978). *Social work practice under capitalism: A Marxist approach.* London, UK: Macmillan.

Crenshaw, K. (1991). Demarginalizing the intersection of race and sex: A black feminist critique of antidiscrimination doctrine, feminist theory, and antiracist politics. In K. T. Bartlett & R. Kennedy (Eds.), *Feminist legal theory* (pp. 57–80). Boulder, CO: Westview Press.

Creswell, J. (2014). *Research design: Qualitative, quantitative and mixed methods approaches* (4th ed.). Los Angeles, CA: SAGE Publications.

Dhamoon, R. (2011). Considerations on mainsteaming intersectionality. *Political Research Quarterly, 64*(1), 230–243.

Dominelli, L. (2002a). *Anti-oppressive social work theory and practice.* New York, NY: Palgrave.

Dominelli, L. (2002b). *Feminist social work theory and practice.* Basingstoke, UK: Palgrave.

Dominelli, L. (2011). Anti-oppressive practice. In M. Gray, J. Midgely, & S. Webb (Eds.), *The SAGE handbook of social work* (pp. 328–340). London, UK: SAGE Publications.

Dietz, M. (1987). Context is all: Feminism and theories of citizenship. *Daedalus, 116*(4), 1–24.

Dustin, D., & Montgomery, M. (2010). The use of social theory in reflecting on anti-oppressive practice with final year BSc social work students. *Social Work Education: The International Journal, 29*(4), 386–401.

Fishkin, J. S. (1996). *The dialogue of justice: Toward a self-reflective society.* New Haven, CT: Yale University Press.

Friere, P. (1970). *Cultural action for freedom.* Cambridge, MA: Harvard Educational Review.

Fook, J. (2002). *Social work: Critical theory and practice.* London, UK: SAGE Publications.

Foucault, M. (1980). *The history of sexuality.* New York, NY: Vintage Books.

Gilligan, C. (1982). *In a different voice.* Cambridge, MA: Harvard University Press.

Gramsci, A. (1971). *Selections from the prison notebooks* (Q. Hoare & G. Nowell Smith, Eds. and Trans.). London, UK: Lawrence and Wishart.

Hankivisky, O. (2004). *Social policy and the ethic of care*. Vancouver, BC: University of British Columbia Press.

Hall, S. (1996). *Questions of cultural identity*. London, UK: SAGE Publications.

Hall, S., & Held, D. (1989). Citizens and citizenship. In S. Hall & M. Jacques (Eds.), *New times: The changing face of politics in the 1990's* (pp. 173–188). New York, NY: Verso.

Harding, S. (Ed.). (1987). *Feminism and methodology: Social science issues*. Bloomington, IN: Indiana University Press.

Haraway, D. (2003). Situated knowledges: The science question in feminism and the privilege of partial perspective. In Y. Lincoln and N. Denzin (Eds.), *Turning points in qualitative research: Tying knots in a handkerchief* (pp. 21–46). Walter Creek, CA: AltMira Press.

Hill-Collins, P. (2000). *Black feminist thought: Knowledge, consciousness and the politics of empowerment* (2nd ed.). New York, NY: Routledge.

Hill-Collins, P. (2005). *Black sexual politics: African-Americans, gender, and new racism*. New York, NY: Routledge.

Hines, J. (2012). Using an anti-oppressive framework in social work practice with lesbians. *Journal of Gay & Lesbian Social Services, 24*(1), 23–39.

hooks, b. (1989). *Talking back: Thinking feminist, thinking Black*. Boston, MA: South End Press.

hooks, b. (1990). *Yearning: Race, gender & cultural politics*. Boston, MA: South End Press.

hooks, b. (1994). *Teaching to transgress: Education as the practice of freedom*. New York, NY: Routledge.

Huyssen, A. (1990). Mapping the postmodern. In L. Nicholson (Ed.), *Feminism/postmodernism* (pp. 234–280). New York, NY: Routledge.

Kincheloe, J., & McLaren, P. (2002). Rethinking critical theory and qualitative research. In Y. Zou & E. Trueba (Eds.), *Ethnography and schools: Qualitative approaches to the study of education* (pp. 87–100). Oxford, UK: Rowman and Littlefield Publishers.

Kymlicka, W. (2001). *Politics in the vernacular: Nationalism, multiculturalism, and citizenship*. Oxford, UK: Oxford University Press.

Kymlicka, W. (2012). *Multiculturalism: Success, failure and the future*. Washington, D.C.: Transatlantic Council on Migration, Migration Policy Institute.

Lather, P. (1991). *Getting smart: Feminist research and pedagogy with/in the postmodern*. New York, NY: Routledge.

Lister, R. (2003) *Citizenship: Feminist perspectives* (2nd ed.). New York, NY: Palgrave-Macmillan.

Mackinnon, C. (1990). *Toward a feminist theory of state.* Cambridge, MA: Harvard University Press.

Mohanty, C. (1991). *Under Western eyes: Feminist scholarship and colonial discourse.* Bloomington, IN: Indiana University Press.

Mookherjee, M. (2011). *Democracy, religion and the liberal dilemma of accommodation.* Dordrecht, Netherlands: Springer Netherlands.

Moosa-Mitha, M. (2009). Social citizenship rights of Canadian Muslim youth: Youth resiliencies and the claims for social inclusion. *Arab Studies Quarterly, 31*(1 & 2), 121–140.

Mouffe, C. (Ed.). (1992). *Dimensions of democracy.* London, UK: Verso.

Mullaly, R. (2002). *Challenging oppression: A critical social work approach.* Toronto, ON: Oxford University Press.

Mullaly, R. (2007). *The new structural social work: Ideology, theory, practice.* Toronto, ON: Oxford University Press.

Offen, K. (1992). Defining feminism: A comparative historical approach. In G. Bock & S. James (Eds.), *Beyond equality and difference: Citizenship, feminist politics and female subjectivity* (pp. 69–88). London, UK: Routledge.

Okin, S. (1989). *Justice, gender and the family.* New York, NY: Basic Books.

Pateman, C. (1992). Equality, difference, subordination: The politics of motherhood and women's citizenship. In G. Bock & S. James (Eds.), *Beyond equality and difference: Citizenship, feminist politics and female subjectivity* (pp. 17–31). London, UK: Routledge.

Pease, B., & Fook, J. (1999). *Transforming social work practice: Postmodern critical perspectives.* London, UK: Routledge.

Phelan, S. (2001). *Sexual strangers: Gays, lesbians and dilemmas of citizenship.* Philadelphia, PA: Temple University Press.

Phoenix, A. (2004). *Theorisation of difference in psychology.* Paper presented at the Psychology of Women Conference, Brighton, UK.

Rawls, J. (1971). *A theory of justice.* Cambridge, MA: Harvard University Press.

Razack, S. (1998). *Looking white people in the eye.* Toronto, ON: University of Toronto Press.

Roberts, D. J., & Mahtani, M. (2010). Neoliberalizing race, racing neoliberalism: Placing "race" in neoliberal discourses. *Antipode, 42*(2), 248–257.

Rogers, J. (2012). Anti-oppressive social work research: Reflections on power in the creation of knowledge. *Social Work Education: The International Journal, 31*(7), pp. 866–879.

Rorty, R. (1998). *Truth and progress.* Cambridge, UK: Cambridge University Press.

Said, E. (1986). *After the last sky: Palestinian lives.* New York, NY: Pantheon Books.

Said, E., & Hitchens, C. (1988). *Blaming the victims: Spurious scholarship and the Palestinian question.* New York, NY: Verso.

Sheurich, J. (2001). *Research method in the postmodern.* London, UK: Routledge.

Smith, D. (1990). *The conceptual practices of power: A feminist sociology of knowledge.* Boston, MA: Northeastern University Press.

Spivak, G. (1987). *In other worlds: Essays in cultural politics.* New York: Methuen.

Staeheli, L. (2013). The 2011 Antipode AAG Lecture: Whose responsibility is it? Obligation, citizenship and social welfare. *Antipode, 45*(3), 521–540.

Stanley, L. (Ed.). (2013). *Feminist praxis (RLE feminist theory): Research, theory and epistemology in feminist sociology.* New York, NY: Routledge.

Stanley, L., & Wise, S. (1983). *Breaking out: Feminist consciousness and feminist research.* London, UK: Routledge & Kegan Paul.

Stasilius, D. (2002). The active child citizen: Lessons from Canadian policy and the children's movement. *Citizenship Studies, 6*(4), 507–538.

Taylor, C. (2004). *Modern social imaginaries.* Durham, NC: Duke University Press.

Trinder, L. (2000). Reading the texts: Postmodern feminism and the "doing" of research. In B. Fawcett, B. Featherstone, J. Fook, & A. Rossiter (Eds.), *Practice and research in social work: Postmodern feminist perspectives* (pp. 39–61). London: Routledge.

Tronto, J. (2010). Creating caring institutions: Politics, plurality, and purpose. *Ethics and Social Welfare, 4*(2), 158–171.

Vaid, U. (1995). *Virtual equality: The mainstreaming of gay and lesbian liberation.* New York, NY: Anchor Books.

Weedon, C. (1997). Principles of post-structuralism. In C. Weedon (Ed.), *Feminist practice and post-structuralist theory* (pp. 12–41). Cambridge, UK: Blackwell Publishers.

Weedon, C. (2004). *Identity and culture: Narratives of difference and belonging.* Berkshire, UK: Open University Press.

Wendell, S. (1996). Who is disabled? Defining disability. In S. Wendell (Ed.), *The rejected body: Feminist philosophical reflections on disability* (pp. 11–41). London, UK: Routledge.

Williams, P. (1998). *The alchemy of race and rights: Diary of a law professor.* Cambridge, MA: Harvard University Press.

Young, I. M. (1997). *Intersecting voices, dilemmas of gender, political philosophy, and policy.* Princeton, NJ: Princeton University Press.

Yuval-Davis, N. (1999). Ethnicity, gender relations and multiculturalism. In R. Torres, L. Mirón, & J. Inda (Eds.), *Race, identity and citizenship: A reader.* (pp. 112–125). Oxford, UK: Blackwell.

Chapter Four

# Our Community Action Research Project: A Blueprint for Resistance

## Jenny Holder

## INTRODUCTION

Throughout my graduate social work education, I developed a keen interest in community-based research. My commitment to community research was solidified as I explored the possibilities of promoting social justice through community action research (CAR). Given the immense privilege I hold as a White, educated social worker, it is important that I harness my privilege to address social justice issues. As a graduate student, this means that my access to the resources of the academy, knowledge, and power be shared where possible in order to increase community capacity for resistance to oppression. With this in mind, I approached Bridges for Women Society (hereafter Bridges) to inquire if there was a meaningful project that would benefit the agency and the community they serve.

The purpose of this chapter is to tell the story of a CAR project deemed successful by the research participants, the researchers, and the community partner agency (Bridges). As a grad student researching CAR in preparation for conducting this project, I found very few examples of CAR projects where the participants or researchers clearly outlined the success of the project. This chapter offers an alternative perspective, highlighting the complexity of engaging in ethical research that encourages true community ownership and participation through detailing issues of informed consent, confidentiality, and my overlapping roles of researcher, research participant, and staff supervisor at Bridges. Ethical considerations are discussed, with close attention to the fact that the project was conducted in a small, interconnected community. Exploring the complexity of CAR as a methodological tool for social justice, this chapter documents Bridges' anti-oppressive, consensus-based process of co-creating knowledge. The story told here marks how the research participant group collectively produced an ethics document and a set of recommendations for action through formulating and implementing a workshop series. I offer reflections regarding the unpredictable process of engaging in CAR research and share lessons learned.

## COMMUNITY ACTION RESEARCH AT BRIDGES

Bridges is located in Victoria, BC. This feminist non-profit agency formed 25 years ago in response to the community need for specialized employment programming for women who have experienced violence, abuse, and trauma, such as intimate partner violence, childhood sexual abuse, adult sexual assault, hate crimes, and other forms of racial and gendered violence. Bridges is a gutsy, innovative community agency that delivers employment training, supportive programs, and counselling to women affected by violence, abuse, or trauma. Bridges was part of a BC-wide program called the Bridging Employment Programs of BC, along with 33 other agencies providing similar specialized employment services to abused women.

In the face of a major funding and program model change, Bridges identified the importance of retaining its ethical practices to ensure the continuation of services, as defined by non-profit, feminist, anti-oppressive perspectives. Through a process of consensus, Bridges decided that a collective research approach be adopted to explore the agency's practice ethics and ensure the preservation of Bridges' ethical values, principles, and anti-oppressive practices. This project therefore explored the following question: What are the core ethical values at Bridges for Women Society that are central to practice and constitute anti-oppressive practice when working with women who have experienced violence?

The collective process of documenting practice ethics, values, and principles had the ultimate goal of preserving the high quality of Bridges' programming, which was under threat of being remodelled under the new Employment Program of BC (EPBC) funding and program structure changes. The generic EPBC model of service does not adequately address the specialized needs and services required for survivors of violence who seek employment services. The BC government's implementation of EPBC gave private corporations control of bridging employment services across the province. Bridges wanted to continue offering accessible, community-based anti-violence employment programming, and so determined that it had to take control of defining ethical practice to mitigate the changes and avoid being redefined by the government's new service delivery agenda. Bridges maintained that without a collective blueprint detailing ethical practice, their women-centred anti-violence services were at risk of erasure. The CAR project enabled the successful documentation of Bridges' ethical values, principles, and anti-oppressive practices, offering a blueprint for community action and resistance for social justice during a time of threat to the existence of the continuation of ethical services.

## FINDING MY WAY THROUGH ETHICS APPROVAL

Before beginning data collection for this project, I applied for and received ethics approval from the University of Victoria Human Research Ethics Board (HREB) to conduct research with human participants. The process of formulating my ethics application and examining the ethical issues within the project proved to be an arduous undertaking. At first glance, my supervisor was not clear as to how I would conduct this research in my workplace, as an employee with supervisory power over some of the potential research participants. Additionally, the question arose as to how I could be a researcher and research participant in my own project, given the complex overlapping relationships and roles. Although these factors were complex, I was determined to find a way to explain to HREB and to my supervisory committee how these ethical considerations were intertwined with the methodology of community action research.

In order to respond to Bridges' requests for community-based research on the topic of ethics and practice, I needed to strongly consider their perspective that I be involved as a participant in the research, given that I had been with the agency for over 10 years. This was not conceived of as a research project where there was a specific, calculated distance between the researcher and the research participants. Rather, the pre-existing relationships, political context, and values at Bridges were central to the project design. Hesse-Biber,

Leavy, and Yaiser (2004) affirm this sentiment, arguing, "The denial of values, biases, and politics is unrealistic and undesirable. Emotions and values often serve as an impetus to a research endeavor" (p. 12).

I went directly to HREB staff to ask how to move forward with my ethics application. Their initial response was that it is generally frowned upon to conduct research in one's own place of work, as it was seen to be a sign of convenience and a possible misuse of power. The second consultation with HREB staff was also very interesting, because when I asked about the dual role of being a researcher and a research participant in my own project, the person I spoke to had never known a research process where this was the case and so took it back to a supervisor for consultation. In the end, the message was positive. I was given the green light to approach the ethics application as a researcher/research participant in my place of work, given I was using CAR as my methodology. However, due to the overlapping relationships, I was strongly cautioned to display clearly how I would attend to power relationships. In my ethics application, I emphasized the importance of utilizing an external third-party recruiter for the project. This recruitment process demonstrated to HREB that the power I held as a supervisor of some of the potential research participants was being taken seriously and mitigated. I detailed the external third-party recruitment process, highlighting that I was not engaging in direct participant recruitment. I made it clear that this was to allow potential participants to choose freely whether or not to participate. Additionally, I outlined the letter from Bridges to the possible research participants that stated that participation or non-participation in the research was unrelated to the assessment of their work performance. This was particularly important given that the research was conducted in their current place of employment. I explained that the letter was to be given to all potential research participants by the executive director at Bridges in advance of the actual research participant recruitment process.

The above two examples were central to explaining to HREB exactly how I would attend to power relationships in the research process. There were many intricate details included in my ethics application that addressed issues of power-over and power relationships. Working in close proximity with my community demanded that I pay close attention to issues of power as a matter of ethics. Even though this was a very time-consuming process, I believe it formed the foundation for the success of the research, as it set the stage for anti-oppressive practice.

The HREB was satisfied that I had sufficiently addressed the larger issues associated with my overall approach and approved my application as a minimum-risk project, given that I was conducting research with adults who were working as social service professionals. It was determined that the possible harm to the participants (myself included) was no greater than that from performing their professional work activities. It is important to draw attention to the fact that if I had been working with a vulnerable population in a dual role as researcher and participant, this would have been a much more complex ethics approval process. It was very clear going through this process that CAR had not always been acknowledged as a legitimate research methodology.

## WHY CAR METHODOLOGY? INTEGRATING FEMINIST AND ANTI-OPPRESSIVE PERSPECTIVES

It was vital that a feminist, anti-oppressive, non-hierarchical collective process be upheld throughout this project. The design of the project was therefore grounded in a collective process of knowledge production, preserving the value of community working together for social change.

This CAR project was directed from the community, for the community, and with intensive community participation. It thus follows the precepts of CAR as outlined by Brown and Reitsma-Street (2003): "Research practitioners and students who are beginning to use CAR or name what they do as CAR do so while inside a project, or as a member of a community seeking change, or upon the invitation of the group" (p. 69).

CAR projects are often constructed with "an explicit social change agenda, and work from the belief that the very process of participating in constructing knowledge about one's own context has the potential to redress power imbalance" (Boser, 2006, p. 11). In the face of the government forming a strong, non-negotiable stance on service delivery, Bridges sought to identify and solidify the practice ethics, values, and principles that were fundamental in carrying out their work with women. A CAR methodology was seen as the means to meet the goals, standards, and requirements Bridges set out.

The importance of intertwining feminist and anti-oppressive perspectives with the CAR methodology became clear in the early stages of the project. Notably, a "consensus model" is very important to Bridges, as it is used as a framework for communication and decision-making at all levels in the agency. Bridges' use of a consensus model is strongly linked to Hesse-Biber et al. (2004), who cite that in non-feminist positivist research, "by privileging the researcher as the knowing party a hierarchy paralleling that of patriarchal culture is reproduced" (p. 12). In order to engage in a research framework that did not reinforce hierarchy, the Bridges model of consensus decision-making was adopted as central to the research, in order to allow the participants' voices to be considered in the research design at all stages. This situated the research participants as co-creators of knowledge and countered the possibility of unequal power relationships between the researcher and the research participants.

In order to follow the principle of community ownership that is central to CAR, an anti-oppressive practice (AOP) framework was integrated into the methodology. According to Potts and Brown (2005), AOP research "means making the commitment to the people you are working with personally and professionally in order to mutually foster conditions for social justice and research" (p. 255). The high level of commitment to working toward social justice on the part of the agency, the research participants, and the project advisory group was the key to implementing AOP in this project. There was an incredible collective will to focus as a group on the documentation of practice ethics in order to create a just alternative to the oppressive government practices and policies regarding specialized employment services for women in BC. In this way, the project used AOP research as a "method of intervention" (Potts & Brown, 2005, p. 258) as well as a platform for the research process itself. Bridges' CAR project was set up to foster community connectedness and ownership of the research process and product. From the outset, each participant committed to working respectfully and collaboratively, with the understanding that attention to relationships of power and difference among the research group as a whole was vital to realizing AOP. In making visible the intricate relationships of power, and viewing dissidence as an essential part of the research methodology, the conditions for social justice and research were achieved using an AOP framework. As well as being a product of the University of Victoria, the research is owned by and utilized at Bridges to advance the social justice work of supporting women affected by violence and trauma in their healing and helping them take steps toward increased safety and economic security.

CAR is value-driven research, relying heavily on the integration of these values into the research process (Brown & Reitsma-Street, 2003).

At the outset of the project design, I suggested the CAR values articulated by Brown and Reitsma-Street (2003)—"*social justice, agency, community connectedness and critical curiosity*" (p. 63, italics added)—to the project advisory group and the research participants as a framework for conducting the research project. The intent of utilizing these identified values was to allow for a basic values structure from which to build the CAR project. Early on in the process, it became very clear that given the time constraints, the limited resources, and the collective nature of the project, we needed a structure to guide us and act as a beginning point. The research group thoroughly reviewed the values and adopted them, adding the value of resistance to the mix.

## THE RESEARCH PROCESS

In this section, I explain CAR by detailing how the principles of the methodology were embedded in all of the research stages. In order to illustrate the interconnection between the values, principles, and research practices, this section focuses on the actual steps involved in the research process, illustrating how each step links to the values and principles of CAR identified above.

### Working Alongside a Project Advisory Group: Seeking Counsel

The project advisory group (PAG) was formed to guide the research process and ensure that the needs of the community group were being attended to. Additionally, this group provided feedback, direction, and practical assistance with workshop facilitation, data collection and analysis, conflict resolution, and overall design of the research project. The PAG was made up of four Bridges members, one of the original founding mothers of Bridges, two former Bridges employees, and myself (a current employee and student researcher). The composition of this group was very intentional. To avoid any other (besides myself) overlapping relations of power-over the research participants, only past employees were selected. Additionally, in order to draw on the history of ethical values and practices, these women were all considered Bridges elders, as they had worked for many years in leadership in the agency.

This group was formed as a "touchstone" for the values, goals, direction, and design of the project. Brown and Reitsma-Street (2003) identify that it is common for community-based research approaches to "select mature, skillful researchers or community members to serve as touchstones to a project" (p. 73). Having the PAG as a touchstone allowed for the project to stay grounded in Bridges' herstory and wove together the past and the present. By maintaining the focus on the values of CAR, the advisory group provided direction and consultation to Bridges, the research participants involved, and me. It was the forming of and participation in the PAG that ensured the research process followed the CAR value of community connectedness, as it truly served to connect the Bridges community together throughout the entire research process.

The PAG members were women who were intimately connected with Bridges, and this was key to the high level of engagement in and attachment to the research. The collective ownership of the research design allowed the research to emerge within a consensus process, which fostered creativity, connectedness, and community ownership. According to Boser (2006), community action research "aims to provide holistic knowledge, integrating tacit knowledge and multiple perspectives" (p. 11). This project followed this articulation, as the PAG played a key role in the research design through multiple perspectives while folding tacit knowledge into the core of the design. The long history that each PAG member had with Bridges and one another allowed for the integration of unspoken understandings and the collective oral herstory of Bridges' 25-year trauma-informed knowledge base. These ways of being and knowing cannot be captured in words, but can only be experienced as relational manifestations of community connectedness in the struggle to end violence against women. The CAR value of community connectedness was alive in the formation and engagement of the PAG at every step of the research process. It is important to stress that without the keen participation of PAG members, the collective nature of the project would have been dulled. Instead, the PAG was vibrant, actively serving as the backbone for this complex project.

## Research Participant Recruitment

The intention of the project was to focus on the *current practice ethics* at Bridges. The Bridges executive director and PAG determined the scope of the research participant recruitment. It was decided that participants would be recruited from the current staff pool at Bridges, and as such, the research participants were limited to nine (including myself) at the outset of the project. The research project was conducted in my current place of employment, where I hold a position of power-over some of the research participants with whom I work at Bridges. Given that the project drew from a very specific, interconnected, and small group of participants, attention to existing power relationships was essential to ethical recruitment practices. At the time of the research, I was the employment program manager and supervised five staff. In order to address some of the ethical issues of power-over in this situation, the PAG identified that an external third-party recruiter was necessary to recruit the participants in this project.

The relationships with my colleagues are of the utmost importance to me, and the preservation and strengthening of these relationships was key to designing this project alongside the PAG. In my dual role as a student researcher and staff supervisor, it was unethical for me to approach staff (potential research participants) directly due to the power differential, real or perceived, arising from my authority. It was essential that communication regarding recruitment was carried out without pressure or obligation in order to allow participants to freely choose to participate or abstain. As a researcher, even though I could not completely ensure that staff did not feel obligated to participate, I aimed to give the utmost care and attention to this ethical concern. The use of an external third-party recruiter provided distance between me and the potential research participants during the recruitment phase. This was essential, because even though there were informal conversations and meetings with Bridges staff that entailed planning the initial focus of the research project, this was a planning phase and clearly not a recruitment phase. The distinction between these two phases in CAR allows for participants to freely choose to participate or abstain, even if they were involved in the initial planning phase as community members. This follows the CAR value of community connectedness by allowing for community members to participate and contribute to the research from conception without holding them to participation past the initial planning stages (community meetings) to determine the focus of the research.

Because the research participants were recruited at their place of work, for a project which concerned their work, the recruitment information given to the participants clearly outlined that participation or non-participation in the research would not be used in any way to assess their work performance. It is important to note that before the recruitment process officially began, the executive director of Bridges sent out a letter to all potential research participants stating that the upcoming project was in no way a stipulation of employment or related to job performance on any level. The letter laid out the research as separate and distinct from work duties and clearly stated that all participants were free to withdraw from the research project without any consequence to their employment status at Bridges.

## Planning for Conflict

Because collective community work is rarely conflict-free, preplanning for conflict management and navigation is a necessary step. Inevitably, conflicts arose during the collective process. The PAG played a key role in conflict management throughout the project. Conflicts included disagreements about the structure and flow of the workshops, different understandings of key concepts that emerged in the data analysis, and conflicting interpretations of some of the ethical values identified. For example, deciding on a definition of anti-oppressive practice created much debate in the group. Although the participants were all current Bridges staff, their individual politics, values, and places of privilege, oppression, and difference were made visible during the research process. The CAR value of critical curiosity was applied in the research process through valuing the diversity of perspectives and allowing the research process to be curious about all perspectives, while using an AOP critical lens. Members of the project advisory group were able to facilitate conversations to assist the group in coming to consensus. The research participants, along with the PAG, determined a process for managing conflict while remaining critically curious about all participants' perspectives. This placed the PAG in a central mediation and facilitation role, where they were responsible for assisting in resolving issues with the group during the research process. Conflict can halt or destroy community research efforts. I believe that the success of this project hinged on the formulation of a conflict resolution process and recommend that anyone conducting CAR strongly consider how conflict will be resolved.

## Data Collection and Analysis: A Collective Process

The PAG and Bridges' executive director requested that I contribute to the research as a participant as well as a researcher. I am a longstanding member of the Bridges community. The PAG and I discussed this request and determined that my participation was important in order to conduct this collaborative research project. Initially, it was a challenge to shift from a role as strictly researcher to researcher and research participant. A series of conversations took place, during which the implications of my dual role were assessed. In order for me to fulfill this dual role, the PAG assumed responsibility for workshop planning, facilitation, data collection, and data analysis. In each group session, members of the PAG took on direct roles. There were two facilitators and two data recorders in each session. Although I was the constant co-facilitator in all sessions, I was not primarily responsible for workshop planning, facilitation, data collection, or analysis of any one session. This shared responsibility created space for my role as a research participant. The true spirit of the CAR value of community connectedness manifested in this process as shared collective responsibility and connection. One drawback was that I had to balance my responsibility of co-facilitation with that of giving my own feedback during the sessions. It was difficult to remember to incorporate my perspectives because I was so focused on facilitating. In between sessions, I was able to add my contributions to the data where it was missed due to these constraints. The data was then sent out to all participants clearly indicating my additions so that the group could specifically review and comment on them, as they were made outside of the workshop process.

## Building the Workshop Series

This project was a collaborative process, and, as such, data collection and analysis were collective processes in which participants, the PAG, and I worked to collect and analyze the data in a fluid and iterative manner. The data collection methods were structured to encourage myself, as a researcher, to be attached to and active with other participants in the process of knowledge creation.

A workshop format was implemented as the primary site of data collection and analysis. The back-and-forth process of learning and teaching in the workshops proved to be vital for the research project as it allowed for genuine interaction between participants, rather than a contrived or highly structured space. The workshops were group sessions for collective knowledge production and analysis for the research project. According to Boser (2006), action research approaches in social research "include the researched in defining the questions, in data collection and analysis, and in interpreting and taking action based on research findings. The objective is co-generating knowledge" (p. 9). Similarly, this project follows Boser's articulation of action research, where data collection and analysis are participant driven and focused on community action. Four workshops were conducted, each for a duration of two and a half hours, in order to develop ideas, analysis, and group processes. The attendance of the nine participants ranged from six to nine attendees over the four workshop sessions, which we marked as successful.

The overall goal of the workshops was to explore and collectively define the values, principles, and practices contributing to ethical practice. This process demanded that an ongoing analysis of the data be conducted in the workshops as we co-created knowledge. This consistent and iterative review process ensured that the research group shared data analysis and interpretation. According to Boser (2006), "community-based co-researchers often gather data and participate in analysis" (p. 13).

The PAG consulted about the accuracy of the data collected in the workshop summary reports written after each workshop. The research participants and the PAG used the summary as a tool to determine the next steps of the research process. This process allowed for a high level of accountability and accuracy in the data collection because the group reviewed all data along the way, which allowed for changes and points of discussion to be brought back to the larger group for clarification. Given the iterative process of data collection, it was vital that after each session the PAG formulated the focus for the following workshop based on the direction of the research participants. The CAR value of agency was clearly embedded in the process, as research participants and the PAG designed the research process step by step according to what they perceived as their best options for effectively moving the process forward. This process involved incremental developments based on the collaboration and input from the research participants and the PAG.

Once the workshop summary report was approved and edited by the PAG, the focus of the next workshop was solidified. At the beginning of each workshop, the research participants reviewed the workshop summary reports for previous sessions and adjusted the reports accordingly. It is important to note here that at the end of each workshop, participants were asked to identify the next steps in the research, and these steps were integrated into the planning for the upcoming workshops. Community action research process "typically take[s] place in iterative cycles of research, action and reflection within a democratic process" (Boser, 2006, p. 11). Grounded in an iterative research process, this project maintained the collective nature of the process by providing time for individuals to reflect on the group's work (namely, reflecting on values, principles, and practices that contribute to ethics at Bridges) in order to bring forward corrections, additions, questions, and suggestions to the group. Participants were welcome to withdraw information they contributed to the process at any time, and this reflection period at the beginning of each workshop provided participants with a space to do so before re-engaging in the next workshop session. Some ideas were retracted and others were rewritten to better capture the meaning in an alternate translation. This process made it clear that the level of community ownership over the research process was high. This critical reflection process demanded that the data accurately reflect the voices of the participants as we moved through the research process.

The ideas for how to conduct each session came from a collaborative process between the research participants and the PAG. The exercises and ideas for discussions evolved as the project progressed. The CAR value of social justice was central to the development of the workshop series because it was the driving force behind most of the decisions regarding how to structure the workshops. The structure was linked to the goal of seeking social justice through defining anti-oppressive practice and documenting ethical practice at Bridges. The exception to this was the introductory workshop. This workshop was planned by the PAG, as the participants were not engaged in the research at the point of planning the initial workshop. However, during this workshop the participants clearly led the way, and the PAG and I followed their lead within the structure provided. There was a strong focus on the research question in this workshop, and the initial goals of the research project were solidified.

The focus of the remainder of the workshops (two through four) was determined through a collaborative process between the research participants, the PAG, and myself. The structure of each workshop was based on the content of the previous workshops (the research findings), as was the direction for upcoming workshops. The process was literally built from workshop to workshop. Similarly, Boser (2006) cites that "community-based research seeks to share power in knowledge generation" (p. 10). The intention in formulating the workshops this way was to allow for a fluid process in which ideas, strategies, and areas of focus could evolve. This approach facilitated sharing power within the group so that everyone had a chance to contribute and co-create knowledge. This consensus decision-making process determined the direction of each workshop. The focus and goals of the workshops always strongly related to the research question, namely identifying the central ethical practices, values, and principles involved in the work at Bridges.

The fourth workshop was conducted as a feedback and research product planning session. The result of this session was a set of recommendations regarding the ethics document and community action strategies. The intensive focus on these strategies was a sign that the CAR process was truly facilitating community ownership of the research. Although there was a plan to make recommendations in this session, the depth and breadth of the resulting recommendations exceeded far beyond anything I had imagined.

In general, my role was to facilitate the data collection and analysis so as to engage the participants in a transparent, collective research process. There was a clear role that I took on to transcribe and organize the data in between sessions. The research participants and PAG ultimately determined if the interpretation of the data that I presented was accurate and valuable from which to move forward. This was a very time-consuming process and took intense dedication on the part of all involved in the research process. The group determined the themes and the definitions of ethical values, and the anti-oppressive practices that accompanied them. In order for the community to truly drive and own this research, the time dedicated by all participants was critical.

## UNANTICIPATED LEARNING: REFLECTIONS ON THE CAR PROCESS

### Informed Consent to a CAR Process

This CAR project was outlined to the research participants as a collective, iterative process. This raises the question: Can a research participant give informed consent to engage in a CAR project? According to Boser (2006), when conducting community action research, participants cannot give informed consent to research activities in advance because the full scope of the process of research is not determined in advance by one individual. Rather, research activities are typically negotiated by participants at each stage of the action research cycle (p. 12).

Considering this, it is important to acknowledge that the recruitment process has specific limitations intertwined with the methodology of CAR. In conventional research, where the research process is predetermined and therefore predictable, research participants consent to a known process or structure. In CAR, this does not exist in the same manner. To address this dilemma, the consent form and recruitment letter given to participants in this project included an emphasis on the ability to withdraw from the research project without consequence at any point. This was emphasized in recognition of the need for ongoing consent throughout the project, given the dynamic nature of the CAR process.

The option to remove data contributions at any stage of the research also assisted in mitigating this ethical issue of informed consent. This way, the participant had control over her choice to withdraw from the process entirely, or to withdraw data from the project at any point of contribution. In addition, the collective nature of data collection in this project made it difficult to assign any specific data contributions to any specific participant. However, it was made clear to the participants that they could choose to withdraw any data they felt was identifying to them personally, regardless of the collective process of data collection. Conversely, this also assisted to mitigate issues of confidentiality in the research process, as the results of the project were attributed to the entire research group.

Upon reflection, it is possible that the process of CAR could have been described more fully in the recruitment materials to better inform participants about the activities to which they were consenting. This may have given them a clearer understanding that they were consenting to participate in a largely unpredictable process involving a continually developing project. Although participants communicated no concerns related to this issue, the ethical responsibility to fully inform participants about the research is critical, both for participation in the research and for increasing the possibility of participants giving informed consent in CAR. It is also important to note that as an inexperienced researcher in the area of CAR, I did not fully understand that the research would be as dynamic and full of change as it turned out to be. Going forward, I now better understand the shifting meaning of a participant-led, community-owned research process.

## Confidentiality in a Group Process

All data collected in the research was stored in a confidential manner, using password-protected documents on a computer in a locked office at Bridges. All research participants were asked to sign a confidentiality form, which obligated them to keep the information shared in the research process confidential, and outlined that the research would be conducted in a group setting. Beyond that, issues of confidentiality were not straightforward in this project.

The data collection was done in a group setting, where limits of confidentiality are bound by each participant's willingness to maintain it. Agreeing to participate in the research meant understanding that confidentiality could not be guaranteed due to the nature of the group workshop format that was central to the design of the project. Given the open group process structure of the project and the promise of participant involvement in data collection and analysis, confidentiality within the research group was essentially nonexistent. However, it can be argued that in another way, the collective nature of the data collection offered more confidentiality, because all data was formulated collectively; no one idea or concept would be assigned to a particular research participant. Further to the confidentiality forms signed by all participants was the verbal confidentiality agreement that all participants gave to one another in the first workshop and each workshop thereafter.

In the process of attending to pre-existing power relationships and the possible risks for the participants and myself in a dual role, I developed a process with the PAG where feedback could be given confidentially to the PAG by the individual research participants. This provided an option for those who wanted to contribute data in a more confidential way, outside of the collective workshop setting. I put this option in place to acknowledge that there may have been things participants felt uneasy contributing in front of other colleagues, and particularly in my presence, given my dual role. Additionally, this gave me, as a researcher in a dual role, the ability to contribute confidentially to the PAG as well. This was a very important part of creating a safe and trusting environment for the research participants, given the pre-existing power relationships in the group. In the end, no one used this method of contributing to the data, but many participants commented how important it was that the option existed. The presence of an alternative confidential option for contribution to the data was in itself a way to acknowledge and address issues of power by equalizing the power relationships.

### Consider Time

CAR takes time. One of the most significant lessons learned from this project was the reality of the commitment when engaging in a community-driven research process. The traditional approach of neatly packaging the research participants' hours of commitment into a box of no more than a certain amount was a complete trap. As a researcher and participant in the project, I grossly underestimated the commitment I made in this dual role. Time was largely spent communicating with the PAG between sessions and transcribing and condensing the notes taken during the session. At the beginning of each workshop, the participants had a chance to review the data from the previous session to check for accuracy and make further contributions. Also, because each workshop was built upon the previous workshop, considering the participants' feedback as to what step to take next in the process and then consulting with the PAG about this step consumed a considerable number of hours. I came to understand that there was a lack of preparedness on my part where time was concerned. Upon reflection, it would have been helpful to plan for increased time to engage in group processes, make adjustments, consider alternatives, analyze data collectively, plan the phases of the research process, and generally debrief and journal my personal journey in the research process. In this project, the agency's desire to conduct the research in a community-based manner assisted with the time commitment that was asked of the participants and the PAG. The group was well established and consisted of long-time colleagues, which greatly contributed to the commitment they showed. If this had not been the case, I can see how a different compilation of research participants could have greatly slowed the research process. Collaboration takes an incredible amount of physical and psychological time, and unless this is taken into consideration in the research planning stages, it could be a determining factor in the success of a CAR project. I caution those considering this methodology to dive deep into the issue of the time needed to engage in a truly community-led and -owned process. It is a major commitment.

## Embrace Community Ownership

There is no prescriptive, step-by-step process in CAR. While holding the research space as unknown and moving forward with the drive and will of the community, I found myself shrink in significance in relation to the whole of the research group's navigation of choices. At the outset of the project, I had a conceptual understanding of what taking direction and moving alongside a collective research process could look like. As a feminist, I have designed numerous projects in largely consensus-based decision-making models on collaborative teams, and I initially felt that my experiences and perspectives prepared me to engage in a CAR project. As the research progressed, this confidence dropped off dramatically. I could not have been prepared for the humbling learning experience of being part of such a powerful research group, who together worked out what actions to take, when, why, and with what outcome in mind. Even after all of my critical social work education and personal and professional experience working from a feminist anti-oppressive perspective, the dominance of traditional positivist research methodology clouded my thinking. I found it difficult to separate my feelings of ownership over my graduate education from the research process and outcome. This was particularly highlighted when fear set in as I anticipated how the research outcomes could affect my academic career.

The importance of being prepared for the unexpected outcomes and the unanticipated path forged by the research group cannot be stressed enough when considering engaging in CAR. It was the moment when the research group challenged me and determined that the knowledge produced and analyzed through the collective process would stand on its own, without my further individual analysis, categorizing, or wordsmithing, that I realized the true meaning of CAR. It was in that moment that I understood I was a participant/researcher with one voice in the collective, rather than a participant/researcher with the power to define the voice of the collective. Looking back, it seems so obvious that the structure was set up to have the community group control the project, but I was not prepared for the lack of control I had as a researcher over the final ethics document produced by the group. I engaged in a process of intense self-reflection and journalling to assist in working out my need for control and contextualizing why the dominant narrative—that as the researcher, surely I needed to perfect the research product—kept running through my mind. It was critical for me to learn, as an anti-oppressive researcher and as a social worker, to internalize that the process, structure, and the products were undeniably that of the entire research group.

I realized that, much like AOP social work practice, the CAR process required me to be a witness and a supporter on a journey, rather than directing, judging, and owning the outcome as my personal accomplishment when remarkable change happened. Participating in the CAR process changed me. Witnessing community ownership brought meaning to the methodology of CAR on a cellular level for me, and took it from a concept to a state of being. Even with the warnings I had received from others about the workload involved and the unpredictability, I could not have prepared myself for this process. It was one of the most rewarding and challenging things I have ever been a part of.

## CONCLUSIONS

In the end of the project, we came to the conclusion that the research process and the products developed as a result of the project were of great value to Bridges, the research participants, and the PAG. The strengths of the research project parallel strengths in CAR as a methodology. CAR, when conducted in a legitimately community-centred way, creates meaningful and socially just community actions (Brown & Reitsma-Street, 2003). By engaging the values of CAR and keeping the community that initiated the research in control of the research process, outcomes, and products, this project produced many useful outcomes. As we moved through the research process, a significant shift emerged. This shift was marked by a politicization of the research participants; they became driven to move beyond contributing to the research by discussing and defining ethics, to strategizing about community action concerning the change in the funding model. Potts and Brown (2005) argue, "Being an anti-oppressive researcher means that there is political purpose and action to your research work" (p. 255). By this definition, this research project was anti-oppressive as it took on a two-part focus: one part focused on the ethics and practices within Bridges as an agency, and the other on the larger community impacts of the new funding model.

According to Strega, "We must assess the political implications and the usefulness of what we produce for progressive, anti-oppressive politics in marginalized communities" (p. 145, this volume). Clearly, the research resulted in a set of strategies for community action, growth, and resistance. The research group engaged in assessing both the usefulness and the political implications of the research outcomes. I witnessed the research group engage in anti-oppressive CAR as they took control of the process, moulding the outcomes in response to the political context that allowed for the dismantling of the provincial bridging employment program.

With the understanding that Bridges had strong ownership over the research from the beginning of the project, I inferred that the process of building community and strengthening relationships among colleagues would also be a central research outcome. Relationships were formed, strengthened, and renewed during the research process. As one participant commented, "Knowing ourselves as women and as ethical practitioners gives us the power to create change" (Workshop session #4). Although I anticipated that relationships would form and strengthen during the research process, the way that the community building organically evolved into a major research outcome was something I did not anticipate. This collective strengthening was demonstrated by the will of the group to move forward together, mobilizing to take action and implement the research recommendations. This was a tremendous indication that relationship building was a major outcome of the research process.

The main limitation of the research was the inability to engage more of a variety and higher numbers of participants in the process. Given the scope of our small research project, we could not design the project to be as inclusive as it could have been. Only current Bridges staff working directly with the employment program clients were invited to participate. This excluded administrative staff, contract workers, staff in other Bridges programs, and past staff from contributing to the research. This particular scope limited the outcome of the research because it did not consider the perspectives of past employees or volunteers working directly and indirectly with clients. In essence, only a select group was asked to define the current ethical values, principles, and practices at Bridges. In this way, the project was not inclusive of the entire Bridges community. Further to this, the client perspective on ethical values and practices was not included in this research; this was also a limitation, as the voices of those who receive service at Bridges were not directly represented.

I believe the most useful and beautiful part of the research process was that the research itself became a form of resistance and solace for the research participants. A research participant described the project as "a place to think clearly and come back to knowing who we are and why we exist for women in the community" (Workshop session #1). Another participant stated, "This project gives me hope that we can resist together and come up with strategies to educate the government about how important our values and ethics are" (Workshop session #2). From the beginning of the project, it was clear that the research process facilitated something beyond the collective formulation of an ethics document. It was a place for connection, reflection, rejuvenation, and strategy.

# REFERENCES

Boser, S. (2006). Ethics and power in community-campus partnerships for research. *Action Research, 4*(1), 9–21.

Brown, L., & Reitsma-Street, M. (2003). The values of community action research. *Canadian Social Work Review, 20*(1), 61–78.

Hesse-Biber, S. N., Leavy, P., & Yaiser, M. L. (2004). Feminist approaches to research as a process: Reconceptualizing epistemology, methodology, and method. In S. N. Hesse-Biber, P. Leavy, & M. L. Yaiser (Eds.), *Feminist perspectives on social research* (pp. 2–26). New York, NY: Oxford University Press.

Potts, K., & Brown, L. (2005). Becoming an anti-oppressive researcher. In L. Brown & S. Strega (Eds.), *Research as resistance: Critical, Indigenous and anti-oppressive approaches* (pp. 255–286). Toronto, ON: Canadian Scholars' Press.

# Chapter Five

# The View from the Poststructural Margins: Epistemology and Methodology Reconsidered

## Susan Strega[1]

The master's tools will never dismantle the master's house.
—Audre Lorde

The master's house will only be dismantled with the master's tools.
—Henry Louis Gates Jr.

These alternative visions, separated by gender and almost a generation, offer some insight to the quandaries faced by marginalized researchers and social justice scholars. The goal of destroying the master's house necessarily leads researchers to the question of how best to go about doing so. The research "tools" that might be employed in this endeavour are not just particular data collection and analysis methods, but the methodologies that frame these methods, and their epistemological and ontological foundations. The researcher who asks herself at the inception of a research project: "How can I best capture the complexities and contradictions of the worlds, experiences, or texts I am studying; whose voices will my research represent; whose interests will it serve; how can I tell if my research is good research?" is asking questions about the ontological and epistemological foundations of her work. For social justice researchers, the answers represent not only methodological choices, but choices about resistance and allegiance to the hegemony of Eurocentric thought and research traditions: the master's tools.

From my position as a marginalized researcher who is committed to furthering social justice in my work, there are compelling reasons to resist using the master's methodologies. I have long been an activist involved with, among other causes, anti-racism and the elimination of violence against women. In the years that I have been concerned with these problems, I have heard and read a great deal of explanation about them, much of it attached to how they might be solved or at least ameliorated. The research that I have read has encompassed both quantitative and qualitative methodologies, and has claimed to prove a number of theories about how and why these problems have arisen and how they might be solved. I contend, though, that none of the research to date, nor the programs and policies it has engendered, has made significant radical change in the world. Thus, like Lorde, I came to the position that we must use different tools if we wish our research to further social justice goals, because I believe there is a relationship between producing knowledge or meanings about the world and the actual practice of doing research.

In this chapter, I take up and support Lorde's contention in two ways. First, I critique the existing "tools" of traditional social science research by examining their ontological and epistemological foundations, explaining how and why most challenges to mainstream approaches have failed, and discussing whether traditional social science can or ought to be transformed. Secondly, I take a critical look at the progressive possibilities of one methodology—feminist poststructuralism—that I believe offers a useful approach for social justice research. As I will explain, feminist poststructuralism requires that researchers examine relationships of power and how they operate through discourse and subjectivity. Through this examination, more effective means of resistance to inequity and injustice may be uncovered.

## ONTOLOGIES, EPISTEMOLOGIES, AND SOCIAL JUSTICE

The ontologies and epistemologies of different research traditions reflect very different ideas about how knowledge about social phenomena can and should be acquired. Each approach carries specific instructions about what should be studied; why and how it should be studied; how the data generated through that study should be analyzed; how research should be assessed; and what ought to be done with research findings. As O'Connor (2001) notes, "These ideas are not simply theoretical musings, they have pragmatic and ethical relevance" (p. 155).

An ontology is a theory about what the world is like—what the world consists of, and why. Another way of thinking about ontology is as a worldview. The worldview of the researcher shapes a research project at every level, because it shapes the researcher's epistemological foundation. An epistemology is a philosophy that explains what counts as knowledge and "truth"; it is a strategy by which beliefs are justified. Epistemologies are theories of knowledge that answer questions about who can be a "knower"; what tests beliefs and information must pass in order to be given the status of "knowledge"; and what kinds of things can be known. All research methodologies rest on ontological and epistemological foundations. Marginalized researchers and researchers committed to social justice, concerned with the inability of traditional research methodologies to bring about social change or further social justice efforts, challenge not only research methods, but also the ontological and epistemological foundations of these methods. As critical race scholar Ladson-Billings (2000) notes, taking up this challenge can be difficult:

> How one views the world is influenced by what knowledge one possesses, and what knowledge one is capable of possessing is influenced deeply by one's worldview ... The conditions under which people live and learn shape both their knowledge and their worldviews. The process of developing a worldview that differs from the dominant worldview requires active intellectual work on the part of the knower, because schools, society, and the structure and production of knowledge are designed to create individuals who internalize the dominant worldview and knowledge production and acquisition processes. (p. 258)

The dominant worldview is not just one way to view the world; it is positioned as the most legitimate way to view the world, and as such, it is difficult to resist. But the existence of non-Eurocentric worldviews that resist the Western world's hierarchical dualism, that alternatively posit that both existence and knowledge are contingent on others, the world, and other living entities, has important implications for researchers. For example, most Indigenous cultures define the basis of all knowledge as relationship: everyone and everything in the world is connected, and understanding these connections is the beginning of knowledge. Similarly, the Afrocentric worldview *Ubuntu*, or "I am because we are," is about knowledge arising from relationship (Ladson-Billings, 2000).

Most of us who have been educated in the White, Western world have been socialized into the ontological and epistemological framework that arose during the period in Eurocentric thought known as the Enlightenment. During the Enlightenment, *science* and *knowledge* began to have the same meaning, and a clear demarcation was established between science and non-science. This binary division between scientific knowledge and all other types of knowledge is hierarchical. Non-scientific sources of knowledge, such as philosophy, folklore, mythology, old wives' tales, and oral traditions, are understood to be less valuable than science because they measure their usefulness through means other than scientific standards of reliability and verifiability. These ways of knowing fail to follow the one "true" path to knowledge prescribed by the Enlightenment: rigorous scientific methodology applied by a rational, neutral, and objective subject to the study of an object clearly positioned outside of himself. Thus, only science is positioned as capable of producing "truth."

Science is said to produce truth through the stringent application of various verification methods, including observation, mathematical calculation, experiment, and replication. Only propositions that can be empirically tested and replicated (by competent scientists) achieve the status of "objective truth." Applying rigorous scientific methods derived from mathematical logic is understood to ensure objectivity, neutrality, and the absence of bias. Objectivity is achieved by separating the "knowing subject" from the "object of knowledge"; can only be achieved through the application of reason; and can therefore only be applied by those who are rational. The scientific method I have described, which was first applied to the study of the natural sciences and has been more recently applied to the social sciences, is alleged to bring about the discovery of knowledge unattached to ideology or power—knowledge that is, in Jane Flax's (1992) phrase, "innocent knowledge." Because scientific knowledge is promoted as bias-free, it has been positioned as the best kind of knowledge for tasks that require prediction and control, such as making law and policy. Law's reliance on apparently neutral knowledge substantiates its claims to impartiality, making it very difficult to challenge the role of law in creating and maintaining inequalities. Similarly, evidence-based practice approaches are appealing for practice professions, such as nursing and social work (McSherry, Simmons, & Abbot, 2002; Otto, Polutta, & Ziegler, 2009), although they have been critiqued (see, for example, Hammersley, 2013) because they enable practitioners to step away from considering how they are implicated in inequality and injustice. As Flax (1992) points out, "Those whose actions are grounded in or informed by such truth will also have their innocence guaranteed. They can only do good, and not harm, to others" (p. 47).

Indigenous scholars, critical race theorists, and feminists have all raised important questions about knowledge production grounded in Enlightenment epistemology and the positioning of science as a superior form of knowledge, asking: Who is entitled to or allowed to create meanings about the world; what criteria are used to decide what constitutes valid truth; and how do gender, class, and race factor into this? As Tuhiwai Smith (2001) points out, "Research [is] a significant site of struggle between the interests and ways of knowing of the West and the interests and ways of resisting of the Other" (p. 2). The idea that there is only one path to truth, that the discovery of truth is guaranteed by objectivity and the rigorous application of a scientific methodology by a rational subject, disguises the gendered, racialized, and classed nature of this discourse and its privileging of White elite masculinity. Science not only guarantees truth, but positions only men (or those who act like them) as capable of finding the truth—through the implication that there is a particular (White) male way of thinking that is critical to scientific method. As Usher (1997) notes:

> A commitment to reason, perspectiveless truth, objective and neutral forms of knowledge, separation of the subject from the object of knowledge are all commitments to the production of [White] male theory in which reason surreptitiously defines itself by excluding categories associated with femininity [and racialized peoples]—subjectivity, the emotions, desire and specificity. (pp. 46–47)

Enlightenment epistemology rests on a hierarchical dualism, in which qualities such as rationality, reason, objectivity, and impartiality are privileged over and opposed to irrationality, emotion, subjectivity, and partiality. This dualism is everywhere in Western/Eurocentric thought, and it is always oppositional and hierarchical, never neutral. It "maintains its position by its capacity to define itself as a universal standard against which the subjective, the emotional, the aesthetic, the natural, the [coloured, classed] feminine must be judged" (Usher, 1997, p. 45).

The Enlightenment, in Eurocentric history, marks the beginning of the "modern" era, and Enlightenment epistemology is thus sometimes known as "modernism." After the Enlightenment, the experimental method became the research norm and the means through which knowledge could be legitimized—that is, accorded the status of truth. Thus, in order to position their research as legitimate, those working in the emerging fields of social science also adopted this approach. Modernist ontology and epistemology continue to inform both quantitative and qualitative social science methodologies, and instruct both quantitative and qualitative researchers. While qualitative and critical social scientists have sometimes critiqued modernism's epistemological foundations, they have not necessarily challenged them. Attempts to be objective in a subjective kind of way have perhaps even reinforced the scientific method as the gold standard against which all ways of creating knowledge continue to be assessed.

The defining characteristics of modernism include the notions that knowledge can be (and is, if the rules are followed) objective, impartial, innocent in intention and affect, and neutrally discovered; that there is only one true method by which knowledge is acquired; and that knowledge can be discovered by a rational subject who is distanced from her or his object of investigation and who separates her or himself from emotions, self-interest, and political values. Information gathered through other methods, and by researchers who socially and politically locate themselves, fails to attain the status of knowledge. Knowledge has function as well as status; in modernism, knowledge is a tool for satisfying needs and controlling the physical and social environment. The idea that human life improves in a progressive fashion through the discovery, acquisition, and application of knowledge is central to modernism.

While feminist critics have stressed gender as the fundamental dualism in Enlightenment thought, another and equally important hierarchical division, that of race, is also apparent. The connection between "light" and knowledge lies within the word *Enlightenment* itself, and provided the explorers, colonizers, and slaveholders of Enlightenment times—and people in centuries to come—a rationale for conquering, subjugating, and civilizing the "dark" peoples of the world. Today, it provides a rationale for ongoing colonialism and the assimilation of Indigenous and racialized people into White Western ways of knowing, being, and doing. As Tuhiwai Smith (2001) notes:

> Research is one of the ways in which the underlying code of imperialism and colonialism is both regulated and realized. It is regulated through the formal rules of individual scholarly disciplines and scientific paradigms, and the institutions that support them (including the state). (p. 8)

The irrational is fundamentally associated not only with the feminine, but also with darkness—whether darkness of night or darkness of skin—and, further, with "magical", "superstitious," and unscientific ways of knowing. Thus, the dominant pattern imposed by Enlightenment epistemology is a hierarchical, gendered, raced, and classed dualism, an asymmetrical division in which the White and male side is valued over the dark and female side.

## MODERNIST METHODOLOGIES

Enlightenment epistemology is the foundation for the three major methodological approaches in the social sciences: positivism (quantitative approaches), interpretivism (qualitative approaches), and critical social science. Although there are significant differences between the approaches, there are also significant commonalities, including the belief that the meaning of social phenomena can be uncovered or discovered, humanist values, and a belief in progress.

Positivist approaches assume the existence of a rational, knowing subject who can recognize the truth about an object of investigation and distinguish it from falsehood through the application of reason. Positivism continues to be positioned as not just the best way but the only way to discover social science "truth." Other, inferior approaches might yield information from various sources (anecdotal evidence, personal experience, stories), but this information is understood to be unreliable. Positivist explanations must be provable and contain no logical contradictions; a fact, even when provisional, is still a fact, and if people disagree about facts, additional measurements and further observation can and will confirm one set of facts over another. Criticism of "facts" derived from the application of positivist methods can be and is routinely dismissed as irrational: the inappropriate imposition of subjective judgments or personal opinions. Other research methodologies—other ways of arriving at facts—are similarly dismissed as irrational, illegitimate, or biased.

On the other hand, qualitative theorists question the value of quantitative methodologies for investigating social phenomena and human behaviour. Their central question is whether the allegedly objective measures used to study the natural sciences can or should be applied to studying the social. Qualitative approaches are intended to arrive at understandings, rather than facts, about the social world and social beings. There are a variety of qualitative methodologies, such as grounded theory, hermeneutics, phenomenology, case study, narrative analysis, and ethnography. What they have in common, according to Neuman and Kreuger (2003), is "the systematic analysis of socially meaningful action through the direct, detailed observation of people in natural settings in order to arrive at understandings and interpretations of how people create and maintain their social worlds" (p. 78). Some qualitative methodologies (such as grounded theory) are more closely aligned with positivism, while others (such as ethnography) are located within a critical or social constructivist paradigm. Each methodology has slightly different definitions of what constitutes data, how data should be gathered, and how data should be analyzed. All share the goal of understanding social life and uncovering how people create meaning in natural settings: What do their words and actions mean to the people who engage in them? How do people define and understand what they are doing? What is relevant? What do they believe is true?

One intention of qualitative research is to give those who read the research a feel for the social reality of others by revealing or illuminating the meanings, values, interpretive systems, and rules of living they apply. From a qualitative perspective, "truth" has been found if the researcher's description and conclusions make sense to those being studied (and others like them), and if they allow others to understand this reality. The researcher's analysis or description is accurate if the researcher conveys a deep understanding of how those who are being studied think, feel, believe, reason, and perceive reality. In interpretivism, reality is about the meanings people create in the course of their social interactions; the world is about not facts, but the meaning attached to facts, and people negotiate and create meaning. Facts are context-specific actions that depend on the interpretations of particular people in a particular setting. Understanding the social context of actions and words is a crucial part of analyzing these interpretations.

Experiences, processes, and phenomena are always contextual, and analyses of them must be grounded in the experience of those who have participated in the experience, process, or phenomenon. Rich, thick description deepens and complicates these understandings.

Although many qualitative researchers believe that completely value-free science is impossible, some qualitative methodologies require that researchers separate from or "bracket" their biases and assumptions. The researcher is instructed to notice, acknowledge, and be reflexive about her biases and values, and hold these separate from the data in order to accurately interpret the material being gathered. Reflection and analysis of the researcher's own thoughts and feelings are considered not only important parts of research, but also an indication of interpretivism's ability to be as rigorous in its methods as positivism, and thus an equally legitimate means by which to generate knowledge. These attempts to redefine objectivity—to, as Con Davis (1990, cited in Lather, 1993) says, "do the police in other voices" (p. 674)—have failed to dislodge positivism as the standard against which all other social science methodologies are evaluated. Arguing that qualitative methodologies can be as rigorous and valid as quantitative approaches serves to reinforce the dualism that constitutes them as inferior.

Critical researchers contend that while positivism works in the service of existing power structures, interpretivism fails to acknowledge the extensive influence of these inequitable structures, leading to the individualization of social problems. Yet in many ways, critical social science is epistemologically aligned with positivism. For example, critical researchers generally believe that there is a "reality" that can be discovered or uncovered. Where they differ from positivists is in their belief that realities are shaped or constructed by social, political, cultural, and other forces. In critical social science, while facts exist, they are always historically, socially, and culturally constituted. Because facts are contingent rather than neutral, they must be interpreted from a value basis—an ideological position. For critical researchers, sites of conflict, contradiction, and paradox are the best places to do research, because these are most likely to reveal what "true" reality is underneath its surface presentation.

Critical researchers make an explicit commitment to social justice. Critical social science is intended to be emancipatory, directed at redressing structural inequalities and transforming existing social relations. Critical researchers want to uncover myths, reveal hidden truths, and help people change the world for themselves. They recognize that knowledge is linked to power, meaning that researchers must think about whether their work is likely to support or challenge existing power structures. Critical research involves two essential steps: accurately describing reality, and then applying that accurate description to suggest, support, or undertake action. In critical social science, these processes are called *praxis*. Explanations are valued when they help people to understand the world and take action to change it.

In the critical paradigm, research is intended to empower the marginalized and promote action against inequities. Questions about the relationship between the researcher and the researched are highlighted, as is the question of whose voice(s) the research (re)presents. Critical social science asks questions, exposes hypocrisy, and investigates social conditions to encourage grassroots action. It is avowedly and clearly political in intention and in process. The meaning that people make of situations is important, but there are real, observable structures to be discovered; these "unseen forces" are what the critical social scientist is interested in. Despite its commitment to social justice, critical social science relies on Enlightenment epistemology through its continuing commitment to the idea that "reality" can be discovered. Thus, it implicitly continues to support hierarchical dualism and the inequities it engenders.

Feminism has mounted significant challenges to the privileging of positivism. Historically, feminists deployed their efforts along three strategic courses. First, they dared to attack positivist science on its own terms, critiquing the methodology by accusing it of falling short of "good" scientific practice, implying that better applications of method might yield different findings. But, as Hekman (1990) notes:

> If the canons of scientific method as they have been defined by
> the dominant tradition since Bacon are inherently sexist, then
> adherence to these methods, no matter how rigorous, will not
> produce results that will fundamentally alter the sexist charac-
> ter of scientific discourse. (p. 124)

A second strategy, one that has been employed primarily by liberal feminists, demands that women be allowed entry "into the sphere of rationality as it has been defined by men" (Hekman, 1990, p. 40). This approach accepts the definition and the privileging of the rational Enlightenment (White, male) subject and seeks to earn that privilege for women by demonstrating that women can be like men. Feminists from Mary Wollstonecraft through to recent second-wave feminists have suggested that, if women are allowed the same educational and life chances as men, they too can become "rational subjects" capable of "creating knowledge." By erasing their differences from men, women can abandon the inferior status of "Other" and thus achieve "the Truth that is accessible to the ideally rational man" (Hekman, 1999, p. 91). Some racialized people have also embraced this position, and it is this thinking that has largely informed affirmative action programs. But, as Catherine MacKinnon (1987) has pointed out, equality between sexes and races is predicated on the ability of "Others" to successfully emulate the qualities valued, and exhibited, by White elite men and meet the standards developed and set by them, and thus leaves the hierarchical dualism at the heart of Enlightenment epistemology intact.

A third feminist route has involved accepting the dualism as an accurate or semi-accurate reflection of the "essential" natures of men and women, while attempting to privilege "woman's nature" through valorizing "essential" feminine qualities, such as intuition, and women's ways of knowing, such as "experiential" knowledge. This strategy has included both the idea of complementarity (that men and women represent "two halves of a whole," and that both ways of "knowing" the world are needed) and the radical feminist suggestion that feminine qualities and values are superior and should be embraced by all, men and women alike. For example, feminist theorists Mary Daly (1978) and Susan Griffin (1982) suggest that "male" qualities, such as rationality and emotional distance, must be displaced by the womanly attributes of intuition, irrationality, and emotionality. But by accepting rather than repudiating an essential female "nature," such a position reinforces a hierarchical dualism. As Hekman (1990) points out, "much as we might laud the 'feminine' values the radicals proclaim, these values will continue to be viewed as inferior until the dichotomy itself is displaced" (p. 41). Further, the radical feminist position has been critiqued by racialized women and some lesbians, who have noted that this stance fails to account for differences within the category "woman" while reversing and thus maintaining a dualistic hierarchy of difference. It also fails to contend with the symbiotic relationship between sexism and racism, through which racism sustains and rearticulates sexism, and sexism sustains and rearticulates racism.

Given the sexual and racial violence and inequity that structure the world, the Enlightenment contention that "truth" can be discovered, and that such discoveries provide for progress, is seductive. Part of what is so alluring in the possibility of discovering incontrovertible "proofs" that sexism and racism are wrong is that it allows women and the marginalized to locate this contention outside of themselves, and thus avoid the retribution deployed against those who take moral and political positions that name these injustices and notice that White, elite men benefit from them.

It is also difficult to challenge Enlightenment epistemology because "the belief that coherent political action must be grounded in absolutes is deeply rooted in feminist as well as modernist thought" (Hekman, 1990, p. 186). The roots of feminism, like those of many emancipatory struggles, such as the civil rights movement, lie in an Enlightenment discourse of rights, equality, freedom, and justice, and various strains of feminism have seized upon these ideas in particular ways, attempting to make them serve feminist agendas. Even Marxist or socialist feminism, which rejects most liberal feminist and liberal humanist ideology, is an emancipatory movement, rife with rights rhetoric and having at its foundation a dualism and a belief in absolutes. But, as a number of feminist and critical race theorists (MacKinnon, 1987; Razack, 1998; Williams, 1991; Young, 1990) have pointed out, the rhetoric of rights and equality masks substantive inequality because it fails to adequately account for difference.

Enlightenment epistemology inscribes a hierarchical dualism that positions women and other marginalized peoples as inferior and served to justify racial subjugation, violence, and inequity. Tuhiwai Smith (2001) positions resistance to dominant epistemology as a matter of survival for Indigenous peoples: "To acquiesce is to lose ourselves entirely and implicitly agree with all that has been said about us. To resist is to retrench in the margins, retrieve what we were and remake ourselves" (p. 4). In a similar fashion, Hekman (1990) notes that "feminists cannot overcome the privileging of the male and the devaluing of the female until they reject the epistemology that created these categories" (p. 8). As racialized women have made clear, researchers must work with epistemologies and methodologies that can make sense of differences, locating themselves within an epistemology of "truths" rather than "Truth," because "Truth" has failed to account for racialized ontologies, women's ways of knowing, and other subjugated knowledges. These are not abstract philosophical issues. The failure of Enlightenment-based methodologies to challenge what Ladson-Billings (2000) calls the "status quo relations of power and inequities" (p. 263), and their basis in racist and sexist thought, means that researchers committed to social justice must challenge, discard, or transcend Enlightenment epistemology and instead locate themselves within an epistemology of multiple and partial perspectives. For some researchers, including myself, this means working at the intersection of radical feminism and poststructuralism, a position that breaks with Enlightenment epistemology and can support the political purposes of social justice researchers. At the same time, I acknowledge that methodological choices are complex, and that we may, for various reasons and at various times, use quantitative, critical, or qualitative approaches. In these situations, feminist poststructural theory can, I believe, help researchers expand their methodology to encompass social justice concerns.

## FEMINIST POSTSTRUCTURALISM AND THE CHALLENGE TO MODERNISM

Enlightenment epistemology categorizes both knowledge and knowers in ways that legitimize the ideas of White men while casting doubt on the ideas of women and racialized people. As Gunew (1990) notes, "Certain kinds of truth or science came to appear as 'legitimate' at the same time that certain specific groups were authorised to articulate these truths" (p. 21). Poststructuralists reject dualisms, such as rational/irrational and subject/object, and challenge the idea that there is one right or best way to create knowledge (Hekman, 1990, p. 9). Feminist theorists reject the hierarchical dualism of masculine/feminine, challenging established ideas about who can be a knower.

There are some obvious alliances between poststructural and feminist thought. Through feminist standpoint theories (Harding, 1987; Hartsock, 1987) and the sociology of knowledge (Smith, 1990), feminists pointed out the role of the social, the experiential, and the discursive in knowledge acquisition. Similarly, poststructuralists posit that all knowledge is contextual, historical, and, ultimately, produced by rather than reflected in language. Second-wave feminists demonstrated how everyday language use materially harms women (see, for example, Kitzinger & Thomas, 1995; Penelope, 1990; Spender, 1980). French feminist theorists Irigaray (1985) and Cixous and Clement (1986) contended that women's oppression is rooted in language. Still, when I first considered combining feminist and poststructural theories to guide my research, I was struck by the critique implied in Sneja Gunew's (1990) question: "Do feminists have any use for a body of theory which has largely misrepresented and/or excluded women?" (p. 13). It is clear that theories about the role in of language in dominance and subordination, and the links between knowledge and power, have acquired a new legitimacy since their "authorization" by White male theorists such as Foucault. For example, many poststructural insights about language and discourse echo those already proposed by feminist and critical race theorists such as Brossard (1988), Hill Collins (2000), Penelope (1990), Spender (1980), Williams (1991), and Wittig (1992). Similarly, as Ladson-Billings (2000) notes, African-American scholars such as W. E. B. du Bois and Carter Woodson challenged modernism at about the same time as critical scholars of the Frankfurt school, but Woodson's and du Bois's work is largely unacknowledged outside of critical race scholarship. The refusal within poststructuralism to engage with or acknowledge the legacy of critical race theory and feminism makes its appropriation by marginalized scholars problematic, because this refusal implicitly restates the Enlightenment idea that only certain kinds of minds (White, male, privileged) can create knowledge. Indigenous scholar Linda Tuhiwai Smith (2001) contends that poststructuralism and postmodernism are convenient inventions of White, Western intellectuals that serve to reinscribe their power (and right) to define the world.

Another significant critique of poststructuralism targets the idea of multiple, perspectival "truths." Feminist standpoint theory, which also posits knowledge as contextual, historical, and discursive, privileges the perspective of women. Similarly, racialized women, understanding the danger inherent in the notion that all visions are equal, insist on the epistemic privilege of the oppressed (Hill Collins, 2000; Narayan, 1988). Some feminist poststructural theorists, such as Hekman (1999), contend that no perspective can be privileged: "If material life structures consciousness, if the different experiences of different groups create different realities, then this must hold for the oppressed as well as the oppressor" (p. 34). But if we accept the idea that all truth claims are perspectival and partial, how can research provide a secure rationale for progressive politics? I believe that socially just researchers must align themselves with the idea of epistemic privilege; as Ladson-Billings (2000) contends, while the view from the margins "is not a privileged position, it is an advantaged one" (p. 271). When we privilege knowledge, and knowledge construction, along marginalized gender, race, or class lines (to name a few), then we are finally able to speak this truth:

we live in a system of domination and subordination that differentially benefits most White men over most women and most racialized people, and that privileges the White, Western world over the global south.

Despite my hesitations about feminist poststructuralism, I have used it in much of my research work (see, for example, Strega et al., 2014; Brown, Strega, Callahan, Dominelli, & Walmsley, 2009). I have done so in part because I agree with Hekman's (1999) declaration that "we must first alter the criteria of what it makes sense to say before we can proclaim another 'truth' and expect it to be heard" (p. 137). I also locate myself here because I believe that we must unapologetically challenge the epistemologies and methodologies that are used to dehumanize and depersonalize the marginalized, and justify injustice and inequality. I do not have a definitive answer as to which epistemologies and methodologies best serve social justice intentions, but I believe that feminism and poststructuralism working together raise useful questions about knowledge, power, truth, difference, and the constitution of the self that make material contributions to challenging the status quo. In the remainder of this chapter, I discuss three key poststructural concepts (discourse, power, and subjectivity), and conclude with some thoughts about evaluating research.

## DISCOURSE

In its modernist conception, discourse is understood as a way of circumscribing a discussion, as in "the discourse about the economy," or as a way to delineate the manner in which a topic is discussed, as in "scientific discourse." Such usage is directly related to an understanding of language as transparent and expressive, and of words as representative of or signifying the objects or concepts to which they refer. Discourse, in this conception, is also understood to be functional, arising necessarily to allow for the possibility of discussing a particular topic. Any curiosity about "where words come from" or "what words mean" (beyond their dictionary definitions) is, in this understanding, a purely etymological concern, and thus, "the social and ideological 'work' that language does in producing, reproducing or transforming social structures, relations and identities is routinely 'overlooked'" (Fairclough, 1992, p. 211). Transformations in language and the development of new discourses are ascribed to progress or the need to develop new and more accurate ways to describe new discoveries, understandings, or areas of interest. Thus, language and discourse are dissociated from power and ideology, and instead conceptualized as "natural" products of common-sense usage or progress. Modernism positions the individual sovereign subject as the originator of meaning, able to both convey and control meaning by the "correct" selection and arrangement of words. However, a woman's ability to be a subject and authorize language or discourse has been complicated by the hierarchical dichotomy of Enlightenment thought, which has positioned her as "object" due to her imputed inability to be rational. Racialized people are similarly positioned by ascriptions of intellectual inferiority and irrationality.

Before poststructuralism, structuralists challenged the idea that language and discourse are transparent, functional, and progressive. Saussure (1974, cited in Featherstone & Fawcett, 1995) argued that language is socially and historically specific and that the meaning of words is constructed rather than pre-existing. Althusser (1984) described language as a social product that reinforces and reproduces ideology; as a Marxist, he was particularly concerned with how language is instantiated through "ideological state apparatuses," such as educational institutions and the church. Although the significant break with modernist ideas about language and discourse is credited to poststructuralists, feminist and critical race theorists challenged these ideas first, exploring the complex relationships that exist between power, ideology, language, and discourse in some depth. They proposed that language constructs and constitutes reality rather than merely describing it, insofar as we can only apprehend, understand, and describe events and experiences through the words, language, and discourses that are available to us. Further, they contend that the availability of words, language, and discourse is constrained by the workings of power and ideology, rather than progress. For example, in *Speaking Freely: Unlearning the Lies of the Father's Tongue*, linguist and radical feminist Julia Penelope (1990) dissected what she called PUD: the patriarchal universe of discourse. In addition to examining how the inferiority of women, lesbians, people of colour, and people with disabilities, and the concomitant superiority of White, heterosexual, able-bodied men, is constructed through language and discourse, Penelope mapped the discursive processes through which the marginalized unintentionally participate in constructing their own subjugated identities. Other examples include feminist examinations of language and discourse in psychology (Broverman, 1970; Weisstein,

1971); violence against women (Walker, 1990); and moral theory (Gilligan, 1982).

Similarly, critical race theorists such as Hill Collins (2000), Razack (1998), Said (1993), and Trinh (1989) mapped the construction of race and racism through language and discourse in diverse ways. For example, Sherene Razack (1998, 2002, 2004) has delineated how the liberal, humanist discourse of justice, rights, and equality simultaneously masks and constructs relations of domination and subordination along lines of gender, race, and class. Critical race theorists were also among the first (see, for example, du Bois, 1903) to interrogate the idea that we are ideally unitary, rational beings, through problematizing the notion that we originate and control meaning by our choice of words and concepts. As radical feminist Monique Wittig (1992) pointed out, our minds are also colonized territories.

Poststructural researchers analyze not only how particular discourses work; they also focus on the all-encompassing nature of discourse, as the constructor and constituter not just of "reality" but also of our "selves." It is this last idea that so clearly breaks with the Enlightenment idea of the rational, meaning-making subject and the modernist conception of the self. Poststructuralists like Bronwyn Davies (1991) contend that "our existence as persons has no fundamental essence, we can only ever speak ourselves or be spoken into existence within the terms of available discourses" (p. 42). Among poststructural theorists, it is Foucault who is most associated with the idea of discourse as all-encompassing, although it is important to note that Foucault has no definitive theory of discourse; his work contains various and sometimes contradictory ideas. In his early work *The Archaeology of Knowledge* (1972), Foucault described discourse as the principal organizing force of all relations and proposed "archaeology" as a means through which discourse could be exposed in terms of *how* it functioned rather than *why* it functioned. What is consistent across Foucault's theorizations is his interest in understanding how, at historically specific points, language, power, and institutional practices coalesce to produce particular ways of thinking, understanding, being, and doing. He was particularly interested in the relationship between power, knowledge, discourse, and "truth," and *Power/Knowledge* (1980, p. 131) contains an often-quoted description:

> Each society has its regime of truth, its "general politics" of truth: that is, the types of discourse which it accepts and makes function as true; the mechanisms and instances which

enable one to distinguish true and false statements, the means by which each is sanctified; the techniques and procedures accorded value in the acquisition of truth; the status of those who are charged with saying what counts as true.

In Foucault's theory of discourse, knowledge and power are inseparable and are both productive of and constraining of "truth"; power is so co-extensive with knowledge that only an expression such as "power/knowledge" can describe it. Foucault saw interactions between power/knowledge and discourse as recursive, working together to produce what may be understood and allowed to be "truth" at any particular time. In poststructural theory, knowledge is not discovered but emerges from the discursive struggle over which (and whose) perspective or understanding is the one that "counts"— the one that has the power to organize relations. According to Ramazanoglu (1993), a feminist Foucauldian theorist, "There is no single truth ... but many different truths situated in different discourses, some of which are more powerful than others" (p. 21).

As Weedon (1997) notes, most discourses "deny their own partiality. They fail to acknowledge that they are but possible versions of meaning rather than 'truth' itself and that they represent particular interests" (p. 94). Discourses organize social relations as power relations while simultaneously masking these workings of power. Discourses accomplish this through how they organize and constitute inclusions and exclusions; some forms of knowledge are noticed and valued, while others are obscured and devalued. Mills (1997) explains, "A discourse is a set of sanctioned statements which have some institutionalised force, which means that they have a profound influence on the way that individuals act and think" (p. 62). Sanctioning occurs in a number of ways: for example, through what media present or represent as "reality"; through what is taught; and through the penalties that are imposed for attempting to circulate an unsanctioned discourse. For example, the psychiatrist Thomas Szasz (1970) suggested that a biological basis for mental illness was a myth that masked psychiatry's function as an instrument of social control; he has been ridiculed, vilified, and physically assaulted for these ideas. As Usher (1997) notes, "Not only does a discourse permit certain statements to be regarded as the truth but the rules which govern a discourse also determine who may speak, what conventions they need to use and with what authority they may speak" (p. 48).

Hegemonic or dominant discourses and subjugated or illegitimate discourses are produced by processes such as the sanctioning, including, excluding, valuing, and devaluing of certain concepts, ideas, language, and words. Earlier, I described the continuing dominance of Enlightenment epistemology in shaping our understanding of what "knowledge" is and how it can be produced, referring to positivism as the "gold standard" by which knowledge claims are assessed, and the positioning of the rational (White, male) subject as the ideal knower. Those discourses that reflect, promote, and ally with the discourse of Enlightenment epistemology are thus most able to both conceal their partiality and position themselves as "the truth." But processes of exclusion make even dominant discourses vulnerable. As Hekman (1990) suggests, "The gaps, silences and ambiguities of discourses provide the possibility for resistance, for a questioning of the dominant discourse, its revision and mutation" (p. 189). They provide the terrain on which alternative, oppositional, and counter-discourses might emerge.

Subjugated knowledges and the possibilities of other "truths" that might break the hold of hegemonic discourse are of particular interest to feminists and critical race theorists, because of the role that dominant discourse has in rationalizing the inequitable position of women and racialized people. Feminism has, for example, looked to women's experience as a source and guarantor of knowledge, as that experience was shared in consciousness-raising and then became the focus of research through various qualitative methodologies and the promotion of feminist standpoint theory. While a great deal of information has been generated in these ways, most women's lives are not substantially different now than they were before these efforts; as McNeil (1993) notes, "The more we know about patriarchy, the harder it seems to change it" (p. 164). This conundrum brings me to a consideration of a concept central to poststructuralist theory, and regarded with much hesitation by those on the margins: subjectivity.

## SUBJECTIVITY

Enlightenment epistemology describes a subject (a self) that is autonomous, rational, neutral, unitary, and abstracted from its context. Liberal humanism, rooted in Enlightenment epistemology, similarly posits a subject that has agency; this agentic self is "self-conscious," in control of itself, and able and required to create an identity from an apparently unlimited range of choices. As I discussed earlier, these understandings are gendered, classed, and raced; the qualities associated with the Enlightenment, humanist self are those qualities associated with White, elite men. There have been three main challenges to this notion of the self from feminists and critical race scholars. One has been to insist that women and racialized people can also become rational subjects by producing themselves as invested with qualities associated with the modernist subject—becoming like White men. One complication of this notion is that, unless we are to insist that women and racialized people consciously and persistently make choices that are not in their own interests, it fails to adequately account for people's suffering under White patriarchy. As Weedon (1997) notes, "The structural and institutional oppression of women disappears behind the belief that if I, as a rational sovereign subject, freely choose my way of life on the basis of my individual rational consciousness which gives me knowledge of the world, then I am not oppressed" (p. 81).

Various analyses have attempted to account for this contradiction. Structuralism, Marxism, and feminism all propose the existence of "false consciousness": an individual can be, and sometimes is, deceived into complicity with oppression, and she will therefore unintentionally think and behave in ways that harm her self. Consciousness must therefore be "raised" or undergo what Friere (1973) called a process of "conscientization" so that an individual can better understand the external forces that oppress her and perhaps resist them. Alternatively, feminist and humanist psychology have suggested that the complicity of women and racialized people with oppression results from the damage inflicted on their psyches through living under oppression, and might be resolved through therapeutic interventions. These theories encourage us to accept that "the political is personal" and abandon our insistence that "the personal is political." In other words, we can become rational subjects if we accept analyses, generated by those more aware or advanced than us, about the ways in which we are oppressed and participate in our own oppression. But conscientization, consciousness-raising, and therapy have all been markedly unsuccessful in materially changing the conditions of most oppressed people's lives. Another strategy problematizes the Enlightenment subject by valorizing rather than discarding "essential" feminine attributes, such as emotionality and relationality, positing a complementary subject that can be valued equally with (or, as some theorists suggest, more highly than) the rational, White male subject. In this analysis, women's choices are not "bad" or "unconscious," but related to their womanly nature, and oppression will disappear as essential female qualities, and the women who embody them, are more valued. Similarly, attempts have been made to position some practices of Indigenous peoples, notably their spirituality, and some practices of racialized people, notably their creative and artistic endeavours, as equal in importance to White patriarchal theories and ideologies. These strategies have also failed to substantively redress inequality and injustice.

Poststructuralists, most notably Foucault, reject outright the notion of an autonomous, essential self who freely chooses. For Foucault, the self is a subjectivity produced as an effect of discourse. Subjectivities are historically and socially situated, constituted, and constructed in and through discourse and discursive practices. Weedon (1997) describes subjectivity as "precarious, contradictory and in process, constantly being reconstituted in discourse each time we think or speak" (p. 32), rather than stationary or evolving in a progressive or unified way. Understanding the self through the theory of subjectivity leads to an alternative reading of "choice." In the analysis of feminist poststructuralist Bronwyn Davies (1991),

> choices are understood as more akin to "forced choices" since the subject's positioning within particular discourses makes the "chosen" line of action the only possible action, not because there are no other lines of action but because one has been subjectively constituted through one's placement within that discourse to want that line of action. (p. 46)

Thus, poststructural theory supports the exploration of how and why we are being complicit without pathologizing our behaviour or attributing it to an underdeveloped consciousness.

But poststructuralist theories of the self pose some quandaries, not the least of which is that the decentred, unstable, contradictory poststructuralist subject sounds suspiciously like the emotional, irrational, inferior (dark) female subject of Enlightenment epistemology. Such a subject can be easily dismissed. Feminists and other marginalized peoples also note that the call to "abandon the subject" comes at a time when the marginalized are actively taking up the project of theorizing their selves/subjectivity. Fortunately, some feminist poststructuralists have proposed alternative and politically useful ways to think about our selves, our choices, and our complicity while still maintaining a sense of agency. Davies (1991)

suggests, for example, that "agency is never freedom from discursive constitution of the self but the capacity to recognise that constitution and to
resist, subvert and change the discourses themselves through which one
is being constituted" (p. 51). This acknowledges that our choices are constructed for us through discursive practices, and that we can only choose
from these discursively constituted choices, but suggests that it is our
understanding of these options that guides conscious choices of how we
position ourselves. When there are no alternatives available that do not
in some measure harm us, choosing the construction that is least harmful can be a strategy of resistance. Another choice, which is commonly
exercised by those who occupy already devalued subjectivities, is to position oneself as different from others who share the devalued subjectivity,
while at the same time accepting the general devaluing of the subjectivity.
Thus, a gay man might describe himself as "gay but not promiscuous,"
or a single mother on welfare might explain that she does not smoke or
drink or use drugs. The idea that we are choosing from a range of cir-
cumscribed choices allows for a more accurate assessment of possibilities
for resistance, although these may be on a small scale. Understanding the
range of subjectivities on offer brings not just the possibility of choice
but an increased awareness of the mechanisms by which our selves—our
subjectivities—are created, disciplined, and under surveillance.

Feminists and other marginalized theorists are also justifiably concerned
that accepting the idea that our selves, our subjectivities, are constituted
solely as an effect of discourse means that we must abandon the importance of experiential knowledge. Having lived so long in a world in which
White, elite, heterosexual, and able-bodied men define their experience as
the totality of reality, it has been critical for women and subjugated Others to explore our "realities." Feminist standpoint theory and the notion of
epistemic privilege (Narayan, 1988) have been critical in supporting the
marginalized to move beyond exploring their realities to interrogating and
theorizing them. These theorists are as insistent as any poststructuralist that
knowledge is situated and perspectival, and that there are multiple stand-
points from which knowledge is and can be produced. But they disagree
with the contention of a few poststructuralists that all accounts are therefore equally valid.

Earlier, I noted my agreement with Ladson-Billing's (2000) contention
that the view from the bottom is fuller, and often more accurate, at least
with certain proscribed areas. As Fine (1998) has noted, "in colonizing

relations ... dominant-subordinate relations, subordinates spend much time studying the Other" (p. 146), because our survival depends on doing so. For example, I know a great deal about what White, heterosexual men think, feel, and imagine about lesbians in particular and the world in general, because my economic, academic, and, too frequently, my physical survival has depended on this knowledge and on my ability to be silent about it. I would also contend, since I have had it frequently demonstrated to me, that most White, heterosexual men know little about what lesbians think, feel, and imagine about White, heterosexual men in particular and the world in general, although they apparently feel free to speak and write as if they do. I have essentialized here because I want to make the point that, in the context of the system of domination and subordination in which we live, the marginalized cannot and must not completely abandon the knowledge arising from their experiences.

Alternatively, positioning experience as knowledge fails to take into account that experience is also structured by discourse: we can only understand, apprehend, or explain our experiences within the discourses and subjectivities available to us. Poststructural theory contributes to our understanding of how experience and the knowledge that arises from it are constructed. It allows researchers to consider how particular constitutions of subjectivity, experience, and knowledge function in discursively constituted power relations. As Haraway (1991, cited in Hekman, 1999) points out, in her critique of feminist standpoint theory, "Women's experience is constructed. Like every other aspect of our lives, it is apprehended through concepts that are not of our making" (p. 49). We can only describe our experiences through the discourses available at each historically specific moment. Do women experience domestic violence, family violence, violence against women, or male violence against women, and what are the material consequences of each interpretation? Or are women experiencing essentially "normal" relations between men and women, and what are the consequences of experiencing or interpreting or knowing this violence as "normal"?

As these conflicting and contradictory choices suggest, "individuals are both the *site* and *subjects* of discursive struggle for their identity" (Weedon, 1997, p. 93, italics in the original). What I am suggesting is that everything we as women do or do not do, say or do not say, write or do not write signifies our compliance with or resistance to what Weedon (1997) has described as the "dominant norms of what it is to be a woman" (p. 83). The range of subject positions available to women also turns on dimensions of race, class, age, ethnicity, dis/ability, sexual orientation, and cultural background. Subjectivities are positioned in power relations through discourse. Each positioning has consequences and effects; as Weedon (1997) notes, "Forms of subjectivity which challenge the power of the dominant discourses at any particular time are carefully policed. Often they are marginalized as mad or criminal" (p. 87). For example, as criminologist Adrian Howe (2009) demonstrates, women are routinely vilified for naming men as the originators of most violence toward women, whether it is an individual man or men as a group. Our "selves," our subjectivities, are not acted upon by discourse, but are instead an effect of discourse, and thus an effect of power.

## POWER

Poststructural theories of power differ significantly from modernist interpretations. Foucault (1978) theorized that power was productive and relational, circulated and dispersed throughout society rather than being held exclusively or primarily by certain individuals or groups. But Foucault also acknowledged patterns of domination and subordination, positing that although power is never fixed and stable, power relations are "embodied in the state apparatus, in the formulation of the law, and in the various social hegemonies" (1978, p. 3). Thus, power is exercised and relational rather than merely oppressive or repressive. As individuals, we are not acted upon by power: we are positioned within power.

The notion that there is no ultimate determining factor related to power, such as race, class, or gender, and no ultimate holder of power, such as the state, sometimes makes poststructural ideas about power an anathema to researchers concerned with the very real material inequalities that exist in society. Alternatively, when poststructural analysis is informed by the progressive politics of feminism or critical race theory, I believe that it has more to offer researchers committed to social justice than do analyses based on hierarchies of oppression, which inevitably pit those on the margins against one another. If, as Foucault (1981, cited in Weedon, 1997) suggests, "power is tolerable only on condition that it mask a substantial part of itself. Its success is proportional to its ability to hide its own mechanisms" (p. 117), then analyses directed at uncovering these mechanisms and delineating how they operate within us and in the minutiae of our daily existence present us with better rationales for resistance than do grand narratives, which both obscure difference and require massive mobilization to bring about change. If, as Gunew (1990) suggests, "power [is] a network which operates everywhere in contradictory ways and can therefore be strategically resisted everywhere" (p. 23), then poststructural theory can direct us to opportunities for resistance. Foucauldian ideas have proved useful, for example, to Indigenous scholars studying colonial relations (Deloria, 2004; Alfred, 2009). Delineating the material effects of discourses provides a powerful basis for challenging not only language but also the practices that are attached to and shaped by it.

Foucauldian theories about disciplinary knowledges and their role in producing internally governed individuals are particularly useful for practice professions, such as social work or education. In *Discipline and Punish*, Foucault (1995) delineates the shift in societal governance from mechanisms of external surveillance and punishment meted out on the body of the wrongdoer to the present situation, in which individuals, guided by disciplinary knowledges such as psychiatry, psychology, education, and social work, police themselves. As Usher and Edwards (1994) note, "When discipline is effective, power operates through persons rather than upon them" (p. 92). Similarly, Gunew (1990) points out, "Power is reproduced in discursive networks at every point where someone who 'knows' is instructing someone who doesn't know" (p. 23). While the possibility exists that we can, if necessary, be externally disciplined—those defined as "mad," for example, are still routinely locked up—the internalization of disciplinary knowledges is generally effective and, in fact, eagerly pursued: bookstore sections, and sometimes entire bookstores, are devoted to "self-help." As self-discipline is embraced, the repressive and coercive aspects of power are obscured, and when self-discipline needs shoring up, those with expertise in disciplinary knowledges (psychiatrists, psychologists, social workers, teachers) provide further instruction. Engaging in research as a practice of resistance requires us to challenge these instructions and the ways they shape our research projects and us as researchers. Usher (1997) advises that

> the researcher should develop a self-reflexive stance towards his/her own relation to their research: she/he must be accountable for her/his own cultural prejudices and disciplinary allegiance and be alert to how these implicate themselves in the choices made in research practice. (p. 53)

All of the poststructural ideas that I have discussed—discourse, knowledge, power, and subjectivity—also come into play when research (and the researcher who has produced it) is assessed and evaluated. As I have noted, traditional social science has been structured around epistemological assumptions about who is best suited to produce knowledge, how it can be created, and how it ought to be evaluated. Working in transgressive methodologies requires that we develop transgressive standards by which to assess our work, a matter I discuss briefly below.

## SOCIALLY JUST ASSESSMENT AND EVALUATION

My suggestions for how research that is socially just in its intentions might be assessed start with acknowledging the difficulty of steering a course between the conflicting demands of personal, political, and community commitments and the academic and professional standards to which we make ourselves subject if we choose to pursue our work within the university or other mainstream structures. As Ladson-Billings (2000) notes, "Mechanisms for scholarly recognition, promotion, tenure and publication are controlled by the dominant ideology. [The marginalized] are simultaneously being trained in this dominant tradition and trying to break free of it" (p. 267). Often, our research must be constructed in certain ways so that we can obtain approval for it from various authorities, notably academic institutions, funding bodies, and government and agency officials who control access to funds, documents, and research participants. While feminists, critical race theorists, and Indigenous scholars have managed to open space in the academy, particularly in the social sciences, historical and critical analysis of the role of research in marginalized lives makes us aware that these institutions are also deeply implicated in maintaining and rationalizing inequities. For researchers committed to social justice, these can be confounding issues. As Foucault (1981) notes, "It is always possible that one might speak the truth in the space of a wild exteriority, but one is 'in the true' only by obeying the rules of a discursive 'policing' which one has to reactivate in each of one's discourses" (p. 61).

Under the dominant paradigm of positivism, quantitative measures of rigour and validity are the "gold standard" through which "proof" is established and information attains the status of knowledge. Qualitative research has attempted to make the case that it is as good as quantitative research by offering any number of "alternative" measures through which it might be evaluated; for example, Denzin and Lincoln (1998) position triangulation as "an alternative to validation" (p. 4). But because the very use of the word "alternative" indicates a continuing allegiance to the notion of epistemological guarantees, such alternative measures are not always useful for researchers whose epistemological stance positions "truth" as multiple, partial, and perspectival.

Nonetheless, it is necessary to provide some criteria that allow the reader to make connections between our analyses and the worlds, texts, people, and experiences that we write about. I believe we must start by discarding standard measures of rigour and validity, in either their quantitative or qualitative guise, as evaluation criteria. The dictionary definition of *valid* is instructive here: "Valid implies being supported by objective truth or generally accepted authority" (*Webster's*, 1993, p. 1304). We must ask what use the notion of validity is to research that discards the notion of objective truth and researchers who wish their work to be valuable to those who are neither accepted nor accorded status as authorities. As Cameron (1998) has noted about feminist attempts to position their work as "rigorous" and "valid," "This is a game that no one engaged in what Gill (1995) calls 'passionately interested inquiry' can win, and it is not clear to me why feminists should want to play" (p. 970).

I suggest three standards by which we might assess feminist poststructural research; these ideas might also be useful for researchers who appropriate some poststructural theory even when working in other methodologies. First, we must assess the political implications and usefulness of what we produce for progressive, anti-oppressive politics in marginalized communities. Deyhle and Swisher (1997), in their discussion of Native American research, call this *social justice validity*. Thus, the standards and needs of the community in which the research is being conducted or from which participants are recruited is crucial to evaluation. Our work must therefore be reconstructive as well as deconstructive. Secondly, we must ask ourselves not just "About whom?" but also "For whom?" Hill Collins (2000) suggests that we must adhere to an ethic of caring and personal accountability as researchers. Tuhiwai Smith (2001) recommends that the results of our studies be "disseminated back to the people in culturally appropriate ways and in a language that can be understood" (p. 15). African American scholar bell hooks (1990) sounds an important caution about poststructuralism, noting that

the contemporary discourse which talks the most about het-
erogeneity, the decentered subject, declaring breakthroughs
that allow recognition of otherness, still directs its critical voice
primarily to a specialized audience, one that shares a common
language rooted in the very master narratives it claims to challenge. (p. 11)

Thus, as researchers, we must assess whether we have managed to speak
truth to power in accessible languages and formats.

Finally, we must measure the extent to which we have been critically
reflexive, including the extent to which we have considered our own complicity in systems of inequality. Critical reflection and complicity are political
concerns; I note Lal's (1996) comment that "a reflexive and self-critical methodological stance can become meaningful only when it engages in the politics
of reality and intervenes in it in some significant way" (p. 207). The nature
and extent of our critical reflexivity is a useful measure for a number of reasons. It highlights rather than obscures the participation of the researcher in
the research process. It makes clear that interpretation is taking place, and by
implication calls into question the alleged neutrality and objectivity of other
research/researchers, thus offering an important political and methodological
challenge to standard research practices. It calls into question whether standard means of assessing rigour and validity are the "proper" or best means
by which to assess research. Have we laid out our processes of inquiry, and
considered the effects of our positionality on the research? While we need
to continuously interrogate our perceptions and embedded ideologies, these
matters must never take centre stage. Our positionalities as researchers must
be noticed, questioned, and taken up, but they ought not to be the purpose
or focus of our work, for the simple reason that this is unlikely, on its own, to
contribute to political change. Critical reflection must not be the sole focus of
our research: the reader must still learn more about the puzzle or experience
being analyzed than about the researcher.

Complicity is an important criterion for me as a feminist, grounded as
it is in my belief that patriarchy continues to exist because women support
it, to a greater or lesser extent, through their own complicity. Resisting
complicity is complicated by the ability of discourse to "account for" such
resistance. Regina Austin (1989, cited in Fine, 1998, pp. 143–144) makes
the observation that her insights have been met with the response that

> you are too angry, too emotional, too subjective, too pessimis-
> tic, too political, too anecdotal and too instinctive ... I suspect
> that what my critics really want to say is that I am too self con-
> sciously black (brown, yellow, red) and/or female to suit their
> tastes and should "lighten up" because I am making them very
> uncomfortable, and that is not nice.

While I am not vulnerable to such dismissals on the ground of race, being a lesbian can have the same effects. But my positionality must also be acknowledged, because to some extent it affords me the luxury of speaking that which most heterosexual women do not dare to say or "know."

Penalties for failures in complicity are both commonplace and familiar to feminists: tenure denied, employment lost, or funding withdrawn. Walker (1990) describes how the Canadian women's movement relinquished its characterization of battering as "men's violence against women" once organizations were threatened with the denial of state support for transition houses and counselling services. More strenuous refusals to be complicit, as in the case of Aileen Wuornos, a sex worker who killed her abusive customers in self-defence, provoke more severe consequences (Chesler, 1994); Wuornos was executed in 2002. Despite the proliferation of equity policies, most women in academia, heterosexual and lesbian, know and fear the power of being labelled a dyke/man-hater/feminazi. We also fear that our work might be dismissed; as Mills (1997) points out, "Even if your research work is factually accurate or insightful, if it does not accord with the form and content of particular disciplines it is likely to be disregarded or to be regard as non-academic or popular" (p. 69). These disciplining activities instruct us in complicity, and yet complicating and challenging complicity are essential for creating political change. As Mills (1997) has noted, "All knowledge is determined by a combination of social, institutional and discursive practices, and theoretical knowledge is no exception. Some of this knowledge will challenge dominant discourses and some will be complicit with them" (p. 33). Thus, a critical measure by which our work needs to be assessed is the extent to which we are complicit with or challenging of dominant discourses.

While we might accept that "truth is plural and relative, historical and particular" (Hekman, 1999, p. 24), we must nonetheless justify the particular truths at which we arrive. Are the questions we pose as a result of our research interesting, challenging, and different from those usually asked? Finally, in a world in which the violence of the dominant toward the marginalized is at one and the same time the context for daily life and a set of invisible facts, have we managed to "make strange that which appears familiar, and make familiar that which appears strange"[1](Hekman, 1999, p. 138)?

## NOTE

1. This chapter owes much to Pat Usher at the University of Southampton, who challenged me to deepen my understandings of both feminism and poststructuralism.

## REFERENCES

Alfred, T. (2009). *Peace, power, righteousness: An Indigenous manifesto*. Toronto, ON: Oxford University Press.

Althusser, L. (1984). Ideology and ideological state apparatuses (Notes towards an investigation). In L. Althusser, *Essays on Ideology* (pp. 1-60). London: Verso.

Brossard, N. (1988). *The aerial letter* (M. Wildman, Trans.). Toronto, ON: Women's Press.

Broverman, I. (1970), Sex-role stereotypes and clinical judgments of mental health. *Journal of Consulting and Clinical Psychology, 34*(1), 1–7.

Brown, L., Strega, S., Callahan, M., Dominelli, L., & Walmsley, C. (2009). Manufacturing ghost fathers: The paradox of father presence and absence in child welfare. *Child and Family Social Work, 14,* 25–34.

Cameron, D. (1998). Gender, language and discourse: A review essay. *Signs: Journal of Women in Culture and Society, 23*(4), 945–973.

Chesler, P. (1994). *Patriarchy: Notes of an expert witness*. Munroe, ME: Common Courage Press.

Cixous, H., & Clement, C. (1986). *The newly-born woman* (B. Wing, Trans.). Manchester, UK: Manchester University Press.

Daly, M. (1978). *Gyn/ecology*. Boston, MA: Beacon Press.

Davies, B. (1991). The concept of agency: A feminist poststructural analysis. *Postmodern Critical Theorizing—Social Analysis Series, 30,* 42–53.

Deloria, P. J. (2004). *Indians in unexpected places*. Lawrence, KS: University Press of Kansas.

Denzin, N. & Lincoln, Y. (1998). *Strategies of qualitative inquiry.* Thousand Oaks, CA: Sage.

Deyhle, D., & Swisher, K. (1997). Research in American Indian and Alaska Native education: From assimilation to self-determination. *Review of Research in Education, 22,* 113–194.

du Bois, W. E. B. (1903). *The souls of black folk.* London, UK: Oxford University Press.

Fairclough, N. (1992). Discourse and text: Linguistic and intertextual analysis within discourse analysis. *Discourse and Society, 3*(2), 193–217.

Featherstone, B., & Fawcett, B. (1995). Oh no! Not more isms: Feminism, postmodernism, poststructuralism and social work education. *Social Work Education, 14*(3), 25–43.

Fine, M. (1998). Working the hyphens: Reinventing self and other in qualitative research. In N. Denzin & Y. Lincoln (Eds.), *The landscape of qualitative research: Theories and issue*s (pp. 130–155). London, UK: Sage.

Flax, J. (1992). The end of innocence. In J. Butler & J. Scott (Eds.), *Feminists theorise the political* (pp. 445–463). London, UK: Routledge.

Foucault, M. (1972). *The archaeology of knowledge.* London, UK: Tavistock.

Foucault, M. (1978). *The history of sexuality (Vol. 1: An introduction)* (R. Hurley, Trans.). New York, NY: Pantheon

Foucault, M. (1980). *Power/knowledge: Selected interviews and other writings, 1972-1977.* New York: Pantheon.

Foucault, M. (1981). The order of discourse. In R. Young (Ed.), *Untying the text: A post-structuralist reader* (pp. 48–68). Boston, MA: Routledge and Kegan Paul.

Foucault, M. (1995). *Discipline and punish: The birth of the prison* (2nd ed.) (A. Sheridan, 1977, Trans.). New York, NY: Vintage Books.

Friere, P. (1973). *Pedagogy of the oppressed.* New York, NY: Seabury Press.

Gilligan, C. (1982). *In a different voice.* Cambridge, MA: Harvard University Press.

Gill, R. (1995). Relativism, reflexivity and politics: Interrogating discourse analysis from a feminist perspective. In S. Wilkinson & C. Kitzinger (Eds.), *Feminism and discourse* (pp. 165–186). London, UK: Sage.

Griffin, S. (1982). *Made from this earth: An anthology of writings by Susan Griffin.* New York, NY: Harper and Row.

Gunew, S. (1990). Feminist knowledge: Critique and construct. In S. Gunew (Ed.), *Feminist knowledge: Critique and construct* (pp. 13–33. London, UK: Routledge.

Hammersley, M. (2013). *The myth of research-based policy and practice.* Thousand Oaks, CA: Sage.

Harding, S. (1987). *Feminism and methodology.* Bloomington: Indiana University Press.

Hartsock, N. (1987). Rethinking modernism: Minority vs. majority theories. *Cultural Critique, 7,* 187–206.

Hekman, S. (1990). *Gender and knowledge: Elements of a postmodern feminism.* Cambridge, MA: Polity Press.

Hekman, S. (1999). *The future of differences: Truth and method in feminist theory.* Cambridge, MA: Polity Press.

Hill Collins, P. (2000). *Black feminist thought* (2nd edition). New York, NY: Routledge.

hooks, b. (1990). Postmodern Blackness. *Postmodern culture, 1*(1), 11

Howe, A. (2009). *Sex, violence and crime: Foucault and the "man" question.* London, UK: Routledge.

Irigaray, L. (1985). *Speculum of the other woman* (G. Gill, Trans.). Ithaca, NY: Cornell University Press.

Kitzinger, C., & Thomas, A. (1995). Sexual harassment: A discursive approach. In S. Wilkinson & C. Kitzinger (Eds.), *Feminism and discourse* (pp. 32–48). London, UK: Sage.

Ladson-Billings, G. (2000). Racialised discourses and ethnic epistemologies. In N. Denzin & Y. Lincoln (Eds.), *Handbook of qualitative research* (2nd ed.) (pp. 257–277). Thousand Oaks, CA: Sage.

Lal, J. (1996). Situating locations: The politics of self, identity and "other" in living and writing the text. In D. Wolf (Ed.), *Feminist dilemmas in fieldwork* (pp. 185–214). Boulder, CO: Westview Press.

Lather, P. (1993). Fertile obsession: Validity after poststructuralism. *The Sociological Quarterly, 34*(4), 673–693.

MacKinnon, C. (1987). *Feminism unmodified.* Cambridge, MA: Harvard University Press.

McNeil, M. (1993). Dancing with Foucault: Feminism and power/knowledge. In Ramazanoglu, C. (Ed.), *Up against Foucault: Explorations of some tensions between Foucault and feminism* (pp. 147–175). London: Routledge.

McSherry, R., Simmons, M., & Abbot, P. (Eds.). (2002). *Evidence-informed nursing: A guide for clinical nurses.* London, UK: Routledge.

Mills, S. (1997). *Discourse.* London, UK: Routledge.

Narayan, U. (1988). Working together across differences: Some considerations on emotions and political practice. *Hypatia, 3*(2), 31–47.

Neuman, W. L., & Kreuger, L. (2003). *Social work research methods: Qualitative and quantitative approaches.* Boston: Allyn and Bacon.

O'Connor, D. (2001). Journeying the quagmire: Exploring the discourses that shape the qualitative research process. *Affilia, 16*(2), 138–158.

Otto, H-U., Polutta, A., & Ziegler, H. (Eds.) (2009). *Evidence-based practice: Modernizing the knowledge base of social work?* Opladen, Germany: Barbara Budrich.

Penelope, J. (1990). *Speaking freely: Unlearning the lies of the fathers' tongue.* Elmsford, NY: Pergamon Press.

Ramazanoglu, C. (Ed.). (1993). *Up against Foucault: Explorations of some tensions between Foucault and feminism.* London: Routledge.

Razack, S. (1998). *Looking white people in the eye: Gender, race, and culture in courtrooms and classrooms.* Toronto, ON: University of Toronto Press.

Razack, S. (2002). Gendered racial violence and spatialized justice: The murder of Pamela George. In S. Razack (Ed.), *Race, space, and the law: Unmapping a white settler society* (pp. 122–156). Toronto, ON: Between the Lines.

Razack, S. (2004). *Dark threats and white knights: The Somalia affair, peacekeeping, and the new imperialism.* Toronto, ON: University of Toronto Press.

Said, E. (1993). *Culture and imperialism.* New York, NY: Knopf.

Smith, D. (1990). *The conceptual practices of power: A feminist sociology of knowledge.* Boston, MA: Northeastern University Press.

Spender, D. (1980). *Man made language.* London, UK: Routledge and Kegan Paul.

Strega, S., Janzen, C., Brown, L., Carriere, J., Morgan, N. J., & Thomas, R. (2014). Never innocent victims: Street sex workers in Canadian print media. *Violence against Women, 20*(1), 6–25.

Szasz, T. (1970). *The myth of mental illness.* New York, NY: Harper and Row.

Trinh, M. T. (1989). *Woman, native, other: Writing postcoloniality and feminism.* Bloomington: Indiana University Press.

Tuhiwai Smith, L. (2001). *Decolonising methodologies: Research and Indigenous peoples.* Dunedin, NZ: University of Otago Press.

Usher, P. (1997). Challenging the power of rationality. In G. McKenzie, J. Powell, & R. Usher (Eds.), *Understanding social research: Perspectives on methodology and practice* (pp. 42–55). London, UK: The Falmer Press.

Usher, R., & Edwards, R. (1994). *Postmodernism and education.* London, UK: Routledge.

Walker, G. (1990). *Family violence and the women's movement: The conceptual politics of struggle.* Toronto, ON: University of Toronto Press.

*Webster's Third New International Dictionary of the English Language, Unabridged.* (1993). Springfield, Mass: G. & C. Merriam Co.

Weedon, C. (1997). *Feminist practice and poststructuralist theory.* Oxford, UK: Blackwell.

Weisstein, N. (1971). Psychology constructs the female. In V. Gornick, & B. Moran (Eds.), *Women in sexist society: Studies in power and powerlessness* (pp. 207–224). New York, NY: Basic Books.

Williams, P. (1991). *The alchemy of race and rights*. Cambridge, MA: Harvard University Press.

Wittig, M. (1992). The straight mind. In M. Wittig, *The straight mind and other essays* (pp. 21–32). Boston, MA: Beacon Press.

Young, I. (1990). *Justice and the politics of difference*. Princeton, NJ: Princeton University Press.

# Chapter Six

# Narrative Research and Resistance: A Cautionary Tale

## Heather Fraser and Michele Jarldorn

From a critical perspective, research must be about empowering the marginalized and promoting action against inequities
Strega, 2005, p. 208

Social scientists [should] not merely ... endorse the values of that culture but scrutinize the special value accorded the interview and the narrative study of lives
Atkinson & Silverman, 1997, p. 313

The aim of this chapter is to consider some of the emotional and political complexities of using narrative research to show some of the reactions to, and impacts of, violence, especially for women. Specifically, we focus on the potential influence of researchers' responses to participants' stories. We tell the tale of two feminist social work researchers (see also Seymour, 2012) who found themselves emotionally triggered by an interview. We illustrate how even those committed to social justice can find their thinking clouded by emotions that belong more to the researchers' own biographies than they do to the research participant's narration of experience. This leads to a longer discussion of how intense emotions, unacknowledged or uninspected, threatened to distort our judgment and distract us from our social justice agendas.

We have organized this chapter into three main sections. In the first section, we provide background material about narrative research and Michele's thesis. In the second section, we map aspects of "Jane's" interview using 20 excerpts from her transcript. All names used are pseudonyms. We have called Jane's first daughter Sarah and her second daughter Linda. Sarah's father is referred to as Malcolm. Here we discuss: (a) Jane's early years; (b) Jane's life after Sarah is born; and (c) Jane's life after Linda is born. We have chosen to present so many chronologically ordered excerpts from Jane's transcript with very little narrative analysis so as to not block or distract from the full extent of the violence Jane has experienced. In the third and largest section, we work our way through the seven (overlapping) phases of narrative analysis (Fraser, 2004). We identify the key issues we faced at each phase as we analyzed Jane's transcript.

For us, it is a risk to discuss this topic. We would prefer to concentrate on the many instances we have felt and conveyed empathy—times when we have "looked good." We are resisting this urge because we know that learning does not only happen through easy experiences or moments of triumph. As we confront some of the awkward, painful, and disorienting aspects of qualitative research processes, we appreciate the need to unearth insights not only about ourselves as researchers, but also about the social problems we are committed to addressing. Part of the process of anti-oppressive social work is to notice how dominant discourses can infiltrate and distort our thinking. Yet, we hope we have found ways to discuss our concerns while dignifying Jane as a person. We know that the cautionary tale we tell here is more about us, as researchers resisting the temptation to individualize people's experiences, than it is about Jane. We tell this tale in the hope that it might be useful to other anti-oppressive social work researchers.

## PART 1: DOING NARRATIVE RESEARCH

Narrative research is a systematic approach to studying stories in context (Mishler, 1995). Stories have plots, characters, actions, and contexts (Daiute & Lightfoot, 2004). They have a point, a theme, or a moral tale (Riessman, 1994, 2003). Studying narratives can involve examining storytellers' attempts to manage problems or resolve tensions or dilemmas, with a view to reconciling anomalies, contradictions, or departures from the conventional (Kimpson, 2005; Plummer, 1995; Riessman, 1994). Stories can reveal a great deal, whether they are big or small (Georgakopoulou, 2006; Plummer, 1995; Riessman 1994).

Even when they do not mean to, stories provide evidence of time, place, and social conventions (Franzosi, 1998; Riessman, 1994, 2003). They can be interpreted in multiple and sometimes surprisingly different ways (Daiute & Lightfoot, 2004; Plummer, 1995). Intended interpretations, or those meanings the storyteller is trying to convey, may not be shared between participants or members of the audience (Franzosi, 1998). While storytelling can be used to achieve consensus, narrative research is not necessarily about reaching agreement. It will depend on the aim or purpose of the study.

The main models of narrative analysis are: 1) *thematic analysis,* which emphasizes what is said; 2) *structural analysis,* which emphasizes how stories are told; and 3) *interactional analysis,* which emphasizes "the dialogic process between teller and listener" (Riessman, 2003, p. 4). In this work, thematic and interactional analyses are our focus as we work through the seven (overlapping) phases of narrative analysis (Fraser, 2004):

1. *Hear the emotions*—not just those expressed by participants but also those felt (expressed, repressed, or ignored) by researchers, at the time of the interview and in subsequent replaying;

2. *Transcribe the interview material*—even if a professional transcriber is used, researchers need to pay close attention to the clustering of talk, delineation of sentencing, and grammatical and emotional signage;

3. *Interpret individual transcripts*—carefully analyze each participant's transcript in their own light, in relation to their own specificities and idiosyncrasies;

4. *Scan across different domains of experience*—including those relating to the intrapersonal, interpersonal, cultural, and structural. Be careful not to inadvertently fixate on only one dimension of the person's stories;

5. *Link the personal with the political*—this includes noticing references (explicit or latent) to popular or dominant discourses. In our case, we examine the politics of "failure to protect" and the unwritten script we hold about "good women domestic violence survivors," both of which initially infiltrated our thinking;

6.  *Look for commonalities and differences among participants*—literally undertaken by comparing and contrasting participants' experiences and methods of conveying and constructing those experiences; and
7.  *Write academic narratives*—recognize the differences in style, format, purpose, and function between academic and personal stories. Researchers take authorial responsibility for the production of academic narratives.

## Michele's Thesis

*Five Australian women over 40 years talk about their past experiences of intimate partner violence* (Jarldorn, 2011) was a social work honours thesis about intimate partner violence, power, substance use, effects on children, staying/leaving, and rebuilding new lives. Ethics approval was granted in May 2011 under the condition that the project was closely supervised. Before each interview, issues of confidentiality were discussed and consent forms signed. The participants chose their own pseudonyms. All agreed to the interviews being audiotaped and transcribed verbatim, with identifying names and places changed or omitted.

Unlike most research about intimate partner violence, which focuses on women in crisis (Waldrop & Resick, 2004), the participants of this study were each at least eight years out of an abusive or violent relationship. Of the five women, only one had received any specific interventions for intimate partner violence. Yet, they had all managed to rebuild their lives after the violence. Contrary to the gender norms they grew up with, all five women found that spending time single helped them "recover" and begin to trust their own judgment. To different degrees, all the women reported still struggling with trusting others. The implications for social work are plentiful, including understanding the enormity of leaving an abusive intimate and the difficulties associated with "moving on."

## PART 2: JANE'S INTERVIEW

Prior to honours, I (Michele) had conducted only one research interview. I had done so on field placement, in the presence of my supervisor, and in a clinical setting. This time I was on my own, in the home of one of the participants in a country town in South Australia. With three other White, working-class, middle-aged women, we sat around the kitchen table as we shared coffee, cake, and then lunch over the course of the day. The atmosphere was friendly and we had a few laughs. Before each interview I felt apprehensive, but also confident. In part, my confidence came from all of us having survived intimate partner violence.

Jane was the second woman I interviewed that day. At the time of the interview, Jane was married and in her early fifties. Born into a working-class family, Jane grew up in a small town in Australia in the 1960s. Across the course of her life, she was exposed to a great deal of violence and abuse.

## Violence and Abuse in Jane's Childhood
Early on in the interview, while reflecting on her childhood, Jane wrestled with the concept of violence:

> It wasn't a very happy household. Mum was a very emotional person; dad was a very cold person, so, a lot of arguments. *But no violence*—as in physical. Mum had a lot of mental abuse where she was told she was dumb all the time, only capable of doing so much—all that stuff. But I grew up in a little country town [where] everything was basically confined to the home. You never talked about it. You never spoke to anybody else about it. Cos dad was, *dad was a businessman.* (excerpt 1)

Jane went on to describe how her father travelled for work and had sexual affairs, and as he did so, her mother's depression deepened and she took more and more antidepressants:

> He [father] had several affairs that we know of. You know, we protected mum from it ... *mum was the crazy one.* (excerpt 2)

At the age of 11, Jane witnessed a dramatic deterioration in her mother's mental health:

> He [father] left for another woman. I came home one day and mum had tried to kill herself. She had taken an overdose of sleeping tablets. I rang my godfather.... He came and took care of things—put her in hospital. Rang my father and I think that it was only 4–5 months later and they were back together. Things didn't really change. Things got worse actually. (excerpt 3)

By 14, Jane regularly got drunk at the local pub, where she met a boyfriend, "Malcolm." Within months of the beginning of their relationship, Malcolm was beating her:

> **Jane:** The day I got my friendship ring—you got them back in those days.
> **Michele:** Yeah, I had one of them once.
> **Jane:** *That was possession.* You didn't realize it then but *that was possession* ... the day after I took my first smack in the mouth. In the main street—weren't nobody around it was around a corner—that sort of threw me a bit. I threw the ring but you know he could charm me back, and I went back with him. Even my parents wouldn't believe. (excerpt 4)

Sometimes Malcolm beat her in public, turning on anyone who dared to intervene:

> It was a full on. He would tackle anything. And the thing was—nobody ever put him down. *Nobody was ever able to hit him or put him on the ground. He was pretty good.* (excerpt 5)

In her late adolescence, Jane stumbled on evidence that her father was physically assaulting her mother:

> I happened to walk into the bedroom—she was getting changed. She was black and blue down one side. I freaked cos the dad had been violent physically. I asked what happened. She said "Your father and I had a bit of a blue. It's nothing to worry about." Well, I ripped into dad something shocking for that. But it ended up mum was on nerve tablets, she was on sleeping tablets, she was on everything. She was not allowed to work at the shop anymore. (excerpt 6)

Seeing her father's abuse written over her mother's body, Jane made a vow to hit back the next time Malcolm attacked her:

> That's how that all happened. That's when it hit home, you know, that's what you are going to look like—that's reality. So

I started getting a bit of a push in myself now. If anything happened I was gonna hit back because it's not going to happen to me ... this is where I've started protecting myself. I would go hit for hit, *though he always won.* (excerpt 7)

## Jane's Life with Malcolm after Sarah's Birth

Jane was still a teenager when she gave birth to Sarah. Jane's relationship with Malcolm went on much as it had, with Malcolm having sexual liaisons with other women while closely policing Jane's movements. Jane said his violence was brutal and regular, and often involved baby Sarah:

[Sarah] was 9 months old when she was put in hospital with pneumonia. They couldn't understand all the bruising on her head. She would just stand there and bash her head on the back of, in those days, wooden cots. And they went through the drill you know abuse and everything else. But they put her into a wooden cot in hospital and the next day I went in to see her and she was worse ... that was the nerves from her hearing [the violence]. (excerpt 8)

Afterwards, Jane made attempts to break away from Malcolm:

I left [Malcolm] when [Sarah] was 1. I went back to him when she was 2. I left him when she was 3, cos of all the violence. The only way he could get me to do things when he come home drunk was to wake her up, so she heard the violence. She was 9 months old. He would wake her up and bring her out into the lounge room and she would just hear it all and see the physical violence. She—it was—yeah—and that's what kept me under control. I'd get up and do what he wanted—just to shut him up. So, she heard the violence. (excerpt 9)

Even so, Jane believed men "spoiled" Sarah "rotten":

[Jane's father] just idolised her, spoiled her rotten. [Sarah] was spoiled rotten by most males. It was just the way she was, blue eyes, blond hair, get the picture. (excerpt 10)

Malcolm's attacks became increasingly life threatening, as did Jane's retaliation:

> I had no control.... When he broke his leg, he hit me. [He] threw a little radiator at me. I picked his crutch up and smashed it against his plaster, and broke his leg again. (excerpt 11)

> He jumped on me and went to hit me. I picked up whatever I could find on the floor and it happened to be a pair of scissors. I stabbed him in the back—missed his spine by a quarter of an inch. When they [scissors] came out they had a broken end.... To this day he still carries that bit of broken scissors in his back. (excerpt 12)

After the stabbing incident, Jane left Malcolm and moved to a different state. Malcolm periodically came to town and called Jane to bring Sarah to him. She did so, explaining:

> I never stopped my daughter thinking or knowing the good part of her father. Never, ever.... Cos there was a really strong bond there and I wasn't going to break it for anybody. (excerpt 13)

Not even four years old yet, Sarah's closeness to Malcolm did not mean ignoring his violence:

> She hadn't seen him for a year or 18 months. She got off the train and ran straight to him—all these people—and she went straight to him. We got in the car, he went to put his arm on the back seat ... she leans over and says, *"Don't you hit mummy!"* (excerpt 14)

By the time Sarah was four, Jane and Malcolm were living together again. On this particular day, Jane took the day off work to recover from a black eye Malcolm had inflicted the night before. Jane's workmates knew about Malcolm's violence, so they came to check on her:

> Um, this is where the story takes a downfall.... My boss and his cousin were pretty concerned that I wasn't at work. They wanted to see if I was all right—they knew what was going on.

My uncle was in the flat looking after my niece and my daughter, both 4 year olds. So I said to him "Just mind the kids while I just nip across the road." I just ran over to say everything is OK. I'm on the footpath next to his car; [Malcolm] came home, pulled in the driveway, saw me talking to another bloke. He walked in and said to Sarah "Tell your mother to get in here or I'll belt her." Sarah just freaked and ran. *She ran straight out on the road and died.* (excerpt 15)

Jane signalled that she has always blamed Malcolm for Sarah's death:

He has to live with that—that's *domestic violence*—and what it does to a child. My daughter would never cross the road, *never. She knew the rules.* Never, ever has she been out the front. And she just freaked and ran. She was only 4—4 and 10 days. Yeah so um yeah, that was gut wrenching that one. *And I don't know how he ever lived with himself but he blamed me for it.* (excerpt 16)

After attending Sarah's funeral together, Jane and Malcolm separated:

**Jane:** We split up after the funeral. I did it all by the book, you know. "Let's just get through the funeral. Let's just...." The funeral was finished. We get home and um '"Pack your bags and go we are finished. *That's it!* There's *nothing* holding me to you now. There's *nothing* you can come back for—absolutely nothing—so *go.*" And I gave up the flat and moved. And 12 months later…
**Michele:** Back again?
**Jane:** Back again. (excerpt 17)

Still only in her early 20s, Jane reunited with Malcolm, and the frequency and intensity of the violence between them escalated, as did her binge drinking.

If I was driving, he would grab the wheel. If he was driving he would put his foot down [and] head towards a[n] [electricity pole] just to get you to say yes or no, or do whatever. (excerpt 18)

### Jane's Life after Linda's Birth

By her mid-20s, and during one of her very alcohol-dependent periods, Jane conceived another daughter, Linda. Realizing the negative impact it had had on Linda, Jane stopped drinking:

> I hit the bottle worse. My daughter was born with dt's [delirium tremens].... [Then] I was on my own for a long time you know, so I was my own boss. I couldn't go into another relationship; I just could not trust another. Having that time to myself and being my own boss, my own house, my own child. I shared [Linda] with nobody. Nobody had control over this child except me. She doesn't know her father, *I don't know her father.* That's how *bad* the drinking got. I didn't answer to anybody, *absolutely anybody.* (excerpt 19)

In the first year of her sobriety, Jane regained contact with Malcolm. Over time, Linda grew fond of Malcolm and started to rely on his contact, which ended abruptly after Malcolm fathered a child with another woman:

> [Linda] thought the world of [Malcolm]. I said, "You'll get let down darling. Don't be surprised." And he sent her birthday presents, and Christmas presents. But when his daughter came, *that was it.* (excerpt 20)

In subsequent years, Jane partnered and later married a man with whom violence has not been a feature. At the time of the interview, Jane appeared happy and secure. She had regular paid work and was maintaining safe levels of alcohol consumption, both of which are meaningful to her.

## PART 3: NARRATIVELY ANALYZING JANE'S TRANSCRIPT

The actual interview with Jane went well. The conversation flowed, and "rich data" was produced. The unsettling part came while listening back to the recording. For the submission of Michele's thesis, we left these feelings aside. We made time to reflect on what we were feeling and were then invited to write this book chapter, giving us a formal opportunity to study our reactions. Like Dickson-Swift, James, Kippen, and Liamputtong (2009), we have found that qualitative research can surely be *emotion work*.

## Phase 1: Hear the Emotions

While the interview took only 58 minutes, many hours have since been spent trying to understand why we did not readily empathize with Jane. We first noticed the *relative lack of emotions* Jane expressed. Jane did not well up or cry at any point of the interview, such as when she recounted the story of finding her mother after she had attempted suicide (see excerpt 3), her father's assault of her mother (see excerpt 6), or the death of daughter Sarah (see excerpt 15). While telling the story of Sarah's death, Jane kept on track, not changing her tone of voice or pace. She did not mention her daughter by name. There were no real pauses or hesitations, suggesting she may have been recounting a story she had told many times before.

We admit our first inclination was to read Jane's reaction as cold, distant, perhaps even uncaring. Only after that did we challenge ourselves to think this through. Who were we to be the arbiters of Jane's emotions? Even though we identify as feminists and are critical of gender stereotypes, were we using them in relation to Jane? Did all women have to cry when telling sad stories? We called this the "Lindy Chamberlain effect," in reference to the famous Australian case of a dingo taking a baby but her mother (Lindy Chamberlain) being convicted for her murder, more because she remained dry eyed throughout the court case than because of the damning evidence prosecutors had against her (Chamberlain-Creighton, 2010).

*Frustration, disappointment,* and *hope* were other obvious emotions that surfaced. Twenty-five years on from their relationship, Jane's frustration with Malcolm's violence and disappointment with his failure to deliver on the promises he made to her were still clear. What we did not expect was how frustrated and disappointed we would feel toward Jane and what we believed was her naïve hope for Malcolm. Our lack of understanding was not because we failed to relate to the problem of being brutalized by a male "loved one." Both of us have firsthand experiences of intimate partner violence (Michele as an adult, Heather as a child) that have taught us about the web of emotions victims can experience—experiences that fuel our motivation to work in the field of violence and abuse. In this instance, however, our personal biographies did not lead us to compassion for Jane, or hope for Malcolm, so much as personal criticisms of them both.

I (Heather) was triggered by Jane portraying young Sarah as "spoiled rotten" (see excerpt 10) even though the child lived only four years, and during that time was admitted to hospital for pneumonia and repeatedly bashed her head on the cot—a traumatic expression of witnessing her parents' violence (see excerpt 8). Perhaps it was the reference to blonde hair and blue eyes (see excerpt 10), which reminded me of the sugar-coated descriptions my mother would make of our home life, that I found myself overidentifying with Sarah. References to Jane and Malcolm separating and then reuniting (see excerpt 9) also seemed to awaken my own unhappy memories from a distant 30 to 40 years ago. Unlike Jane and Sarah, who left Malcolm periodically, my own parents remained together until I was much older. We did, however, live in fear—and then hope—that we (my mother and sisters) would be leaving the house and his violence. After each violent episode, Mum would vow that we were leaving, "this time for good," and I always seemed to believe her. Within hours this talk would end, and we would again be instructed "not to upset your father," and most of all not "have a long face."

The problem was not simply that I was remembering this. It was the distraction it caused. Rather than maintaining my focus on Jane's experiences, I was preoccupied by my own feelings of frustration and disappointment related to my family, not hers. I am not proposing that it is off-limits to ask critical questions about Jane's stories, but it is important to do so in reference to *her experience and context*—not my own. And there I had been thinking that the extent of my experience working and teaching in the area of intimate partner violence meant that I was somehow beyond being triggered like this.

In contrast, most of my (Michele's) unease could be put down to Jane dealing with her experiences so differently from me. My unease was surprising, given that I usually have no trouble appreciating differences among women. For instance, I could appreciate that less public criticism is sometimes levelled at women, such as Jane, who "stay" with violent men, since they are, at least, "keeping the family together." This made sense to me, even though I had personally chosen to accept the criticisms for leaving—a decision that was not without its own difficulties.

I felt frustrated by the way Jane did not see Malcolm's infidelity as indicative that there was no hope for their relationship. At the end of the interview, Jane revealed that until a week before—decades after they had ended their relationship—they were back in contact via Facebook. Why were they still in contact with each other? Why was Jane so convinced that Malcolm would behave differently with his current partner and daughter? My frustration and disappointment belied my own knowledge of intimate partner violence. I knew what could get in the way of women relinquishing hope for the (violent) men they (may) love (see Fraser, 2005, 2008). I knew that many women want the violence, not their relationships, to end; that while there is still hope, women are likely to accept apologies and believe promises (Fraser, 2005, 2008). Possessing this knowledge did not stop me from wondering why Jane took so long to give up hope that Malcolm would stop being violent. I am disappointed with myself for not acknowledging that losing hope does not necessarily work to a preordained or logical timetable.

Later, I noticed that the only other people Jane referred to in the interview had experienced violence, either as victims, perpetrators, or witnesses. Together with Jane's observations of men's treatment of women—her parents, for example—liberating possibilities for women were not obvious. Jane knew of her father's affairs from an early age. She could see the double standard of men being permitted to have multiple sexual partners, but women needing to remain faithful. Rather than reading Jane as accepting intimate partner violence as a "normal" part of life in Australian families, perhaps she was simply fatalistic about its occurrence. In contrast, I did not grow up with such a miserable or oppressed view of marital relations, and was not aware of anyone else in an abusive relationship. My parents are still together after 50 years, and abuse is not a part of their relationship.

## Phase 2: Transcribe the Interview Material
We knew that our raw emotions could threaten our ability to fairly and critically analyze Jane's stories. We responded by revisiting Jane's transcript over the course of the next six months, long after Michele's thesis had been submitted. We found that working with Jane's written rather than spoken words allowed for some of our stronger (and sometimes misplaced) feelings to simmer down. This allowed us to reorient our analytical efforts—to stop asking how Jane's stories were affecting us personally, and ask instead what her stories reflected about women's changing but still subordinated place in Australian society.

Repeated readings of Jane's transcript reminded us of the extensive and routine violence Jane was exposed to, and from a young age (see, for instance, excerpt 4). Placing these stories in a chronological order (see

Section 2 above) helped to show the repetition of the violence, and the damaging consequences. It was also a way to allow some air between Jane's reported experiences and our reactions to hearing them. Allowing some air is, however, different from any claim to neutrality.

Transcribing interview material and presenting participant quotations is certainly not a neutral activity, free from researcher influence. Deciding where a full stop goes in spoken talk can make a lot of difference to meaning and interpretation (Riessman, 2003). We recognize the role we have played in selecting excerpts from Jane's interview and weaving them into another story—this story about conducting narrative analysis, being tripped up by emotions, and needing to resist individualized explanations for social problems.

## Phase 3: Interpret Individual Transcripts

We became well acquainted with Jane's transcript. We segmented the material and more closely inspected the stories we thought "stood out." We raked over each story for thematic content, but also emotional impact. We did this individually and together, in person and via email. We used Track Changes to make comments or observations. We trusted each other. We told each other our truths about our reactions to Jane's transcript, warts and all. It helped that we had both worked together before, and that we had both experienced intimate partner violence, but also that we were from working-class backgrounds, where straight talk is prized. There were times when we wondered whether we could publicly voice what we were experiencing. The more we worked on it, the more questions emerged.

As social workers and narrative feminist researchers, what do we do when the lines between victim and perpetrator are blurred? What sense do we make of Jane's acts of violent retaliation, including those enacted in front of Sarah? Does it matter that from Jane's account, the aggression she displayed toward Malcolm came after his attacks? Did these acts make Jane a perpetrator too, or should we read them as self-defence? To answer these questions, we kept returning to Jane's transcript.

Jane made many attempts—some of them we believe were self-defeating—to escape the gender constraints of being a girlfriend, partner, and mother. One way she did so was to drink heavily, first at the pub alongside men, but then at home. Another was to admire (rather than criticize) the way men could come and go as they pleased, behaving as they liked, dismissive of any consequences. This was underlined when Jane kept using the expression "no-one could put him [Malcolm] down," which she said in a proud rather than fearful tone (see excerpt 5). Seeing her mother's bruised body was a tipping point (see excerpt 6) and led Jane to fight back (excerpt 6). Nevertheless, Malcolm still "always won" (see excerpt 7). Perhaps that is why, in later years, she started fighting back more aggressively, "like a man," breaking Malcolm's leg (see excerpt 11) and stabbing him with a pair of scissors (see excerpt 12). Trying to understand the logic of Jane's actions is not the same as endorsing or excusing the violence. Then there is the question of whether Jane "failed to protect" Sarah from Malcolm's violence (see excerpts 8 & 9). Should she have protected her second daughter, Linda, from him, too (see excerpt 20)?

*Failure to protect* is a central component of child protection policy and legislation in Australia (Australian Institute of Health and Welfare, 2006) and many other parts of the world (Trepiccione, 2001). The problem is this: While purporting to recognize the seriousness of child abuse and take action to stop it from recurring, the policy discourse of failure to protect uses gender-neutral language but is applied to women far more than men (Edleson, 1998). It is women—as mothers—who are ultimately held responsible for children, while the expectations for men—as fathers—to provide care and protection are significantly lower (Wells & Owen, 2011). Apart from assuming that women *can* protect children from men's violence, it is a paradox that perpetrators of violence and abuse themselves are rarely charged with failure to protect (Kaufman-Kantor & Little, 2003).

While we both usually disavow the legitimacy of discourses such as *failure to protect*, we nevertheless found it lurked overhead. Being emotionally triggered seemed to make us more open to its influence. Unlike critical analyses that do not lose focus of the unfair social systems and cultural conventions that help to produce social problems such as intimate partner violence, discourses like *failure to protect* can appeal because their focus rests on individual and interpersonal readings of the problem. They can be used more specifically to apportion blame.

The irony was that when we returned to the transcript, we could see that Jane made multiple efforts to protect Sarah. Excerpt 9 shows Jane trying to appease Malcolm: how she would "get up and do what [Malcolm] wanted—just to shut him up" to prevent him from escalating the situation and waking Sarah up. There were also the times Jane broke away from Malcolm (see excerpts 9 & 17), all of which involved overcoming significant obstacles, including her own father—a man she held in high esteem—consistently ignoring Malcolm's violence and insisting they stay (or get back) together.

Rather than wondering why Jane "kept returning" to a man who abused her, and deliberately did so in front of their young daughter, the first and more pressing question to ask might be why Malcolm was not required to protect Sarah. Why did he feel so entitled to use violence against Jane and in his daughter's presence, even though he could see its negative effects (see excerpt 8)? Shouldn't Malcolm also be held responsible for "failing to protect his child"? For that matter, might Jane's father be charged as well? He was involved in Sarah's life. Apart from exposing Jane to violence as a child, he pressured Jane to stay with Malcolm, a situation that led to his granddaughter's death. Many other questions are possible. The point is that to position Jane as the main problem is to assume that she is primarily responsible for the violence (see also Magen, 1999).

Questions must continue to be asked about the cultures and societal structures that allow, if not encourage, (heterosexual) male violence against women and children (see Flood & Pease, 2009; Fraser, 2008; Mullaly, 2010). Jane certainly recognized the cultural setting of her life. Without prompting, she explained in excerpt 1 that she "grew up in a little country town [where] everything was basically confined to the home. You never talked about it [intimate partner violence]. You never spoke to anybody else about it."

## Phase 4: Scan across Different Domains of Experience

Focusing on particular episodes of violence and abuse Jane experienced from her childhood has meant that we have only provided a very limited view of Jane's life, and one that is mostly problem-saturated. Viewed from a completely different vantage point—through the other dimensions of Jane's life—are the themes of success and personal strength.

Jane's interview indicated that she has not just survived but triumphed over adversity. No longer addicted to alcohol or dependent on antidepressants, Jane has managed to recover from witnessing her father's abuse of her mother and two decades of her own partner's chronic violence. Most of all, Jane has dealt with the sudden death of her daughter Sarah (see excerpts 15, 16, & 17) and has mothered a now-adult second daughter (see excerpts 19 & 20). She is a woman with a close (and non-violent) partner and many friends, and has meaningful work. Psychologically, she appears motivated and optimistic about the future. This took us time to fully appreciate.

## Phase 5: Link the Personal with the Political

As we worked through the transcript, piece by piece, we cringed when we realized that we had been (unwittingly) applying a stereotypical script or template for the "good" (heterosexual woman) survivor of intimate partner violence. Our reactions to Jane's interview showed us that failure to adhere to this script risked our condemnation, showing just how overlapping the political and the personal can be.

This script goes something like this: "good" (heterosexual woman) victims/survivors of intimate partner violence do what makes popular sense, which is wanting to leave and then stay away from violent men. While they may blame themselves for not seeing the signs, or acting more quickly on the signs that they did see, they learn to be cautious of men. They do not surrender to fairytale romance, or look for "bad boys," however charming they might be. They prize peace, harmony, and gentleness as they forge futures unmarred by men's domination and violence. More inclined now to be women-identified, they join with other women and girls to learn lessons from past hurts. They experience cognitive and spiritual growth, and with the benefit of hindsight, they can see the impact intimate partner violence has on children, if they hadn't already done so. Even though they are not responsible for the violence, they try to compensate for these effects and undergo a process of *healing*. If they re-partner with men, they look for men who are genuinely kind, gentle, and respectful.

*Wow.* Who would have thought that we (feminists) would fall into the trap of such prescriptive and stereotypical thinking? Why were we expecting so much from victims/survivors of abuse like Jane? Isn't this what I (Heather) teach students to watch out for, and wasn't this one of the main points of my book about love and abuse (Fraser, 2008)? And isn't this kind of thinking something I (Michele) deliberately avoided in my direct practice with women offenders? There they were, though: our assumptions about how Jane "should" behave, disaggregated from the cloud of our emotions and out in the open for us both to see.

Without too much self(-indulgent)-flagellation, we moved on to consider the wider politics (and ethics) of criticizing interview material that participants give us as *gifts*. Like many studies of its kind, this study invited the participation of women who knew in advance that while they might have an interesting conversation, their involvement was not likely to bring them any direct benefits. We wondered, then, about the ethics of subjecting participants' stories to any level of criticism, given that they have gifted their stories to us. Might we want to say on future consent forms that we seek the right to critically analyze the stories they tell? Give our prospective participants advance warning that their words might be subject to scrutiny? Among these were questions about how we might produce "critical," "scholarly" research that sheds light on lived experience in a full and uncensored way, and whether doing so always allows for the honouring of voices and experiences of the oppressed. We have no definitive answers. What we do know is that if criticisms are to be made, they need to be made carefully, thoughtfully, and respectfully, reflecting cultural and structural analyses as much as individual and interpersonal ones. They need to warrant the criticism. Which led us back to the question of why we had focused on Jane's actions so much in the first place.

So often in research, we research "down"—that is, we interview the abused, the violated, the addicted, and the stigmatized. We rarely seek or are given the opportunity to research "up," for example with drug dealers or the clients of sex workers (Strega, 2012). This is also true in the area of research into intimate partner violence. It is useful to reflect on the implications of conducting most of the research with victims/survivors and not the perpetrators. One of the drawbacks of studying women's experiences of violence and abuse is that analytical attention can be misdirected to consider the efforts they made to leave "their" perpetrators, protect their children, and/or stop *their partners'* violence.

## Phase 6: Look for Commonalities and Differences among Participants

Just like the other women interviewed, Jane openly revealed many aspects of her life, and did so candidly and generously. The main difference was that no other woman participant reported using so much retaliatory violence toward the men who abused them. No one else watched their child die young. None of the other women gave birth to a child who needed to get help withdrawing from alcohol (as Jane's daughter Linda did). No one else in the study came home to find her mother had attempted suicide. Most importantly, none of the other women approached the interview in quite the same way as Jane.

Jane laid her stories bare. She did not seem to need to try to minimize her actions or (stage) manage other people's responses to her stories. Using a flat, somewhat emotionless tone at times, she pressed on with stories that must have been hard to narrate, particularly in a non-therapeutic setting such as a research interview. She did not hide her feelings, but she did not express them in gender-stereotypical terms. It is us, Michele and Heather, with multiple identities as woman, feminist, mother, daughter, student, teacher, survivor, and researcher, who find ourselves "managing" our reactions, dealing with our emotions as they sit within the context of Jane's story. We often speculate about what we would ask if given the opportunity to interview Jane for a second time, and have considered how we would have approached working with Jane if we heard her story as frontline social workers rather than researchers. Yet, as we wonder this, we also wonder whether we would have the right to ask Jane for another interview, given our reactions to her first.

## Phase 7: Write Academic Narratives

Metaphorically, we liken the writing of this chapter to a set of Russian or matryoshka dolls. Each nested doll, enclosing the next, symbolizes different experiences that narratives try to represent. Our largest doll—and the most public one—was Michele's honours thesis. It was the official story told about the five middle-aged Australian women's experiences of violence. This academic story, written much later, encases other less visible and organized stories about Michele meeting with the women, and talking with them before, during, and after the tape went on. While they influenced Michele's thinking, the stories produced through this talk are not cited directly in the thesis. Inside this doll is Jane's individual situation, as she expressed it on the day of the interview. Inside Jane's testimony is the story of us, Heather and Michele, reacting and responding to the interview contents. Our attention here is on the smallest doll, but one still important to the set.

Patterned across the whole set of dolls are the themes of privilege and oppression. MacIntosh (1988) reminds us that privilege is "like an invisible weightless knapsack of special provisions, maps and passports, codebooks, visas, clothes, tools and blank checks" (p. 1). Privilege allows some groups to escape penalties and dangers that oppressed people often suffer. We have the (class) privilege of being able to author this chapter and take control of how our story is told.

Jane narrated many stories indicative of male privilege. Jane's father and her partner, Malcolm, provide good examples of the relative impunity with which men have historically been able to perpetrate violence against the women they claim to love. Being heterosexual, White men helped them elude scrutiny and evade criminal charges. Overlapping were

Jane's stories about gender oppression. Mullaly (2010) reminds us that *oppression* is a term meaningfully applied to members of *devalued* social groups: groups that are subject to negative stereotypes (see also Shera, 2003). Oppression is not a random or individual experience, nor the distorted perceptions of the overly "dramatic," "sensitive," or "emotional." It is also not a term meaningfully applied to all individuals who experience frustrations, limits, or pain (Mullaly 2010). Oppressed populations are those likely to be subject to denied opportunities, restricted social, economic, and cultural participation, marginalization, exploitation, and violence (Young, 2009). While numerically dominant, women are often described as a "minority group" because of the gender oppression they face. Jane's testimony provides a sobering reminder of this. Not only was she oppressed as a girl and then as an adult woman, but her mother and daughter were, too. And it was this oppression that helped cause Sarah's death (see excerpt 15).

## SUMMARY

Jane was a woman who narrated her stories one day in a kitchen in a small South Australian country town. Our response to Jane's interview reverberated long after. This was not because we doubted the veracity of her stories. To dignify Jane's experience and prevent the fragmentation of her overall story, we used Part 2 of this chapter to illustrate the nature and extent of the violence perpetrated against Jane. In the third section of this chapter, we showed that the shared experience of a social problem is no guarantee of empathy or compassion. We traced the origins and effects of stories that triggered us. We did so to prevent our analyses from being hijacked by unfair dominant discourses, such as *failure to protect*. In the process, we uncovered our (unintended) application of a script for "good (heterosexual women) intimate partner violence victims/survivors," a script full of gender stereotypes, individualistic thinking, and ideas from popular culture.

While our research process was by no means tidy or neat, as the seven phases of narrative analysis (Fraser, 2004) may imply, it was useful to use this framework to stand back and make sense of the various conundrums. We know how important it is for researchers to understand their biases and acknowledge their presence (Pezalla, Pettigrew, & Miller-Day, 2012). Through the narrative analysis processes we deployed, we now feel quite differently about Jane's stories, and about ourselves. We hope it will strengthen our ability to perform anti-oppressive social work research in the future, where our focus will remain on "empowering the marginalized and promoting action against inequities" (Strega, 2005, p. 208).

## REFERENCES

Atkinson, P., & Silverman, D. (1997). Kundera's "Immortality": The interview society and the invention of the self. *Qualitative Inquiry, 3*(3), 304–325.

Australian Institute of Health and Welfare (AIHW). (2006). *Child protection Australia 2004–05.* AIHW cat. no. CWS 26. Canberra: AIHW (Child Welfare Series no. 38).

Chamberlain-Creighton, L. (2010). *Is the media to blame?* Retrieved from http://www.lindychamberlain.com/content/media/blame

Daiute, C., & Lightfoot, C. (2004). *Narrative analysis: Studying the development of individuals in society.* London, UK and Thousand Oaks, CA: Sage.

Dickson-Swift, V., James, E. L., Kippen, S., & Liamputtong, P. (2009). Researching sensitive topics: Qualitative research as emotion work. *Qualitative Research, 9*(1), 61–79.

Edleson, J. L. (1998). Responsible mothers and invisible men: Child protection in the case of adult domestic violence. *Journal of Interpersonal Violence, 13,* 294–298.

Flood, M., & Pease, B. (2009). Factors influencing attitudes to violence against women. *Trauma, Violence and Abuse, 10*(2), 125–142.

Franzosi, R. (1998). Narrative analysis—or why (and how) sociologists should be interested in narrative. *Annual Review of Sociology, 24,* 517–554.

Fraser, H. (2004). Doing narrative research: Analysing personal stories line by line. *Qualitative Social Work, 3*(2), 179–201.

Fraser, H. (2005). 'Women, love and intimacy "gone wrong": Fire, wind and ice. *Affilia, 20*(1), 10–20.

Fraser, H. (2008). *In the name of love: Women's narratives of love and abuse.* Toronto, ON: Women's Press.

Georgakopoulou, A. (2006). Thinking big with small stories in narrative and identity analysis. *Narrative Inquiry, 16*(1), 122–130.

Jarldorn, M. K. (2011). *Five Australian women over 40 years talk about their past experiences of intimate partner violence* (Unpublished thesis). Flinders University, Adelaide, South Australia.

Kaufman-Kantor, G., & Little, L. (2003). Defining the boundaries of child neglect: When does domestic violence equate with parental failure to protect? *Journal of Interpersonal Violence, 18*(4), 338–355.

Kimpson, S. A. (2005). Stepping off the road: A narrative (of) enquiry. In L. Brown & S. Strega (Eds.), *Research as resistance: Critical, Indigenous, and anti-oppressive approaches* (pp. 73–96). Toronto, ON: Canadian Scholars Press.

MacIntosh, P. (1988). *White privilege: Unpacking the invisible knapsack.* Retrieved from http://www.nymbp.org/reference/WhitePrivilege.pdf

Magen, R. H. (1999). In the best interests of battered women: Reconceptualising allegations of failure to protect. *Child Maltreatment, 4*(2), 127–135.

Mishler, E. G. (1995). Models of narrative analysis: A typology. *Journal of Narrative & Life History, 5*(2), 87–123.

Mullaly, R. P. (2010). *Challenging oppression and confronting privilege: A critical social work approach* (2nd ed.). Toronto, ON: Oxford University Press.

Pease, B. (2009). *Undoing privilege: Unearned advantage in a divided world.* London, UK: Zed Books.

Pezalla, A. E., Pettigrew, J., & Miller-Day, M. (2012). Researching the researcher-as-instrument: An exercise in interviewer self-reflexivity. *Qualitative Research, 12*(2), 165–185.

Plummer, K. (1995). *Telling sexual stories: Power, change and social worlds.* London, UK, and New York, NY: Routledge.

Riessman, C. K. (1994). Making sense of marital violence: One woman's narrative. In C. Riessman (Ed.), *Qualitative studies in social work research* (pp. 113–132). Thousand Oaks, CA: Sage Publications.

Riessman, C. K. (2003). Performing identities in illness narrative. *Qualitative Research, 3*(1), 5–34.

Shera, W. (Ed.). (2003). *Emerging perspectives on anti-oppressive practice.* Toronto, ON: Canadian Scholars' Press.

Seymour, K. (2012) Feminist practice: Who I am, or what I do? *Australian Social Work, 65*(1), 21–38.

Strega, S. (2005). The view from the poststructural margins: Epistemology and methodology reconsidered. In L. Brown & S. Strega. *Research as resistance: Critical, Indigenous, and anti-oppressive approaches* (pp. 208–236). Toronto, ON: Canadian Scholars' Press.

Strega, S. (2012, March 28). "Nothing about us without us"—meeting the ethical challenges of research at the margins. Public seminar, State Library, South Australia. Audio recording available at http://www.flinders.edu.au/sabs/saps/

Trepiccione, M. A. (2001). At the crossroads of law and social science: Is charging a mother with failure to protect her child an acceptable solution when her child witnesses domestic violence? *Fordham Law Review, 69(4), 1487–1522.*

Waldrop, A. E., & Resick, P. A. (2004). Coping among adult female victims of domestic violence. *Journal of Family Violence, 19*(5), 291–302.

Wells, S., & Owen, M. A. (2011). *Living without enemies: Being present in the midst of violence.* Downers Grove, IL: IPV Books.

Young, I. (2009). Five faces of oppression. In G. Henderson & M. Waterstone (Eds). *Geographic thought: A praxis perspective* (pp. 55–71). New York, NY: Routledge.

Chapter Seven

# Honouring the Oral Traditions of the Ta't Mustimuxw (Ancestors) through Storytelling

## Qwul'sih'yah'maht (Robina Anne Thomas)[1]

## INTRODUCTION

Every summer, when I find myself in the backyard cleaning and preparing fish for canning, freezing, and smoking, I have a moment when I stop, smile, and remember my grandmother. I remember watching her prepare fish as a child. Now, as an adult, and as I prepare my own fish, I can't help but reflect on Grama. She was an incredible woman, and I think she would be so proud of me (delighted that I have learned the necessary skills to process fish). I wonder, why it is still so important that my grandmother would be proud of me? Why, after all these years, does what she might have thought still matter? It matters because she was a mentor and teacher. Simply by thinking of these questions, I can hear her voice telling me stories. She tells me why it is important to process fish this particular way. She reminds me how important fish was to her, and how it was the main staple food of the Hul'qumi'num people. She remembers times when fish stocks were plentiful, but shares her concern about how depleted the stocks have become. And, oh yes, I can hear her remind me how wasteful it is to throw out the heads and tails when you could brew up the best fish-head soup. How I hated the sight of that soup—or more specifically, the thought of fish heads (eyes and all) floating in that tasteful broth. And, even though she is in the

Spirit World, her voice and stories are still with me. I feel blessed by the Creator that she shared these stories.

Just as my grandmother's stories stick with me, traditionally, storytelling played an essential role in nurturing and educating Indigenous children. I used to only half-listen to the talk of my grandparents, parents, aunties, and uncles and think this type of idle chat was not very important. I now realize the wisdom that made up those stories. Now, as a parent and educator, I find myself taking every possible opportunity to share these important stories and teachings that I once thought insignificant. In fact, not only do I share these stories, but I also now understand that they are vital to the survival of Indigenous people. Mihesuah (2003) believes that "truthful, honest and complete storytelling should be the goal for all of us" (p. 25). Storytelling is and always has been purposeful and intentional. Aunty Ellen White (2006) reminded me "that in traditional teaching, these stories were spoken, not written. So the storyteller had the opportunity to focus on different aspects of the story as needed" (p. 64). This is the beauty of storytelling; the storyteller can emphasize different aspects of the same story a number of times, depending on the circumstances. Despite colonization, I believe storytelling continues to play very important roles in the lives of Indigenous people. I argue that storytelling is essential to the survival of Indigenous people because stories pass on culture, tradition, historical facts, and life lessons. Stories have always done this, and continue to do this.

> Our stories have served and continue to serve very important functions: both the historical and mythical stories provide moral guidelines by which one should live; they teach the young and remind the old what appropriate and inappropriate behavior consists of in our cultures; they provide a sense of identity and belonging, situating community members within their lineage and establishing their relationship to the natural world; and they always serve as a source of entertainment as well as a source of bonding and intimacy between the storyteller and the audience (Waziyatawin, 2005, p. 35).

As with the voice of my grandmother, these stories tell us who we are, leave us with a sense of purpose and pride, and give us guidance and direction—these are stories of survival and resistance. In what follows, I will continue to story tell. By drawing upon previous research, I will look at storytelling as a research methodology, and discuss the joys and challenges of storytelling as a research methodology.

## MY STORYTELLING STORY

My story about storytelling begins at Camosun College, a community college in Victoria, BC. It was my first year of post-secondary education, and I had chosen to do an interview-based essay for my final English assignment. I grew up listening to family and friends chat abstractly about residential schools, and I wondered: What exactly were residential schools? What happened there? And how did they come to be? I took this opportunity to learn a bit more about residential schools. I remember that my friend Alex Nelson always made reference to "St. Mike's." I decided to ask him if he would share his experiences at St. Mike's for this assignment. Alex agreed.

Alex shared his experiences at St. Michael's Residential School in Alert Bay, BC. His story devastated me. I cannot remember the specific details of his story, but the sense of trauma I experienced remains absolutely clear. As well, the sense that this experience was not a thing of the past, but continued to play itself out in Alex's everyday life, was abundantly clear.

After hearing Alex's story, I got down to the business of writing my assignment. I had a nervous anxiousness in the pit of my stomach—that feeling we get when we discover a hidden family secret, but even bigger: a Canadian secret. How is it that this incredibly important person was sent to a place like this? How is it that I, now pursuing my undergraduate degree, knew nothing about these places? Why? Why didn't more people know Alex's story? This was a story that needed to be told—a piece of Canadian history that had been silenced, like so many other stories from the past. Our stories

> needed to be denigrated and suppressed, for they not only connected people to their lands, but they also tended to tell disturbingly "different" stories about the colonial experience, stories which generally contradicted the histories told by the colonizers to glorify and justify the colonial project. (Nicholas, 2008, p. 19)

I never really got over the shock and anger of learning the "disturbingly different story" from Alex, so years later, while doing a graduate degree in social work, I took the opportunity to deepen my understanding of residential schools. Because three generations of my family had attended Kuper Island Residential School, I knew I wanted to research this particular school, which was located on Kuper Island, one of the pristine Gulf Islands off the east coast of Vancouver Island, BC—in the heart of Coast Salish territory. The term *Coast Salish* is an anthropologically/linguistically defined area that includes the southern tip of Vancouver Island over to southwest British Columbia. As a Coast Salish woman (my Grandmother was Snux'ney'muxw, my Grandfather was Sto:olo, and I am Leey'qsun through marriage), understanding the impact of this school located on our traditional territory was significant. Another reason I wanted to research Kuper Island Residential School was that I believed the stories stemming from that place needed to be told. More importantly, these stories will "help us to reclaim our past for ourselves and stand ... as a body of knowledge to be differentiated from that body of knowledge written and understood by the dominant society" (Waziyatawin, 2005, p. 35).

As my writing process always seems to go, I learned more from doing things wrong than from doing them right the first time! There was a time when I was quite anxious to get my thesis proposal done so that I could start the research. I had begun my thesis proposal through my research class. I am not absolutely sure, but I think I was initially proposing to do some kind of qualitative phenomenology. I finished my first proposal and set up an appointment with my thesis supervisor. As supervisors do, she asked me why had I chosen this and why that and on and on. As our appointment went on, she finally asked me one last "why" that I simply could not answer. After a moment of silence (and verging on tears), I looked up at her and said, "All I ever really wanted to do was tell stories." And she replied, "Well, why don't you tell stories?" This is where, for me, storytelling as a research methodology began.

## STORYTELLING AS METHODOLOGY

*Storytelling in the Spirit of Wise Woman: Experiences of Kuper Island Residential School* (2000), my graduate thesis, uses storytelling as the methodology through which to look at the experiences of three former Kuper Island Residential School students. Although the school has been torn down, the memories remain. The thesis was undertaken to shed light on the devastating and catastrophic legacy of the residential school system in Canada. Residential schools have been the single most devastating event to affect Indigenous people since contact. Day to day, many former students continue to live out the horrific impact of these schools.

For guidance and direction, again I draw upon the voices of my grandmothers. They lived, they acquired wisdom, and they were all survivors of their experiences—they had much to share. As I began to ask what is in a story, I once more listened for the voices of these Wise Women for examples.

> Nana:
> "When I was just a young girl we used to live right over there." Nana pointed to the land on the downtown side of the Ellice St. Bridge. "One Christmas Eve, my mother, father, brothers and sisters were going to my uncle's place for dinner. It had snowed so much that day that it seemed like it took us hours to get to their place. They lived down where Uncle's Johnny's place is now. You know, it used to snow lots in those days, not like now."

> Grama:
> "I am so proud that you are practicing some of our old ways," my Grama said. "What is Dylan's name?" "Qwulthelum," I told Gram. "And Paul, what is his name?" "Pahyahutssen." "Did they have the Sxwaixwe dancers there?" "No, Grama, they didn't." "Our family is from the masked dance, you know. I remember years ago, when I was young, when we went to the winter dances, sometimes there would be twenty or more dancers there."

> Amma:
> "Amma, why don't you just throw out those old socks?" "Oh, because that would be such a waste, the tops of the socks are perfectly fine, only the feet need to be replaced. I have wool and know how to knit, why throw the whole sock away?"

What is in a story? Are these simply words? Grandmothers reminiscing? Or, are they stories rich with teachings? Wilson (1998b) states:

> The intimate hours I spend with my grandmother listening to her stories are reflections of more than a simple educational process. The stories handed down from grandmother to granddaughter are rooted in a deep sense of kinship responsibility, a responsibility that relays a culture, an identity, and a sense of belonging essential to my life. (p. 27)

I agree with Wilson. My grandmothers' stories are the essential core of my being. The stories are cultural, traditional, educational, spiritual, and political. Nana's story points to the land where she was raised, that special place where she held memories of her ancestors—her mother, father, grandparents, and siblings. But also, identifying this land as traditional Lekwungun (Songhees) territory is crucial, as the Lekwungun First Nation is currently negotiating their land treaty through the BC Treaty Commission. The land Nana identified is cut-off land that is not a part of the present-day Songhees territory, despite the fact that she was born there.

Gram tells me about the cultural and traditional rights our family has that are handed down from generation to generation. She tells me I have the inherent right to have Sxwaixwe (masked dancers) at all ceremonies our family hosts. This is our most sacred ceremony and is passed down through familial rights. Grama also asks what names were given. Behind a name is history; it brings forward with it the Ta't Mustimuxw (Ancestors) of the past who shared that name and where they were from; it may bring songs, dances, or masks, and other important messages. These teachings are passed along to the ones who carry those names today.

Amma's story teaches about conservation—taking, using, and throwing out only what is necessary. She taught me about taking care of Mother Earth long before anyone else did. As well, she taught me about recycling and composting before these things were trendy.

These stories include important teachings that pass down historical facts and share culture, traditions, and life lessons. Traditionally, stories and storytelling were used for the same reasons: to teach values, beliefs, morals, history, and life skills to youth and adults. Wilson (1998a) claims that

> stories in the oral tradition have served some important functions for Native people: The historical and mythological stories provide moral guidelines by which one should live. They teach the young and remind the old what behavior is appropriate and

> inappropriate in our cultures; they provide a sense of identity
> and belonging, situating community members within their lin-
> eage and establishing their relationship to the rest of the natural
> world. (p. 24)

Storytelling also taught us about resistance to colonization; our people have resisted, even when legislation attempted to assimilate our children. All stories have something to teach us. What is most important is to learn to listen, not simply hear, the words that storytellers have to share. Many stories from Indigenous people tell a counter-story to that of the docu- mented history of Indigenous people in Canada. For example, Alex's story is not the Canadian story of residential schools—the story of education and Christianity. In fact, his is a story of abuse, survival, and resistance, how he fought to survive in a system that abused him and how he resisted this abuse as a means of healing. He lived to tell his story and to share it with all those around him who needed support to begin their healing journeys. His story, and the stories of the three storytellers in my thesis research, are very important because they give us teachings that allow us to continue to hear and document those counter-stories—our truths. A mentor of mine, Seletze Delmar Johnnie, once said that it is such a shame that every time someone who went to residential school dies without telling their stories, our government and the churches look more innocent. As such, telling these stories is a form of resistance to colonization; as one storyteller told me, "Despite all of their (the government and churches') attempts, I am still here. I am Indian and I am proud." These stories simply must be told, because they confirm our belief in our stories, our histories, and our Ta't Mustimuxw (Waziyatawin, 2005, p. 40).

Most Indigenous people come from oral societies. A storytelling meth- odology honours that tradition and the Ta't Mustimuxw. As storytelling was traditionally done orally and in a different language, we must be com- pelled to listen and document stories "in the spirit" of the Ta't Mustimuxw. In other words, I feel that storytelling forces us to keep the teachings and protocols of our Ancestors, culture, and tradition alive (front and centre) throughout the entire research process. Silko (1996) believes that "storytell- ing can procure fleeting moments to experience who they were and how life felt long ago" (p. 42). As we share stories from long ago, we are given an opportunity to go back to that time. What an honour to bring to life a moment from years ago—the voices of our Ta't Mustimuxw.

But for me, there is always the fear of documenting our stories. Will the voices be heard? Will the voices of the storytellers be edited? Document-ing, in and of itself, is a foreign concept. When I began to transcribe the tapes, I even wondered if the oral and written are contradictory. But, as with everything, times change, and in order for Indigenous people to have their stories and voices validated, they have had to adapt and write down their experiences, while at the same time maintaining the integrity of the stories. Again, I am talking about counter-stories—the stories that have never been told by our own People. Storytelling in this sense is an act of resistance. The stories in my thesis are written as they were told and expe-rienced, not edited to parallel the Canadian story; they put voice to a story that has not been fully told. Certainly, the stories of residential schools tell the other story—the story of colonization and genocide. But so do many other stories that Indigenous people have to tell: the stories of land dispos-session. The stories of the 1960s Scoop that saw our children taken from us. These are all resistance stories because they validate the lives and times of our People. They tell stories that have been inaccurately documented in a new way.

The beauty of storytelling is that it allows the storytellers to use their own voices and tell their own stories on their own terms. Cruickshank (1990) states that her work, *Life Lived Like a Story*, is "based on the premise that life-history investigation provides a model for research" (p. 1). In the past, life stories (storytelling) have been viewed as supplementary material to support other forms of research. However, as Cruickshank states, this view is changing. And I believe this view must change. All that is written and researched is someone's interpretation of what happened. In her book *The Social Life of Stories: Narrative and Knowledge in the Yukon Territory*, Cruickshank (1998) questions the dominant voices of history by asking, "Whose voices are included, and whose are left out?"

> Contesting the legitimacy of the dominant discourse is not new, of course. Certainly a concern that many voices are systemati-cally erased from written history has been recognized for a long time now in northern aboriginal communities. As feminists have pointed out, enlarging discourse involves much more than adding and stirring in additional voices, there are fundamental methodological problems involved in rethinking familiar genres of historical narratives. (Cruickshank, 1998, p. 116)

Storytelling is often deemed illegitimate because it is subjective and therefore biased. However, we must consider that in some communities there were little, if any, written records. How are our communities, then, to have our histories recorded? Our history will most often include a very important counter-history, such as the impact that racist legislation like the Indian Act has had, and continues to have, on our communities. Why is it that our only means of recording histories—oral transmission—must be validated by a more "legitimate" research methodology? When we search, we will find that our communities (the Coast Salish) in fact had, and continue to have, very sophisticated traditional ways of documenting important events. I will give you an example.

In 1998 I was given my traditional name: Qwul'sih'yah'maht. This was my grandmother's name and originated from the Snux'ney'muxw people. Prior to receiving this name, protocol required that our family go to the eldest surviving female of my grandmother's family and ensure that it was acceptable for me to be given this name.

At the naming ceremony, we have a system of paying "witnesses"—representatives from different communities who are called upon to witness the event. Witnessing is a significant responsibility because a witness is being asked to pay attention to the all the details of the evening (what the name was, where it originated, and the protocol that was followed to ensure I had the right to use this name, as well as other details). In the Big House, visitors are seated in sections according to what community they are from. Witnesses are selected from every community present. This way, the information is shared throughout Coast Salish territory. If there were concerns or questions about what took place, what my name was, or where it was from, we could ask any of the witnesses. They would have this information because it was their responsibility to pay attention to all the details. This highly sophisticated process of witnessing continues to be central to our traditional ceremonies.

All major events that took place in our community were documented. However, documentation in mainstream research forums seems to refer only to the written. I am suggesting that the level of complexity and sophistication with which major events were witnessed in our communities demands that these oral histories and stories be reconceptualized and viewed as primary sources. These events are our Department of Vital Statistics—they record births, marriages, and deaths, to name a few. Storytelling creates space for the "Other," or those voices that have been excluded or erased, to be included in the dominant discourse. Storytelling has the ability to fill the gaps in the present documentation of the lives of Indigenous people.

Storytelling provides an opportunity for Indigenous people to have their histories documented and included in the written records. In other words, storytelling revises history by naming and including their experiences. Life stories "take seriously what people say about their lives rather than treating their words simply as an illustration of some other process" (Cruickshank, 1990, p. 1). In *Victims of Benevolence: The Dark Legacy of the Williams Lake Residential School*, Furniss (1992) states that "it is critical for these and other stories to continue to be told, and to be heard with an open heart and mind, if we are to prevent the tragedies of history from being repeated" (p. 120). When we listen with open hearts and open minds, we respect and honour the storytellers. I find this process incredibly comforting and respectful. I believe that storytelling respects and honours people while simultaneously documenting their reality.

Storytellers may opt to share their culture and tradition (spiritual), how events made them feel (emotional), what things looked like or how they physically felt (physical), or how this influenced their ways of knowing and being (mental). In this sense, storytelling has the potential to be very holistic. However, as the storytellers are always the authors of their own stories, we cannot always assume the story will be holistic.

Oral histories or life stories "generally range over a wide range of topics, perhaps the person's life from birth to the present" (Reinharz, 1992, p. 130). Because the process of telling the stories is in the hands of the storytellers, they have the opportunity to include that which they wish, that which they perceive as important, and that which they want documented. Storytellers hold the power in this research methodology; they are in control of the story, and the "researcher" becomes the listener or facilitator. Cruickshank (1998) refers to this process as the "open ended possibilities" of oral history (p. 72), because the researcher does not enter the relationship with any preconceived directions that the research will take.

Storytelling provides an opportunity to uncover new ways of knowing. Indigenous people have ways of knowing and being, but for the most part, these ways were stripped from us through the process of colonization. Residential schools are but one example. Indigenous students were forced to speak English and practice Christianity. Our ways of knowing and being were not permitted, and storytelling is a means through which these ways of knowing and being were passed on and a means through which they can be uncovered or reclaimed (Yow, 1994). Passing on knowledge, wisdom, and teachings is how we perpetuate the cycle of teachings from generation to generation, as it was passed on to us.

## PROCESS

Storytelling should always be teller-focused and share what the tellers deem important about their experience, and should not be about studying what the researcher deems important. In order for me to hear what the storytellers in my thesis research wanted to share, we met informally over coffee and tea, and they shared many stories. Some might call this interviewing, but even the word *interview* does not seem appropriate, as it denotes structuring from the researcher. I knew that if I asked specific questions, I would get specific answers. What would happen if I asked the wrong questions? What would my research look like? It would only answer the questions I asked, and as such, I would be structuring the process. I was not the expert; the storytellers were, and I was the learner, listener, recorder, and facilitator.

Unstructured interviews are useful when the research has "no presuppositions about what of importance may be learned" (Patton, 1980, p. 198). It was crucial for me to enter my research with no presuppositions about the experience of attending Kuper Island Residential School. Maintaining maximum flexibility allowed the information to be gathered in whatever direction the conversation went.

Authenticity was a concern for me from the time I started my research. I wanted to authentically tell another's story. That is, I was concerned about how I could tell someone else's story when I was the researcher (both as listener and as writer). How could I ensure that it was their stories and told in their words, and not mine? Because of my concern with authentically representing the storytellers, what worked best for me were series of dialogues. By this I mean that each time we met, the process was more about storytelling and conversation than questions and answers. The dialogues actually came to be only a part of the process. The relationship that transpired between the storytellers and me became very fluid. The storytellers would contact me either over the phone or in person and say, "I just remembered another story," or they would tell me how they felt after the interviews, or how they felt when something else happened. I strongly believe that the relationship that developed was possible because of the nature of the dialogue—storytelling.

> One of the most trenchant observations of contemporary anthropology is that meaning is not fixed, that it must be studied in practice—in the small interactions of everyday life. Such practice is more likely to emerge in dialogue than in a formal interview. (Cruickshank, 1998, p. 41).

To facilitate my desire to capture the essence of experience, I chose to conduct multiple dialogic storytelling sessions. However, there were many conversations where I recorded and listened to the various stories of the particular storytelling session with little interaction, other than the odd "Ahh," "Really," "Wow," "Ha ha ha," and looks (I am sure) of disbelief. Mostly, the dialogues took place before and after the actual recording. Conversations took place over tea or coffee, wherever the storytellers wanted to meet. The interviews were recorded, and at the same time I would take brief notes. These notes often included my observations of the storyteller's physical reactions to their process, as well as my own reactions to the stories. After each conversation, I would listen to the recordings and reread my notes. Because I wanted to authentically share the storytellers' experiences, I felt there was no need for me to ask questions during the sessions. In fact, I worried that if I did ask questions, I would begin to shape the story by stressing the points that I chose to question and delve deeper into. If I did not understand something that was recorded, I would ask for clarification at the next meeting. The process of clarification was brief, and then the stories would begin. The unstructured, dialogical nature of the conversations enhanced the collection of stories.

I found it an interesting process to watch how the storytellers set their boundaries. Initially, storytellers openly shared the easy parts of their stories—that is, the parts of their story they felt safe to discuss. Then, at each subsequent conversation, the storytellers returned to where they had left off and set out on their journey into the more dangerous, less explored territory of their experiences at Kuper. It was after our second meeting that the fluid nature of the process began. After beginning their voyage into the unexplored territory, the storytellers were often inundated with memories, feelings, thoughts, and so on. At this point, I began to receive phone calls at home. On one occasion, a storyteller phoned and asked that I come over that evening and tape; he was ready to tell more stories. I received phone calls saying things like "I remembered more about that time ..." I strongly believe that the flexible and personal nature of my research supported the storytellers during their process of sharing.

As my research focused on former students of Kuper Island Residential School, the participants were specifically selected. Also, they needed to feel safe and strong enough to share intimate parts of their lives in such an open and vulnerable way. Patton (1990) describes this process of selection as "purposeful sampling." Purposeful sampling is a method of selecting "information-rich cases whose study will illuminate the questions under study" (Patton, 1990, p. 169). For the purposes of my research, I selected experts in the field of residential schools. Specifically, the storytellers selected had experience directly with Kuper Island Residential School. Unquestionably, these former students were the experts, because they have special skills related to and knowledge about this experience. Friere (1970) asks, "Who are better prepared than the oppressed to understand the terrible significance of an oppressive society?" (p. 27).

## STORYING

As I had chosen storytelling as my methodology, how the stories were perceived, documented, and written was a crucial point. As I mentioned above, authentically representing the storytellers' experiences was vitally important to me. It was imperative that the stories remain the storytellers' stories and did not become mine. My story needed to remain separate. I realized early on that as the researcher, I had incredible power to shape the final work that I was doing. For example, had I decided to use interview questions, for the most part, the thesis would have covered the areas that I deemed important enough to ask a question about. Another source of power to shape the work occurred once the interviews had been completed. I could have taken the transcriptions, written the stories myself, and finished the work necessary to complete my thesis. But I was determined to authentically represent the voices of the storytellers.

When the storytellers told me they were done sharing, I transcribed the tapes. The written transcriptions were given to the storytellers and I asked them to ensure that what was transcribed was accurate, encouraging them to add, delete, or edit what was written. Only then did I begin to formulate the stories.

The stories had to speak in the voices of the storytellers, not mine. Again, as I wrote the stories, they were passed along to the storytellers to edit. This process was incredibly difficult, as the transcription was not a story told from beginning to end, but the many stories that had shaped their lives. I spent hours listening to the tapes and then re-listening to their voices. I would ask as I was writing, "How would they say this?" My task was to compile all the stories into one story, while at the same time not losing the intent of the many stories. In fact, I had to find the story to tell.

How would this teller begin this story? I would listen and read the interviews over and over again, looking and listening for themes. Was there a phrase or topic that came up consistently that I could form a story around? This process of finding the story was more difficult than I had ever anticipated. Well, actually, I was not really that sure what to anticipate, as storytelling as a research methodology was brand new to me.

What words would they use to transition from one thought to another? Throughout the storywriting process, I used the words of the storytellers directly from the transcripts as much as possible. When I would have to write a transition statement or statements, I would ask, "What words do they use when they naturally transition?" These were areas in the stories that I would highlight and ask them to pay particular attention to. The first time I did this with one of the storytellers, he laughed and said, "Robina, this sounds so much like you!" So we rewrote that section! Really listening to their words and their voices was the only way that I could at all attempt to authentically present the voices of the storytellers. How might this teller end this story? Again, listening and re-listening. Did the storytellers have some closing statements that they might like to say? This was probably the easiest task in the storytelling process. Each of the storytellers naturally had words of wisdom she or he wanted to share. Each had his or her own way of speaking and particular audience he or she wished to address. The storytellers edited the stories into the format in which they were presented in my final thesis.

A final struggle that I want to share about editing is that of determining what to include and what to exclude. It was very difficult to make the decision to cut a piece of the transcript from the story. This too was done in consultation with the storytellers, but it was still tough. Even though my work was striving for authentic voice representation, how influential was I in shaping the story by including some things and excluding others? I have not completely resolved this yet. It should be a struggle; as researchers, we have the power to shape the lives of the storytellers, and this issue should be taken seriously.

## UY'SKWULUWUN

As I proceeded with this work, what became paramount was getting it right. As storywriter, I have the ultimate power to write the story to serve my own purposes. I could even dig through the interviews and find words from the storytellers to justify my arguments. I know that in the past, words of our people have been taken out of context and used to justify another's opinion. I will not do this kind of unethical work. So, what did the storytellers say? I wanted to make the right decision and truly reflect their knowledge and wisdom. I relied heavily on my teachings and understanding of cultural protocols to guide and direct my understanding of the teachings the storytellers shared. As time went on, I also relied on Prayer and the Ta't Mustimuxw to guide and direct this work. This reminded me of Basso's story. I will share it here. After Basso (1996) has mispronounced an Apache word three times, he says,

> "I'm sorry, Charles, I can't get it. I'll work on it later, it's in the machine. It doesn't matter."
>
> "It's matter," Charles says softly to me in English. And then turning to speak to Morley, he addressed him in Western Apache:
>
> "What he's doing isn't right. It's not good. He seems to be in a hurry. Why is he in a hurry? It's disrespectful. Our ancestors made this name. They made it just as it is.... Tell him he's repeating the speech of our ancestors!" (p. 10)

It is critical to get the stories right, especially those stories that share words from the Ta't Mustimuxw. Consequently, I have always had a fear of documenting our stories, because once our words are out there, we can never get them back. Sto:lo author and activist Lee Maracle (1993) advises us, "Everything you do and every word you speak ... either empowers or disempowers" (p. 168). In other words, we must be very mindful of every word we speak. In the same way, we must think about every word we write down. I know my intentions are good and believe my work is empowering, but how can I guarantee that someone will not misinterpret my words—or more importantly, the words of the storytellers? Even though Devon Abbott Mihesuah (2003) believes personal narratives are necessary, she urges us to do the work in a good way, with a good mind and spirit, and to not forego too much of the story or its original intent or meaning (p. 30).

The beauty of storytelling is that it allows the storytellers to use their own voices and words. We as the storywriters must honour those words and write with the teller's intent. The storyteller always holds the power in this research methodology, because it is her narrative. Consequently, the researcher becomes more of a facilitator. Now, having completed this research, I will add that as the researcher, I became the student. I learned so much from every single interview I conducted. I was not the expert; I was first and foremost the learner.

Once when I was sitting with Aunty Ellen, she very gently instructed me. She said that now that she had shared her words, wisdom, and knowledge with me, it was my responsibility to stop and listen. She urged me to be patient and sit with her words. She told me that this is how teachings work; you must sit with them for at least three months. She said that eventually I would make sense of the teachings and what they mean to me. Then, they would become my teachings. I believe this point is critical to storytelling—it is rooted in Indigenous ways of knowing and being, and we must be patient and sit with the words. Yes, I was conducting research. Yes, I was collecting data, using dialogues as my primary research method. And yes, I was calling my research methodology *storytelling*. But whatever the methodology is called, what is most important is that it is rooted in my traditional ways of knowing and being. Even as I write this, I wonder if I'm getting it right. What are the Ta't Mustimuxw thinking?

Some might call this ethics, but it goes beyond traditional ethics. It is what the Hul'qumi'num people call *uy'skwuluwun*—to be of a good mind and a good heart. As a Leey'qsun woman, my responsibility is to the storytellers. As Qwul'sih'yah'maht, my responsibility is also to my grandmother and all of the Ta't Mustimuxw. I was witness to their stories, and as such had the incredible responsibility to ensure that the work done was respecting *uy'skwuluwun*—that I had paid attention to their words, their lives, their stories. Over my life, I have been taught that when you ask someone to share her wisdom, you must respect and honour her teachings. This was the most important ethical responsibility that I had. I had to ensure that while I was storytelling, I simultaneously respected and honoured the storytellers.

## SPIRIT OF ETHICS

Prior to beginning my research, I believed that informed consent and confidentiality would be the most important ethical concerns. As each of my storytellers had agreed before my research that they wanted to be involved, informed consent had already been established when the work began. All the storytellers knew they were going to share their lived experience. There was no room for deception. The participants were involved in all stages of the research, including data analysis, editing, and participating at my thesis defence.

As for confidentiality, two of the storytellers had already publicly identified themselves as having attended Kuper Island. None wanted to be anonymous for the purpose of this research. Lipson (1994) claims that researchers "should do everything in their power to protect the physical, social and psychological welfare of informants and to honor their dignity and privacy" (p. 335), unless they want to be identified. The three participants were Belvie Berber, Seletze Delmar Johnnie, and Herman Thomas.

In a discussion of ethics, Punch (1994) states, "In essence, most concern revolves around issues of harm, consent, deception, privacy, and confidentiality of data" (p. 89). While I certainly agree with these issues, what I experienced was not quite that simple. There were ethical issues that I had not anticipated, and I now call these the Spirit of Ethics. When I began this work, I believed that I was prepared. I had read every book, article, and story pertaining to residential school that I could get my hands on. I had talked to nearly everyone I knew who had attended one of those institutions. But I was far from prepared. I had no idea what obstacles lay ahead on my path.

When I began my research, I thought about working from a place of *uy'skwuluwun* while at the same time being involved in a community where I am well known. What I failed to consider was the emotional impact of listening and sharing stories when the characters are family. Many of the stories I heard included family members. At times, listening to stories of my family caused me a whole lot of sadness. Here I was, as a part of my thesis, learning about my family. Some of the stories were funny, but some of them were so sad and tragic. And this was my family, too.

However, had I not been there, I would not have had the opportunity to learn. Here I was, on this day, listening to stories of the past about my ancestors, grandparents, aunts, uncles, and cousins. I was given a gift of knowledge that I otherwise would not have had. Through this research I was gifted with the opportunity to glimpse into the lives of our Ta't Mustimuxw as well as the lives of the storytellers.

When the storytellers are family, there is little choice but to be a part of the research. Again, being so intimately involved in the research was emotionally draining. Interview after interview, I would leave feeling physically, mentally, spiritually, and emotionally exhausted. I thought that I would do an interview a day, but I never thought about how much time would be needed between interviews to feel balanced and prepared for the next interview.

One day I drove north on Vancouver Island to do an interview with one of the storytellers. The night before, I had interviewed for about five hours. I was thinking about the interview and I began to cry. I almost had to pull over because I had become completely overwhelmed with grief. I learned to pay particular attention to the time necessary to heal between interviews and then to prepare for the next.

On that same day, I wondered about *uy'skwuluwun*. Was asking people to participate in this research and share this grief working from a good mind and heart? I now knew how painful it was for the storytellers to relive those times. I had heard and seen the pain, agony, sadness, and grief the storytellers endured while sharing their stories. For the sake of the research, should I continue? Here I was falling apart, but it was their lives. At that time, I needed to consult as many people as I could. Should I continue? Was this ethical? Is there another way of doing this project?

My conflict was quickly resolved when two storytellers contacted me after really difficult interviews. Both of them shared the agony they had gone through during the interviews, but also the lightness they felt inside when they finally went back to that place and told what really happened. So the research would go on.

With the storytellers' acknowledgement of the healing nature of sharing, I knew the stories would continue. But I also knew that I needed to be aware of my own Spirit. During one interview, the storyteller was sharing an incident of sexual abuse. As I sat and listened, I started feeling physically numb. I had to consciously say to my Spirit, "You must move over here beside me." This needed to be a mental process, because the pain and grief of the story was too harsh for my soul. I would leave and pray to the Creator to make sense of the things I was hearing and feeling.

# HONOURING THE TA'T MUSTIMUXW

Just as I felt this responsibility to the storytellers, I also felt a responsibility to the Ancestors—my grandmothers and grandfathers, and all those residential school students who had gone to the other side. And I wondered: What does it really mean to say that the reason I have chosen storytelling as my research methodology is because it *honours the oral traditions of my Ancestors*?

I have come to realize, more through my inability to write my thesis than through the writing of it, that this process must be real. I was unable to use words such as *honour, tradition*, and *Ancestors* only as token words that glorify or romanticize my academic process of producing a thesis. There was a point in the research where I was unable to write, and I wondered why. As I examined the work closely, I realized that I had, on one hand, the stories—the words that honoured the traditional teachings of my Ancestors. Then, on the other hand, a traditional academic process was shaping the remainder of the thesis. I felt that I was not a part of either. The traditional academic words did not have life; they were not a part of me—of my identity. Nor was this work in any way respecting *uy'skwuluwun*.

As I mentioned above, in 1998 I received my traditional name: Qwul'sih'yah'maht. Aunty Helen wanted me to have a name so that I would always remain grounded in where I am from—a Hul'qumi'num woman, partner, mother, daughter, sister, granddaughter, aunt, friend, and so on. With this name came the responsibility of walking in a good way that honours and respects my grandmother, Lavina Wyse Prest.

The message I received from the Creator and my Ancestors was that I was not to use words that justified the academic process of meeting my thesis requirements, but rather that I needed to believe in and use the integrity of a storytelling approach throughout the thesis. As such, my final thesis was a series of many interconnected stories—no beginning and no end, but rich with teachings and gifts.

Storytelling traditionally was, and still is, a teaching tool. As such, the stories that are told in research will be teaching tools, too. Sharing stories validates the various experiences of the storytellers, but also has the ability to give others with similar stories the strength, encouragement, and support they need to tell their own stories. For example, as more and more former students come forward looking for justice for the crimes of the residential school era, stories shared about others' experiences at residential schools can support them as they tell their own stories. As such, storytelling is also a tool of resistance. This research begins to uncover the genocidal characteristics of residential schools, and by recovering our ways of knowing and being, we will continue to honour the Ta't Mustimuxw and all of the lessons and teachings they left for us.

Many of us have stories in our families that have never been shared. This is in part another impact of colonization. Stories and legends were our culture and tradition, and over the years, these rituals were banned through legislation and then enforced and entrenched through residential schools. We need to go back and collect these stories and share them with our families, friends, and communities. Consequently, another significant gift of storytelling is the ability to share and document missing pieces of our history and pass these teachings on to future generations. As stories continue to be told, we continue to build the strength and capacity to resist colonization and assimilation.

I never dreamed of learning what I learned. I never dreamed of learning to listen in such a powerful way. Despite all the struggles, storytelling made me feel like I absolutely respected and honoured the Ta't Mustimuxw and the Storytellers, while at the same time sharing tragic, traumatic, inhumanly unbelievable truths that our people had endured. It was this level of integrity that was essential to storytelling.

I am not a storytelling expert. No; I see myself as a storyteller-in-training. Having used storytelling as the methodology for my thesis, I will continue the rigorous path required in my training as I see the countless gifts and teachings that storytelling has to offer each of us. When we make what we teach personal, as I see storytelling do, we touch people in a different and more profound way. As I end my storytelling story, I want to thank each of you for being witness to it. And as Thomas King (2003) reminds us, do what you want with my story about stories, "but don't say in years to come that you would have lived your life differently if only you would have heard this story" (p. 29).

## NOTE

1. This chapter draws from teachings provided by Belvie Berber (mentor), Delmar Johnnie (mentor), Val Josephson (grandmother), Mary Moody (grandmother), Alex Nelson (mentor), Lavina Prest (grandmother), and Herman Thomas (mentor). I acknowledge here their significant contributions to my work.

# REFERENCES

Basso, K. H. (1996). *Wisdom sits in places: Landscape and language among the Western Apache.* Albuquerque, NM: University of New Mexico Press.

Cruikshank, J. (1990). *Life lived like a story: Life stories of three Yukon Native Elders in collaboration with Angela Sidney, Kitty Smith & Annie Ned.* Vancouver: University of British Columbia Press.

Cruickshank, J. (1998). *The social life of stories: Narrative and knowledge in the Yukon Territory.* Vancouver, BC: University of British Columbia Press.

Friere, P. (1970). *Pedagogy of the oppressed.* New York, NY: Continuum Publishing Company.

Furniss, E. (1992). *Victims of benevolence: The dark legacy of the Williams Lake Residential School.* Vancouver, BC: Arsenal Pulp Press.

King, T. (2003). *The truth about stories: A Native narrative.* Toronto, ON: Anansi Press.

Lipson, J. (1994). Ethical issues in ethnography. In J. M. Morse (Ed.), *Critical issues in qualitative research methods* (pp. 333–355). Newbury Park, CA: Sage.

Maracle, L. (1993). An infinite number of paths to the centre of the circle. In J. Williamson (Ed.), *Conversations with seventeen Canadian women writers* (pp. 168–178). Toronto, ON: University of Toronto Press.

Mihesuah, D. (2003). *Indigenizing American women: Decolonization, empowerment, activism.* Lincoln: University of Nebraska Press.

Nicholas, A. B. (2008). The assault on Aboriginal oral traditions: Past and present. In R. Hulan & R. Eigenbrod (Eds), *Aboriginal oral traditions: Theory, practice, ethics* (pp. 13–44). Halifax, NS: Fernwood Publishing.

Patton, M. (1980). *Qualitative evaluation methods.* Beverly Hills, CA: Sage.

Patton, M. (1990). *Qualitative evaluation and research methods.* Thousand Oaks, CA: Sage.

Punch, M. (1994). Politics and ethics in qualitative research. In N. K. Denzin and Y. S. Lincoln (Eds.), *Handbook of qualitative research* (pp. 83–97). Thousand Oaks, CA: Sage.

Reinharz, S. (1992). *Feminist methods in social research.* New York, NY: Oxford University Press.

Silko, L. (1996). *Yellow woman and a beauty of the spirit: Essays on Native American life today.* New York, NY: Touchstone.

Thomas, R. (2000). *Storytelling in the spirit of Wise Woman: Experiences of Kuper Island Residential School* (Unpublished master's thesis). University of Victoria, Victoria, BC.

Waziyatawin, A. W. (2005). *Remember this! Dakota decolonization and the Eli Taylor narratives*. Lincoln: University of Nebraska Press.

White, E. R. (Kwulasulwut). (2006). *Legends and teachings of Xeel's, the Creator.* Vancouver, BC: Pacific Education Press.

Wilson, A. (1998a). American Indian history or non-Indian perceptions of American Indian history? In D. Mihesuah (Ed.), *Natives and academics: Researching and writing about American Indians*. Nebraska: University of Nebraska Press (pp. 23–26).

Wilson, A. (1998b). Grandmother to granddaughter: Generations of oral history in a Dakota Family. In D. Mihesuah (Ed.) *Natives and academics: Researching and writing about American Indians* (pp. 27–36). Lincoln: University of Nebraska Press.

Yow, V. (1994). *Recording oral history: A practical guide for social scientists*. Thousand Oaks, CA: Sage.

# Chapter Eight

# AIDS, Men, and Sex: Challenges of a Genderqueer Methodology

## Elizabeth (Eli) Manning

## INTRODUCTION

Here is my confession: I was skeptical of the utility of theory and research before I began my master's degree in social work. As a genderqueer femme, I did not feel that my reality was reflected in either theory or research. I am still skeptical, but in much different ways and with an acquired taste, both sweet and bitter, for these academic tools. I would even venture to say I came to value theory through applying it in my thesis research, because I came to see methodology as the engagement between politics and theory in research practice. My hope is that this chapter offers insight into how I, as a new student researcher, embraced theory and research, utilizing methodology for political, theoretical, and practical purposes. This chapter offers fellow emerging researchers an application of queer theory useful for research purposes, an approach to knowledge production concerns, and an emerging genderqueer methodology informed largely by AIDS activism, queer and trans theories and histories, feminist poststructuralism, and Foucauldian thought. I begin by outlining my methodological framework, focusing on my research ontology and epistemology. Then, I explain how I engaged with men who have sex with men (MSM) discourse through feminist poststructural, genderqueer, and trans perspectives, while also shaping a genderqueer discourse analysis. Finally, I describe how I take up discourse analysis as the primary method through which I explore the question: Who are the men in MSM?

My interest in researching MSM discourse arose from my personal and political commitments. I want to interrogate the "who" in MSM discourse because I am invested in disrupting the hegemonic understandings of sex and gender that are conveyed through the concept of MSM. For me, the political usefulness and theoretical significance of MSM as a concept is undermined because MSM continues to rest on mutually exclusive binaries within sex and gender. My experiences working in HIV and sexual health also influence my interest. Finally, I am part of the community of queers who feel the routine institutional effects of the rigid and constant partitioning of sex and gender categories. I have witnessed the atrocities committed and dangers created when two-spirit, trans, and intersex people are excluded from health care, and have also experienced these firsthand. My research, both in focus and in methodology, reflects that I am invested in myself, the people I love, and those with whom I share the struggle to deconstruct gender and sex discourses, in order that we might sabotage the power of their effects.

## BEGINNING

Dichotomous thinking and being negate queer existences because those who identify as queer live in a liminal space between the binaries within sex, gender, and sexuality. I believe that queer methodologies are vital for exposing hegemonic, linear ways of being and thinking that analyze, categorize, and psychiatrize those outside of binary identities. My goal is not to delimit what queer or genderqueer methodology is, but rather to consider ontology and epistemology, and how queering may shift our gaze in a research inquiry. Ontological and epistemological questions are about what exists and what can be known, respectively. I draw here on Strega's (2005) definition of ontology: "An ontology is a theory about what the world is like—what the world consists of, and why" (p. 201). Her definition highlights that ontology sets out the limits of what exists. Related to ontology, epistemological questions ask, "What is knowledge?" or rather "What can be known?" A genderqueer methodology centres the existence of people who have been known only in particular ways: seen as mystical creatures, ignored, and vilified.

# QUEERING

I use *queer* as a noun to describe a particular group of people who resist or reject dominant heteronormative sex, gender, or sexualities, and I also use *queer* as a verb. To queer something is to question normalcy by problematizing its apparent neutrality and objectivity. Britzman (1998) locates what queer theory can do as a practice: "Queer theory is not an affirmation, but an implication. Its bothersome and unapologetic imperatives are explicitly transgressive, perverse, and political" (p. 82). *Queer* resists definition, uniformity, and cohesion. It examines how normal is made, specifically with regard to sexuality. It is useful to research such as mine that seeks to interrogate and disrupt the normalcy of sex, gender, and sexuality, revealing their seemingly natural constitution.

At the root of queer theory is the idea of heteronormativity, a concept that invites examination of the ways in which heterosexuality positions itself as neutral, normative, and dominant. Similarly, homonormativity, according to Duggan (2003), is a set of "politics that does not contest dominant heteronormative assumptions and institutions but upholds and sustains them" (p. 50). What I mean by homonormativity are practices or ideas that affirm the normalcy of some gay and lesbian people within a capitalist and colonialist framework. For example, gay marriage rests on heteronormative gender and sexuality stereotypes, such as sex binaries and monogamous relationships constituted as units of capitalist production and consumption. Gay men and lesbians accept these ideas for many reasons—for example, as a way to normalize their existences and to gain rights previously available only to heteronormative couples. But heteronormativity and homonormativity both reflect neoliberal ideology, in that they privilege individual over collective needs, assert self-dependency, and foster the privatization of goods and services. For example, critiques of homonormativity argue that "the introduction of lesbian and gay marriage, or other forms of civil recognition, has become a means of not only privatizing gay cultural aspirations, but also shifting the burden of social welfare into the domestic sphere" (Brown, 2009, p. 1499). And normalization is enacted at the expense of queer, trans, intersex, and two-spirit people, constituting us as invisible or deviant. Normalization produces other negative effects, including the marginalization of gender presentations outside of binary norms, the denial of the existence of queer individuals outside of same-sex marriages, and the assimilation of two-spirit people as simply the Indigenous version of gay. In resistance to heteronormativity and homonormativity, I take up *queer* in multiple ways in order to expand on its relationality, disruptions to normalcy, and intrinsic deviance. My intention in doing so is to disrupt the neat and tidy homonormative version of gay and thus promote social justice for those discarded through its imposition.

But queer theory is not without its problems. What is at risk in some of the ways that queer theory is applied is not simply ideas, but our lives. Namaste (2000) identifies how queer theory has centred the conversation on sexuality, with a casual disregard for the deadly implications of contesting and crossing the enforced sex/gender binaries upheld within heteronormativity. She notes:

> Although the violation of compulsory sex/gender relations is one of the topics most frequently addressed within queer theory, this body of knowledge rarely considers the implications of an enforced sex/gender system for people who have defied it, who live outside it, or who have been killed because of it. (2000, p. 9)

Recognizing that discourse is "the violence we do to things," (Foucault, 2010, p. 299), some transgenderists, feminists, and queer theorists (cf. Fausto-Sterling, 1997, 2000; Grosz, 1994, 1995; Namaste, 2000; Stryker, 2006; Wilchins, 2004) push queer theory beyond simply examining the discursive production of sexuality. Where queer theory primarily disrupts the seemingly stable categories of "homosexual" and "heterosexual," gender and transgender theories can take this disruption further by problematizing how sex and gender are socially constructed and required. Gender and transgender theories also tease out neoliberal ideologies embedded in the dominant lesbian, gay, bisexual, and transgender (LGBT) movement. These theories offer ways to make visible and centre intersex, transsexual, transgender, two-spirit, and genderqueer people as subjects within discourses where we have often been objects, and provide a means through which to critique the "natural" construction of sex.

Although articulating a queer methodology is useful, in my own work developing a genderqueer discourse, analysis was necessary for several reasons. First, while many of my epistemological understandings are situated within queer theory, I veer off toward trans and gender theories because they have the capacity to expose dominant understandings of sex and gender constructions beyond the ways made available in most feminist and queer thinking. Second, I am interested in sex, gender, and sexuality and how these three areas depend on one another, a balancing act in which understandings within each serve as underpinnings for the others. By this, I mean that as I explore sexuality (which is consistently negotiated in tandem between desiring subject and objects of desire), I realize how dominant understandings of sex and gender are reified, accepted, and circulated as "truth." As I question these underpinnings, I sense that my work extends beyond what is traditionally seen as queer theory. While my analytical framework in this research project is in many respects queer, it is perhaps better articulated as genderqueer. Through genderqueer analysis, I am able to hone in on understandings specific to sex and gender constructions; this is where my influences from trans and gender theories gain momentum and traction. These influences are particularly important when considering questions of subjectivity, which I define as ways of thinking about how one is situated within a set of power relations. By taking up Foucault's critique of sexuality as a critique of how we articulate our being, queer theory challenges the construction of identity as a normal way of knowing oneself. Yet, for me, it is important to examine subjectivity, because subjectivity differs from identity in ways significant to my research. Whereas the concept of identity implies that identity can be freely self-constructed, the concept of subjectivity is able to account for the roles of historical context and power relations in producing certain subject positions. A genderqueer approach to subjectivity shifts a queer approach to subjectivity by questioning dichotomous understandings of sex and gender, allowing room for people of various sexes and genders that may be liminal or challenge these dominant understandings.

I position genderqueer as a parallel subjectivity that is fluid, shifting, and in need of interrogation rather than as an umbrella term for transgender, transsexual, intersex, and two-spirit people. I partner trans, intersex, and two-spirit critiques with a genderqueer analysis, not in a unifying or colonial sweep, but as a way to show how multiple existences are affected by dominant hetero/homonormative, White, Western, and classed understandings of sex and gender. I foster an overlapping relation between queer and genderqueer. It is on these grounds that I am interested in questioning the sex and gender constructions of men who have sex with men (MSM). Even though I articulate a queer methodology, I wish to refine my analysis to a genderqueer discourse analysis in order to disrupt the construction of sex and gender as well as sexuality, thus bringing my analysis more in line with my politics.

## DISTURBING ONTOLOGY

Research methodologies are grounded in ontology. Modernist ontology, a way of thinking that asserts objectivity, universal truths, natural categories, and dualism, inscribes binary constructs in ways that maintain sexual and gender dominance. For example, modernist ontology would assert that there are only two sexes, which has been proven by objective scientific inquiry. Contesting the certainty of biology's authoritative proclamation of the existence of only two sexes, Fausto-Sterling (1997) argues that science is a form of cultural interpretation rather than the Truth it claims to be. When researchers rely on methodologies grounded in modernist ontology, they fail to question the dualistic nature inherent to them, thus perpetuating these social, physical, and political hierarchies. "Deeply embedded in these [modernist] constructs are systems of classification and representation, which lend themselves easily to binary oppositions, dualisms, and hierarchical orderings of the world" (Tuhiwai Smith, 1999, p. 55). These binary constructs are not limited to sex and sexuality, but also significantly frame constructions of race, ability, and other relations of domination. For example, Somerville (2000) describes how race and sexuality were classified and enmeshed to construct deviant, knowable, and subordinate objects.

In laying claim to queer and genderqueer knowledges previously made deviant and invisible, my specific interest is to expose the techniques and technologies of "making normal" (Brock, 2003). I focus my attention on how "deviant designation can be used to suppress, contain, and stigmatize difference ... how the rules come to be made and who gets to be 'normal'" (Brock, 2003, p. xiii). I am particularly interested in using genderqueer methodologies to examine how those of us with non-normative sexes, genders, and sexualities are discursively produced. My unapologetic and purposeful mission is to poke holes in, deconstruct, and destabilize hegemonic understandings that classify, ignore, persecute, and kill us. Through an analysis of how sex and gender are constructed in MSM discourse, I contribute to destabilizing dominant ways of thinking about queer, trans, intersex, and two-spirit people. My politics of resistance is deeply rooted in my own subjectivity. My experiences of hierarchical sexed and gendered power relations have shaped my ontological perspective, which centres genderqueer, two-spirit, trans, intersex, and non-normative sexed, gendered, and sexual people in the world even while science may try to erase us.

Science has been a tool to carve out the lines of normalcy on multiple bodies, including bodies that fail to adhere to heterosexuality. My critique of science echoes previous feminist, anti-racist, anti-colonial, and post-structural analyses of the effects of scientific discursive productions and material tyranny (see Namaste, 2000; Ramazanoglu & Holland, 2002; Tuhiwai Smith, 1999). For example, as Terry (1995) suggests, "biological arguments about race had long been seen as the handmaidens of racism, just as those about gender were identified to be a central part of the architecture of sexism" (p. 155). Somerville (2000) examines how contingent the making of race and homosexuality are:

> I suggest that the structures and methodologies that drove dominant ideologies of race also fuelled the pursuit of knowledge about the homosexual body: both sympathetic and hostile accounts of homosexuality were steeped in assumptions that had driven previous scientific studies of race. (p. 17)

Foucault (1978) argues that "sex would derive its meaning and its necessity from medical intervention" through the scientific study of sex, "*scientia sexualis*" (p. 67, italics in original). Grundy and Smith (2007) emphasize how social science research raises the "thorny issue of 'ontological politics'" (p. 300) and caution the usefulness of scientifically informed tools, such as evidence-based decision-making models used in "LGBT social science [that] makes some queer realities real at the expense of others" (p. 299). As Grundy and Smith note, the Canadian 2006 census made visible those in heteronormative same-sex relationships, while making invisible transgender, intersex, and transsexual people, as well as LGBT and queer people not in normative same-sex relationships. Only same-sex couples were counted in the census. They point out Cossman's (2002, cited in Grundy & Smith, 2007) contention that

> We have not arrived as individuals, but as relationships. It is not gay men and lesbians who have arrived, but same-sex couples.... It is part of the way in which our membership as sexual

minorities in the Canadian nation is mediated through the lens
of respectable relationships. (p. 303)

Grundy and Smith's argument highlights another characteristic of queer
methodologies—that is, these methodologies reject attempts to legitimize
and solidify existences that are shifting and mobile. In addition, their argument centres on how respectability gets taken up and who gets constructed as
reputable within heteronormative frameworks. This feature of respectability
is one I associate with a homonormative agenda, as it advocates for rights
and benefits for those defined as normal at the expense of those constructed
as deviant. In other words, "proper" gay people are those who subscribe to
monogamous marriage and nuclear families. The homonormative agenda
advocates for the inclusion of gay men and lesbians in this heteronormative
hierarchy. Implicit in this argument is the notion that there are right—and
wrong—ways of being gay. To guard against reconstituting this normative
agenda through our research methodologies, we must ask ontological and
epistemological questions: Who is getting measured and who is not getting
counted? Why is measurement important, and to whom? Can that which
is fluid and shifting be quantified? What are the purposes of quantification?

As I describe above, my application of queer theory includes noticing
how fluid and shifting gender, sex, and sexuality are and interrogating how
sexual deviance came to be labelled as such. While I critique science and
its quantitative methods for its authoritative claim of only two sexes, this
is an easy critique to make. A more challenging critique requires examining how qualitative research also inscribes modernist, and therefore binary,
thinking, thus making its own contribution to circulating hegemonic ideas
about what can exist or be known in the world. Alternatively, poststructuralism supports my genderqueer approach because it challenges absolute
existences, welcomes multiplicity, and deconstructs power relations. These
ideas provide a touchstone for the ontological, epistemological, and methodological foundations of my research project.

## Locating Myself

If I discuss my own subjectivity within this paper, will I reproduce my own
oppression by taking up reverse discourses, which reconstitute dominant
discourses about queers based on the (scientific) knowledge that is used to
exclude us? Speaking specifically about sexuality, Foucault (1978) names
reverse discourse as the way in which "homosexuality began to speak in

its own behalf, to demand that its legitimacy or 'naturality' be acknowledged, often in the same vocabulary, using the same categories by which it was medically disqualified" (p. 101) Audre Lorde is another theorist who saw the irony of using oppressive ideas to build freedom. Although Lorde's (1984) famous quote, "The master's tools will never dismantle the master's house" (p. 112), articulates a specific critique about Black resistances to experiences of slavery and racism, her argument is similar to Foucault's. Yet if I declare myself genderless and sexless, and thus immune to these categorizations, I ignore how sexism, transphobia, heterosexism, and misogyny have forever changed my life and my body. If I locate myself solely within theoretical frameworks of poststructural feminism, and queer and gender theory, will this simply reflect my thinking and not my physical being? As methods are to methodology, so is my body connected to my subjectivity.

Would it suffice to say that I am genderqueer? Likely not. Absent from this declaration are my race, class, age, and ability (or, in the absence of naming them, are they read as dominant in each of these categories?). Nor is my sex or sexuality intact. I have experienced life as a White, lower middle-class, hard of hearing, cisgendered queer femme from English-speaking western and northern Canada. These identities written upon me shape how I experience and understand the world: "We embody the discourses that exist in our culture, our very being is constituted by them, they are a part of us, and thus we cannot simply throw them off" (Sullivan, 2003, p. 41). What is not so clear is that I transgress heterosexual gender norms and that I have also experienced the material consequences of patriarchy, heterosexism, and homonormativity through incest, a detrimentally delayed diagnosis of cervical dysplasia, and intimate partner violence. There are few spaces I exist in where I can definitively mark which category I fit into. Binary systems within sex, gender, and sexuality are problematic for me not only personally, but also politically and theoretically. But I must ask whether articulating myself within the prescribed limits of identity permits me to undo the problems I seek to rupture. These sorts of questions lead me to question how methodologies might be reshaped to serve explicit political purposes.

## (RE)SHAPING METHODOLOGY

Several academics have taken up queer methodologies (see Browne & Nash, 2010; Halberstam, 1998; Holliday, 2000). My goal is to articulate what is unique about a queer methodology and show how I use it in my work. I propose that queer and genderqueer methodologies are shifting, changing, and becoming. I argue that queer methodologies have an interest in centring a particular kind of politics—in other words, a queer ontology. Conceptualizing ways of being beyond the binary systems means certain existences come into view. The goals of my particular queer methodology are several: to challenge the invisibility, normalcy, and stability that are produced by dichotomous understandings; to resist neoliberal assimilation and reverse discourses; and to expose and deconstruct respectability, heteronormativity, and homonormativity. I state these social justice goals not as proprietary claims, but rather in effort to work through what my own goals are. I articulate them so they can be revised, used, and challenged by those interested in taking up genderqueer methodologies. Delineating my rendition of genderqueer methodology engaged me in the process of discerning which theories are useful for my political commitments to social justice. Informing feminist poststructural discourse analysis with queer and trans theories enables me to examine HIV research findings in ways other methodologies prohibit. Specifically, I am able to challenge binary understandings of men's sex and gender in HIV research. I am able to resist dominant understandings of sexuality and sexual practices that take up dominant stratifications. I am able to question if, and how, men who have sex with men are seen as deviant, and conversely who, then, is seen as respectable, and who it serves for MSM to be viewed in this derogatory light.

## PRACTICING A QUEER METHODOLOGY

Queer and genderqueer analyses unearth undercurrents that remain obscured under a normative approach, and partially invisible even through an LGBT lens. In this section, I expand on how a queer methodology can expose, and disrupt, these deadly agendas that have killed those ostracized from normative categories of sex and gender. More precisely, I detail how I apply a genderqueer discourse analysis.

### Identifying Methods

It is more of a question of increasing the *combative power* of potentially subversive forms of knowledge than of simply

> attempting to amplify their "truth-value"; more a tactics of
> sabotage and disruption than a straight-forward head-to-head
> measuring up of supposed truth with a "truer" counter-
> example. (Hook, 2001, p. 536, italics in original)

My queer methodology situates the methods I use to deconstruct the categories of sex and gender in the terminology of MSM. It is influenced by poststructural discourse analysis, a methodology that can expose power relations—an explicitly political action. The disruption to normal that discourse analysis can do fits well with my ontological and epistemological stances and what I want to accomplish through my genderqueer methodology. I also distill a genderqueer discourse analysis, which focuses keenly on the ways in which sex, gender, sexuality, and sexual practices are read and power relations are instantiated, specifically regarding deviance. Similar to how Hook (2001) makes subjugated subject positions visible in his work, I seek to enact this political agenda in my work as well. In what follows, I describe how I answered my research question by using these methods of inquiry/inqueery.

As genderqueer discourse analysis is an emerging methodology, it is important to discuss what I see the nuances of this method doing. With a genderqueer discourse analysis, much like discourse analysis in general, I am interested in power relations, but my attention is specifically focused on how normalizing techniques and technologies are used with regard to sex, gender, sexuality, and sexual practices. My version of discourse analysis is more aligned with feminist poststructural discourse analysis than with critical discourse analysis. I am unequivocally interested in power relations and how they function—their material implications, rather than the textual, more literary details of discourse. My feminist commitments to examining gender and power significantly influence my use of discourse analysis, while my interest in poststructural (constructionist) understandings of gender and sex question some important fundamentals within some (essentialist) feminist thought. Feminist poststructuralism informs my analytical lens, while queer and trans theories propel me further to expose hegemonic, binary, and normative thinking in regards to sex, gender, and sexuality.

## Selecting Text

In selecting data to analyze, I examined a Canadian health policy related to MSM and HIV. My text selection was influenced by my findings about where

MSM is used. By this, I mean that as I examined further how and where MSM has been used, I allowed my research to guide my selection. I am interested in influential pieces of text—texts that have significant material effects on people's lives. Because of my interest and investment in the material consequences of discourse, I reviewed the section of *Canadian Guidelines on Sexually Transmitted Infections*, produced by the Public Health Agency of Canada (PHAC, 2008), entitled "Men Who Have Sex with Men and Women Who Have Sex with Women." This document contains clinical guidelines for how to assess people for STIs, including HIV, and, at the end, a special appendix is included on MSM and women who have sex with women (WSW). I chose to analyze one text in depth so that I could investigate with penetration and fervour the effects of MSM discourse. Selecting one text also allowed me to maintain the scope of a master's thesis.

I selected this section of *Canadian Guidelines on Sexually Transmitted Infections* (PHAC, 2008) for several key reasons. First, federal clinical guidelines are a primary resource for health care practitioners who are conducting sexual health assessments, and this document, produced by the Public Health Agency of Canada, has particular significance for sexual health assessments. Second, I selected this text because it focuses on practice. Chambon (1999) argues, "By examining concrete practices in their most minute details, we can question institutional mechanisms and gain a new understanding" (p. 59). Winch (2005) suggests that "data" should be "drawn from 'practical texts' that provide rules, opinions, and advice on how to behave in a certain fashion ... texts are themselves objects of a 'practice' in that they are designed to underpin everyday conduct" (p. 181). As my interest is in the material consequences of MSM discourse, I wanted to analyze text that spoke to how MSM discourse affects interactions in HIV assessments. Third, as a regulating and governing body, PHAC not only produces clinical guidelines, but also has significant influence over how regional health authorities and health care deliverers provide service. In my experience of working within a health clinic that received funding from PHAC, I witnessed a growing and forceful push to adhere to government standards. Funding became tied to agencies reaching "standards of care" established by regulating health authorities through accreditation processes. In addition to these effects on clinical practice, government significantly influenced funding decisions. Because funding is allocated based on what the government positions as important at any given time, I propose that how the government understands MSM influences which projects get funded, as well as how individual health care providers assess for HIV risk. Bodies such as PHAC have power to not only "guide" direct practice, but also to control what services are available to people affected by HIV/AIDS. For these reasons, I selected the *Canadian Guidelines on STIs* as data because it not only speaks to "advice on how to behave," but because it is a prescriptive guideline of practice drawn up by a governing authority.

## Analyzing Discourse

I am intensely curious about the discursive practices of MSM. I understand discourse to vary from language in a specific way that is critical for me to pay attention to in my analysis. Language refers to the meaning of words, or rather the intention behind the words spoken or written. Language can reveal the intention of the piece, which situates the reader in relation to the writer or speaker.

> When we understand the "intentions" of a piece of language, we interpret it as being in some sense *oriented*, structured to achieve certain effects; and none of this can be grasped apart from the practical conditions in which language operates. It is to see language as a practice rather than an object. (Eagleton, 2008, p. 99, italics in original)

Language is a constituent of discourse; discourse tells language what to do (Gee, 1999). Discourse exemplifies a specific way of thinking that is regarded as normal and does not need explanation. Discourse uses language to do the work of enforcing hegemonic ideas through language practices that ask the interpreter to draw upon "common" knowledge in order for meaning to be made. Discourse varies from language in that discourses work beyond the writer's intention, revealing relations, particularly those between power and knowledge; as Foucault (1978) notes, "It is in discourse that power and knowledge are joined together" (p. 100). Discursive practices focus on "establish[ing]" power relations and truth making (Dreyfus & Rabinow, 1983, p. 63). While language practices are interesting, I am primarily interested in the effects of discourse, as these effects have systemic material consequences.

Discourse names its own objects and prescribes the material effects of these labelling actions. For example, a psychiatric diagnosis is one way in which a discourse claims its object and *does* something to someone.

Those who are subject to this diagnosis are objects of discourse; discourse creates an object (person with a psychiatric diagnosis), a subject (doctor declaring the diagnosis), and subjectivities (for both patient and doctor). Diagnosis may be used to "treat" subjects, which in cases of homosexuality and gender identity dysphoria have included "treatments" such as aversion and electroshock therapy. Hook (2001) states that "once we consider the discursive utterance ... as an action, as a practice ... then this utterance seems to start verging on the territory of materiality and becomes more easily linked to the array of physical activities" (p. 537). As a textual piece of governmental policy comprises my data, discourse analysis is a fitting methodology. I link the use of the term *MSM* and the discourses associated with it with the reproduction of dominant systems of power. The meaning made through the use of MSM is done through language (Gavey, 1989, p. 463) and is situated within a historical, cultural, and political context. The examination of the underpinnings of the term *MSM* has the potential to expose how this term works, what it does, and what assumptions or "discoursal common sense" (Gough & Talbot, 1996, p. 226) must be called upon for MSM to do the work it does. Focusing on the work MSM does is important because "it is through discourse that material power is exercised and that power relations are established and perpetuated" (Gavey, 1989, p. 464). Questions that arise include: What work does naming "men" in MSM do? Whom does it benefit? And at whose expense? What other discourses are drawn upon to make sense of MSM? I looked for how practices get taken up because of the possibilities made available through MSM discourse. I am interested in how MSM discourse functions as a practice, drawing lines for what is possible within the discourse and what is impossible or invisible.

My method of examination consisted of careful and purposeful reading and rereading of these texts, paying attention to multiple effects, such as categorizing, privileging, ignoring, making invisible, making normal, and the like. As my subjectivity and ontology work together (and are contingent upon each other) to make available a certain set of questions, I read these texts to highlight what is troubling about them. I also paid attention to what was not troubling me and probed as to why. Because I see my own subjectivity implicated in my work, I reflected on how I see the discourse matching my own assumptions and understandings. My data analysis began in many ways as I compiled and read for my literature review. I noted my reactions to the texts, noted questions and comments as I read, and reflected on these. I paid attention to phrases that stayed with me after I had read the texts. Often when I read, certain words or concepts surfaced in my thinking and caused me to examine them further. I explored these lingering ideas as points of engagement with the texts that might expose further meanings and inflections. This part of the analysis is intuitive and reflective, based on my own experiences, body, and thinking. How I am situated within this world gives me an ability to read texts in a particular way, exposing some heteronormative and homonormative discourses.

My curiosities led my questioning. I was curious about how MSM discourse arose, how it is used, and the effects of these uses, particularly on the regulation of gender and sex boundaries. I was interested in how MSM is used to impose researchers' understandings of sex and gender regarding a group of people they see sharing the same sex or gender, or both. I am fascinated with points of research and writing that suggest tensions within a binary understanding of gender and sex. How do researchers make sense of trans and intersex people? When do they fall under the category of MSM, and when do they not? Are trans women more likely to be included in MSM, or are trans men? What are the material effects of including and excluding people with non-normative genders and sexes in the category of MSM?

As I read the text, I posed several questions in order to address my curiosity about how men's sex and gender are constructed in MSM:

1. What is required for these texts to be coherent? In other words, what other discourses are required for the reader to draw upon in order to understand where the limits are in the category of "men"?
2. How are people excluded from the category of MSM, and on what grounds?
3. Who is included in the category of MSM, and on what grounds?
4. How might MSM's sexual practices enlighten a researcher's understanding of MSM's sex and gender? Are these discourses of heteronormativity or homonormativity, or both?
5. How might a researcher's understandings of MSM's sexual practices compound or challenge dominant understanding of race, sexuality, sex, and gender?
6. How might the various political and epidemiological reasons MSM has come to be used in HIV work be realized? What are the material effects of these divergent uses of MSM?

These questions helped me to identify how researchers and policy analysts deploy dominant discourses regarding the sexes and genders of MSM.

Two particularly useful techniques in my research were the notion of coherence and a focus on the materiality of discourse. Gough and Talbot (1996) discuss how "coherence is a useful focus of attention in the examination of identity-construction in discourse" (p. 216). Although there are no unified methods in conducting discourse analysis (Potter & Wetherell, 1987, cited in Gavey, 1989, p. 467), I also paid attention to details in the text and read between the lines. I attended to phrases used that required the reader to be complicit in the thinking of the author. This speaks to the need to analyze coherence (Gough & Talbot, 1996). Reading between the lines also connects to the idea that there is "world-knowledge" (Gough & Talbot, 1996, p. 218) required for the pervasiveness and persuasiveness of the discourse to establish, maintain, or perpetuate power-infused meaning. This is important to my work on MSM for several particular reasons. First, coherence speaks to not only the "surface" reading of a text (linguistic specificity, such as syntax, grammar, lexicon, etc.), but also to the "underlying" meanings. These underlying meanings are suspended upon knowledge and discourses that are not necessarily explicitly laid out in the texts, but reference a series of beliefs and assumptions that organize the reader and the writer (as well as the objects/subjects of study) within discourse and, thus, within a set of power relations. Another way to think about these assumptions is as grand narratives—large organizing concepts, such as the notion that heterosexuality is normal or that gender and sex exist as dichotomous binaries. I saw these grander narratives in the text amounting to heteronormative assumptions and gender/sex-dichotomous thinking. These hegemonic discourses situate the writer and anticipated reader as heterosexual and clearly fitting within the dominant gender and sex binary paradigm. I focused on "assumptions about the social world that are set up in such a way that they are not asserted, but readers still need to supply them to read a text as coherent" (Gough & Talbot, 1996, p. 226).

Hook (2001) discusses a significant problem commonly seen within discourse analysis, in focusing simply on the textuality of discourse. He claims that ignoring the "extra-discursive" and discursive practices within discourse undermines and negates the power relations implicit in them. Following Foucault's work, Hook warns against the mere "markings of a textuality" and suggests that specific attention needs to expose the "*physicality* of [discourse's] effects, in the *materiality* of its practices" (p. 537, italics in original). What is particularly useful here is the double meaning of "physicality." Hook speaks to the material consequences and discursive practices that collapse the textual and material realms, and sees them as inseparable and contingent on one another to highlight how discourse brings about action. In my work, I am also interested in looking at how the physicality of discourses creates certain identities, specifically how it constructs sex and gender. Physicality here not only implies discourse, but also highlights how MSM physiology is made visible or invisible through discourse. The use of discourse to create identities rendered visible is an element I paid particular attention to in my readings.

To this end, my findings reveal how two-spirit, trans, and intersex people are erased through MSM discourse. The sex and gender of MSM are collapsed into a particular kind of man through, primarily, discourses of phallocentricity and deviance. Phallocentricity defines a man based on his body, namely his use of his phallic appendage for penetrative sex. Throughout the *Guidelines*, sex roles are described as active and passive, a heteronormative and sexist way to describe sex. Effectively, this articulation structures sex as centred on who is penetrating with a penis and whom the penis is penetrating, all the while without naming the phallus. This exposure of the invisible nature of the phallus implies its power and dominance. Condom discourse engages in phallocentricity in a similar manner by never having to name the penis as the thing that needs to be covered. Stating that you must cover an ejaculatory penis to prevent the spread of STIs and HIV is merely implied, never stated specifically. The *Guidelines* also deploy the discourse of intercourse by segregating sexual activities from "intercourse." By describing intercourse always in reference to the orifice that the penis is penetrating, there is little need to describe what is doing the penetrating. However, there are "other" sexual activities that can transmit HIV and STIs, if precautions are not taken, that are rendered invisible. It is only in these cases that more explicit care is taken to describe what steps would aid in decreasing the risk of contracting STIs. Again, naming specific situations that require "alternative" measures to be taken reinforce the centring of sex on the penis. Phallocentricity explicitly highlights how not only sex, the activity, but also sex, the biological category, is deployed.

The discourse of deviance results in a different effect on the men who are categorized as MSM. Throughout the HIV epidemic, the discourse of deviance has been used to ostracize and exclude people to keep them from being seen as the "innocent victims" of AIDS. The conflation of homosexuality and AIDS reified modern concepts of deviance as appropriately applied to those who are diseased. While MSM discourse attempts to extract men who have sex with men from that construction, the term consistently reaffirms MSM with the diseased. The *Guidelines* deploy deviant and diseased discourses by citing MSM's prevailing list of STIs.

Yet, the diseased discourse is not the only discourse engaged to enlist MSM as deviants. Discourses of sexual deviants, spatial deviants, and criminal deviants solidify MSM as abnormal and as outcasts. MSM are sexual deviants for transgressing lines of heterosexuality (and sometimes venturing back into it after having sex with other men). In addition to this obvious form of sexual deviance, MSM discourse constructs these men as deviant through refined tactics deployed against their sexual behaviour, which is cited for spreading STIs and HIV. Engaging in "barebacking" (the practice of unprotected sexual intercourse), not disclosing STI or HIV status, having multiple sexual partners, and other practices compound the sexual deviant status of MSM. MSM are named as spatial deviants for having sex in untoward places. For example, bathhouses are notorious for being places of ill repute and are therefore often raided by police for the illegal or disreputable sex activities they believe take place there (Haubrich, Myers, Calzavara, Ryder, & Medved, 2004; Hislop, 2000). Naming these places as deplorable sites, along with these acts of surveillance, adds to the reification of these places as deviant spaces and those who visit them as deviants. Criminal deviance has also been employed in MSM discourse through highlighting the engagement of MSM with illegal substances, thus further solidifying the criminal aspect of MSM deviance. While these discourses are drawn on in divergent ways that also divide groups of deviants into those who are heroes and those who are culprits, the irresistible force of deviant discourses enwraps all their subjects in various inescapable effects. Often these effects are compounded systems of oppression that reinforce hegemonic dominance through structures of race, class, nationality, imperialism, and colonization. Indigenous, African-American, and Latino men who reject White, Western constructions of gay identity and the gay community are not only made deviant through homonormativity by the "gay community," but also through the heteronormativity deployed in the *Guidelines*. The overpowering nature of heteronormativity marks MSM as deviant based on their sexual, spatial, criminal, and cultural transgressions.

Although my methods of discourse analysis continue to emerge, I hope I have been able to make explicit not only my reactions to the text, but also the ontological and methodological thinking that underlies my critique and analysis. Hastings (1998) adopts a similar strategy of "present[ing] the data, analysis, and conclusions in such a way that the reader is able to assess the researcher's interpretations and claims" (p. 196). This way of developing my analysis speaks to my current position, as I am also still formulating how to take on a genderqueer methodology within my work through discourse analysis. I argue that genderqueer methodologies provide space for the multiplicity of strangeness to exist, as their disruption of normalcy and Otherness is explicitly political (Kumashiro, 1999). Queer and genderqueer methodologies deconstruct truth claims and question dualistic ontology and queer/straight lines. My articulation of the connections between ontology, epistemology, theory, and politics gives way for an implementation of a genderqueer methodology.

# REFERENCES

Britzman, D. (1998). Queer pedagogy and its strange techniques. In D. Britzman, *Lost subjects, contested objects: Toward a psychoanalytic inquiry of learning* (pp. 79–93). Albany, NY: State University of New York Press.

Brock, D. (2003). Moving beyond deviance: Power, regulation and governmentality. In D. Brock (Ed.), *Making normal: Social regulation in Canada* (pp. ix–xxxii). Scarborough, ON: Nelson Thomson Learning.

Brown, G. (2009). Thinking beyond homonormativity: Performance explorations of diverse gay economies. *Environment and Planning A, 41*, 1496–1510.

Browne, K., & Nash, C. J. (2010). *Queer methods and methodologies: Intersecting queer theories and social science research.* London, UK: Ashgate Publishing.

Chambon, A. (1999). Foucault's approach: Making the familiar visible. In A. Chambon, A. Irving, & L. Epstein (Eds.), *Reading Foucault for social work* (pp. 51–82). New York, NY: Columbia University Press.

Dreyfus, H. L., & Rabinow, P. (1983). *Michael Foucault: Beyond structuralism and hermeneutics* (2nd ed.). Chicago, IL: The University of Chicago Press.

Duggan, L. (2003). Equality, Inc. In L. Duggan, *The twilight of equality* (pp. 43–66). Boston, MA: Beacon Press.

Eagleton, T. (2008). Structuralism and semiotics. In T. Eagleton, *Literary theory: An introduction* (pp. 79–109). Minneapolis, MN: University of Minnesota Press.

Fausto-Sterling, A. (1997). How to build a man. In R. Lancaster & M. di Leonardo (Eds.), *The gender/sexuality reader* (pp. 244–248). New York, NY: Routledge.

Fausto-Sterling, A. (2000). *Sexing the body: Gender politics and the construction of sexuality*. New York, NY: Basic Books.

Foucault, M. (1978). *The history of sexuality: An introduction, Vol. 1*. (R. Hurley, Trans., 1990). New York, NY: Vintage Books.

Foucault, M. (2010). *The archeology of knowledge and the discourse on language* (A. M. Sheridan Smith & R. Sawyer, Trans.). New York, NY: Vintage Books. (Original work published 1969)

Gavey, N. (1989). Feminist poststructuralism and discourse analysis: Contributions to feminist psychology. *Psychology of Women Quarterly, 13*, 459–475.

Gee, J. P. (1999). *An introduction to discourse analysis: Theory and method*. New York, NY: Routledge.

Gough, V., & Talbot, M. (1996). "Guilt over games boys play": Coherence as a focus for examining the constitution of heterosexual subjectivity on a problem page. In C. R. Caldas-Coulthard & M. Coulthard (Eds.), *Texts and practices: Readings in critical discourse analysis* (pp. 214–230). London, UK: Routledge.

Grosz, E. (1994). *Volatile bodies: Towards a corporeal feminism*. Bloomington, IN: Indiana University Press.

Grosz, E. (1995). *Space, time, and perversion: Essays on the politics of bodies*. New York, NY: Routledge.

Grundy, J., & Smith, M. (2007). Activist knowledges in queer politics. *Economy and Society, 36*(2), 294–317.

Haubrich, D. J., Myers, T., Calzavara, L., Ryder, K., & Medved, W. (2004). Gay and bisexual men's experiences of bathhouse culture and sex: "Looking for love in all the wrong places." *Culture, Health & Sexuality, 6*(1), 19–29.

Halberstam, J. (1998). *Female masculinities*. Durham, NC: Duke University Press.

Hastings, A. (1998). Connecting linguistic structures and social practices: A discursive approach to social policy analysis. *International Social Policy, 27*(2), 191–211.

Hislop, G. (2000). The bathhouse raids were a turning point. *Maclean's, 112*(52), 126.

Holliday, R. (2000). We've been framed: Visualizing methodology. *The Sociological Review, 48*(4), 503–521.

Hook, D. (2001). Discourse, knowledge, materiality, history: Foucault and discourse analysis. *Theory & Psychology, 11*(4), 521–547.

Kumashiro, K. (1999). Supplementing normalcy and otherness: Queer Asian American men reflect on stereotypes, identity, and oppression. *Qualitative Studies in Education, 12*(5), 491–508.

Lorde, A. (1984). *Sister outsider: Essay and speeches*. Freedom, CA: The Crossing Press.

Namaste, V. K. (2000). *Invisible lives: The erasure of transsexual and transgendered people*. Chicago, IL: The University of Chicago Press.

Public Health Agency of Canada (PHAC). (revised January 2008). Men who have sex with men and women who have sex with women. In *Canadian Guidelines on Sexually Transmitted Infections*. Ottawa, ON: PHAC. Retrieved from http://www.phac-aspc.gc.ca/std-mts/sti-its/pdf/603msmwsw-harsah-eng.pdf

Ramazanoglu, C., & Holland, J. (2002). *Feminist methodologies: Challenges and choices*. London, UK: Sage.

Somerville, S. (2000). Scientific racism and the invention of the homosexual body. In S. Somerville (Ed.), *Queering the color line—Race and the invention of homosexuality in American culture* (pp. 15–38). Durham, NC: Duke University Press.

Strega, S. (2005). The view from the poststructural margins: Epistemology and methodology reconsidered. In L. Brown & S. Strega (Eds.), *Research as resistance: Critical, Indigenous, and Anti-Oppressive Approaches* (pp. 199–235). Toronto, ON: Canadian Scholars' Press.

Stryker, S. (2006). (De)Subjugated knowledges: An introduction to transgender studies. In S. Stryker & S. Whittle (Eds.), *The transgender studies reader* (pp. 1–17). New York, NY: Routledge.

Sullivan, N. (2003). Queer: A question of being or doing? In N. Sullivan, *A critical introduction to queer theory* (pp. 37–56). Edinburgh, UK: Edinburgh University Press.

Terry, J. (1995). The seductive power of science in the making of deviant subjectivity. In J. Halberstam & I. Livingston (Eds.), *Posthuman bodies* (pp. 135–161). Bloomington, IN: Indiana University Press.

Tuhiwai Smith, L. (1999). *Decolonizing methodologies: Research and Indigenous people*. London, UK: Zed Books.

Wilchins, R. A. (2004). *Queer theory, gender theory: An instant primer*. Los Angeles, CA: Alyson Books.

Winch, S. (2005). Ethics, government and sexual health: Insights from Foucault. *Nursing Ethics, 12*(2), 177–186.

## Chapter Nine

# "On the Footsteps of Foucault": Doing Foucauldian Discourse Analysis in Social Justice Research

## Teresa Macias

## INTRODUCTION

Like many of the students I now encounter in my graduate courses, I stumbled into a graduate program over a decade ago and was confronted with the realization that, while I had an intense need to make sense through research of the historical events that had caused my arrival at that particular time and place, I actually knew next to nothing about research methodologies. I had read theory, as well as research conducted by others, but the actual work of planning and doing research was a mystery. In retrospect, my difficulties in understanding research were caused by the fact that I had not yet identified a research project that could inform my search for a research methodology. Until I found that research issue that captured my curiosity more than any other, all discussions of methodology had the hazardous potential of causing more confusion than clarity.

I usually tell students that the best place to start thinking about social justice research is in the materiality of their own lives: the historical, political, economic, and social conditions that determine their existence and subject position, and the issues or questions about which they feel passionate. It is generally the histories, conditions, or issues that touch our lives that are also likely to fuel our curiosity or spike our outrage. I also tell them that a good research issue, especially when thinking about social justice, is one that implicates us, even if in uncomfortable ways. As authors such as Barbara Heron (2005) have suggested, we are always socially and historically implicated because we all live at the intersection of historical and socio-political power relations that sustain conditions of inequality and privilege and shape our subjectivity. Being implicated in social relations, as I commonly remind my students, is not a matter of good or bad intentions. Simply the fact that we live within social relations that sustain our social position, and that of others, implicate us in the conditions and structures of inequality and privilege that those social relations sustain. While being implicated is not a matter of intentionality, it should, however, be a matter of social responsibility: responsibility that can become a powerful motivator to engage in social justice research. It is in the moments of discomfort, of passionate or even enraged curiosity, and of realization of our social responsibility that the best research questions emerge. In those moments, we may ask questions such as, "How come things are this way?" and "How did we arrive at this moment?" and "Whose voices and experiences are ignored when we unquestioningly accept reality as it is presented to us?" These kinds of questions constitute the starting point for purposeful thinking about research.

Critically situating research in our lives, and situating our lives within research, constitutes—as many of my colleagues in this book suggest—a political and ethical requirement of research, as well as a recognition that research itself is a political and social activity located within social power relations that necessarily implicate us. This idea of research as political, situated, and embedded in life throws traditional notions of research and objectivity into question; it clarifies that all research, even that which alleges objectivity, is socially, historically, and politically situated.

In this chapter, I wish to retrace the steps that brought me to identify the research issue that became the central preoccupation of my doctoral work. I also wish to discuss how this research interest led me to the work of French philosopher Michel Foucault, specifically his work on discourse and its relationship to power, knowledge, and subjectivity. As I make evident in this chapter, Foucault's work, as well as some of the concepts that have been loosely associated with a Foucauldian methodology, opened up for me the possibility of mounting a critique of the historical and political forces and conditions of social injustice that prompted my outraged curiosity. I organize this chapter around that specific moment that brought my research into sharp focus. In so doing, I use this moment as both an example of and a point of entry into a journey into Foucauldian discourse analysis (FDA), in which I follow, at times with more success than others, the footsteps of Foucault through the complexities, challenges, possibilities, and impossibilities of FDA. In this chapter, I walk the reader through the methodological implications of FDA, provide useful, concrete, and practical direction, and explore how a strategic and politically informed application of FDA can assist in social justice research.

My need to understand research methodology and be able to do research with a level of proficiency emerged from a social, political, and historical responsibility I felt to bear witness and make sense of the historical and social forces that had determined the conditions of existence for people who—like me—had lived under regimes of political and social injustice. In more personal terms, I wanted to understand the forces of history that influenced my existence, my history, and my very presence as a racialized woman from the global south in a Canadian university, first as a student and later as an academic. I was born in one of the poorest neighbourhoods on the outskirts of Santiago, Chile, and lived through the repressive years of the authoritarian dictatorship that ruled the country between 1973 and 1990. I became a politically and socially conscious young woman in the resistance and popular movements that fought against that dictatorship, and I eventually joined the flow of refugees from the global south into one of the most diverse cities in Canada. I knew before I entered the university that whatever my PhD project was, it would not stray too far from those historical and political conditions that had influenced my life.

I experienced that moment of enraged and passionate curiosity that brought my research project into focus about a year into my PhD, when I started reading official statements regarding the gross violations of human rights committed under the military dictatorship in Chile. As a survivor of the authoritarian regime, and as someone who lived under its repression, I—like many of my compatriots—was aware of, had witnessed, or had experienced the systemic and organized character of the authoritarian violence. As Chilean scholar Tomas Moulian (1997) argues, the military regime in Chile was a social reorganizing project that required the exercise of power at all levels of personal, social, political, and economic life in order to achieve not only the permanent transformation of the political and economic model into a neoliberal system, but also the intimate transformation and shaping of the Chilean post-authoritarian citizen. The authoritarian regime in Chile organized the systemic persecution, repression, torture, and elimination of anyone considered an enemy of the state. The repression of the regime was not, Moulian continues, an incidental occurrence or simply the result of individual criminality, but rather an organic and integral element of the reorganization project. The military dictatorship in Chile, like many of the authoritarian regimes that ruled Latin America during the 1970s and '80s, left a legacy of about 5,000 dead and executed people. Exact numbers, and the whereabouts of the remains of over a thousand of these victims, remain unknown. Additionally, the Chilean state has recognized that about 37,000 people were tortured under authoritarianism. These numbers do not take into consideration the unknown number of displaced people who, like me, ended up spread out around the world.

Yet, when Chile made a transition to democracy in 1990 and the Chilean nation confronted the imperative to make sense of the atrocities of the regime and to respond to demands for recognition and justice from victims and survivors, the new democratic government engaged in what, at the time, I considered some rather creative storytelling. The official version of the history was one that departed in significant ways from the accounts of repression provided by thousands of victims and survivors. One official statement in regards to the history of authoritarian violence particularly struck me, and in the moment I heard it, the research questions that preoccupied me for the next seven years emerged. In his 1990 inaugural speech before tens of thousands of people at the National Stadium in Santiago, President Patricio Aylwin, Chile's first post-authoritarian democratically elected president, argued that in order to achieve true reconciliation, Chileans should resist the "great temptation" of revenge, and stated:

> The reinstatement of trust and cohabitation between Chileans—
> *regardless of their belief or political ideologies*, whether *they are
> civilians or military—yes compatriots, civilians and military!—*
> means we cannot turn *individual guilt, the result of individual
> actions*, into the guilt, actions and responsibilities of everybody.
> (Aylwin Azocar, 1990, emphasis added)

How could 37,000 victims of torture and over 5,000 dead people be explained as "individual guilt, [and] the result of individual actions"? Why was the post-authoritarian government so invested in making the violence of the regime the result of individual actions? What histories, experiences, and realities were ignored or excluded, and what kinds of state practices in the form of social policies, for example, were authorized by this official account? And, what kind of survivor experiences became un/speakable in this official narrative? Nelly Richard (1998, p. 27) proposes that a central characteristic of post-authoritarian political discourse in Chile is its conciliatory character, resulting in a "democracy of agreements" in which political elites sustain the transfer of power to a civilian government with minimal risk to the social order imposed by the dictatorship. How did this conciliatory discourse, with its emphasis on individual accountability, its implied condoning of the acts of institutions, and its imperative emphasis on national cohabitation and reconciliation, come to be? How is this conciliatory discourse produced in statements such as Aylwin's speech? How is this discourse inscribed in the nation's history, and what social function does it accomplish? While it could be easily argued that the official version of events is simply wrong, what is intriguing and rather unnerving is that Aylwin's version of history systematically became the accepted version: a version repeated many times over by other political and public figures and reproduced in official documents until it became the official truth.

It was at this moment that my need to make sense of the process by which we come to know some things as truth at the expense of other truths became my research project. Foucault's work on discourse provided me with critical direction to explore how power relations shape the production of truth, to critically question and deconstruct statements that are presented to us as truth, and to ask how truth is re/produced in post-authoritarian human rights discourse in Chile.

## FOUCAULDIAN EPISTEMOLOGICAL AND ONTOLOGICAL FRAMEWORK

To argue that President Aylwin's statement is simply untrue, inaccurate, or incomplete, or that other, truer statements can discredit it, would be to deny the power of his words to shape how a whole nation understands its own history. FDA prompts us to ask not whether the statement is true, but rather how it *becomes* truth, and what this truth accomplishes: its social function and social effects. FDA requires us to interrogate how power is at work in the statement in ways that determine what the statement explicitly or implicitly denies, disavows, or excludes, as well as what it accepts, avows, and includes. It also requires that we explore and trace how statements fit within larger systems of thought that together and across history produce truth. Furthermore, FDA directs us to explore how statements capture or fail to capture specific human experiences—for example, what we can and cannot know about victims and perpetrators, and the nature of authoritarian violence—as well as their role in determining and delineating specific outcomes, such as human rights policies and juridical procedures. In this sense, FDA directs us to look for what Foucault called the *biopolitical* effects of the interrelation of knowledge, power, and subjectivity that are at work in the statement (Foucault, 1984b, 1990). In sum, FDA illuminates the truth effects of the statement as well as its biopolitical effects on the material surface of bodies: those captured and produced in the power-knowledge regimes of which the statement is a part, and those who can claim national belonging and subjectivity by participating in the discursive practices that continuously re/produce the power of these and other statements.

This emphasis on the production of truth and its biopolitical effects points to the ontological and epistemological frameworks that inform Foucauldian poststructuralism. Epistemologically, Foucault questions positivist scientific claims that truth and knowledge are unquestionable, metaphysical, and essential conditions that can be objectively attained or discovered through research (see, for example, Foucault, 1984b, 1988, 2003). Rather, Foucault argues that truth is a "thing of this world: it is produced only by virtue of multiple forms of constraint. And it induces regular effects of power" (Foucault, 1984b, p. 72). Truth and power are circularly related in that power produces and sustains truth, while truth sustains and extends power (p. 75). The work of power in the production of truth ultimately informs what we come to accept as knowledge.

Foucault proposes that societies are regulated by power-knowledge regimes: the "general politics," discourses, mechanisms, means, and techniques that determine what counts as truth, who can speak truth, and how truth authorizes specific disciplinary and normalizing actions enacted by social institutions and by individual subjects on themselves and others (Foucault, 1984b, p. 73). Methodologically, Foucault's epistemological claims direct us to look not for truth, but for the processes by which truth is attributed to certain forms of discourse and not to others (Foucault, 1981). In other words, the goal of FDA is to trace, delineate, or map how we come to know something as truth, understanding that truth is produced, as Derek Hook (2001) argues, through processes of inclusion and exclusion that can be traced in discourse. These processes result in the exclusion, inclusion, acceptance, or rejection of certain speeches or ideas through which they become either true or false within a struggle for knowledge that is the result not of a "will to truth," but a "will to power" (p. 524).

Ontologically, FDA is founded on the claim that notions of humanity and human nature—what we may call human life—do not come into social relations fully formed or with an essential nature, but are in fact constantly re/produced in discourse (Foucault, 1997). FDA allows us to explore how power-knowledge regimes work to produce human subjects who are captured in discourse or use discourse to ascertain or claim subjectivity and a place in social power relations. This ontological position means that by using FDA as a methodology, we can uncover how discourse captures human life within power-knowledge regimes in ways that submit it to "explicit calculation[s]" (Foucault, 1990, p. 155). These calculations have biopolitical effects, allowing certain forms of life to become citizens/subjects while legitimizing, sustaining, and enforcing the regulation and discipline of other forms of life. In the case of Aylwin's speech, for example, we can see the biopolitical effect of the statement at two interrelated levels. First, biopolitics plays out not only in the internal structure of the statement and its interrelation with other statements, but also in the manner in which the repetition of the statement and its agential enactment by Aylwin and others allows them to become ideal post-authoritarian subjects who can claim legitimate belonging in the post-authoritarian nation (see, for example, Foucault, 1994, 1997). Secondly, the statement has concrete biopolitical effects on the bodies whose experiences are organized and rendered explicitly and implicitly knowable within the statement. The bodies of victims and their relationship to perpetrators are specifically organized in the statement along lines of individual accountability and guilt. I discuss biopolitics further later in this chapter.

## FOUCAULDIAN DISCOURSE

The concept of discourse remains a rather elusive term in Foucauldian research. While speech, language, text, and talk, as critical discourse analysts argue, can easily be considered discourse (see, for example, van Dijk, 1993, 2003), Foucault is quick to point out that discourse is *more than* simple language. Discourse includes also the social struggles and procedures that control, select, organize, and distribute text and talk while also determining those forms of text and talk that should be averted. Discourse cannot easily be captured in a restricted definition of language to be studied, deconstructed, or pulled apart in order to uncover its hidden meaning, though, as my example suggests, language, text, and talk are a good place to start searching for discourse. Discourse is *not simply* what is said, but also those conditions that determine what can and cannot be said at a particular social and historical moment (Foucault, 1986, p. 149). In this way, discourse extends to the "conditions of possibility" and the conditions of prohibition that determine what can be said, what "we are not free to say," and the relations that determine who possesses "the privilege or exclusive right to speak of a particular subject" (Foucault, 1986, p. 149). This points to another condition of discourse: discourse is not simply utterances authored by a speaker, but also the conditions of recognition that vest a person's speech with the character of more than "mere noise" (p. 150). In other words, discourse is not only what is said, but also what we are able to hear within specific fields of intelligibility.

Discourse is the site of struggle within which truth emerges: the social conditions that determine how certain statements acquire the status of truth and knowledge (Foucault, 1986, p. 151). I mentioned above that Foucault's epistemological claim is that truth is historically and socially produced and informed by a desire or "will to power" (Foucault, 1981, p. 212). This will to power is not necessarily a desire to uncover an unquestionable truth, but rather to invest certain kinds of knowledge with the character of truth. Thus, truth emerges always at the expense, exclusion, and subjugation of other knowledges (Foucault, 1986, p. 151; see also Sharp & Richardson, 2001). Bernard McKenna (2004, p. 11) stresses the importance Foucault attributes to the connection between discourse and material practices external to discourse, observing that discourse occurs within fields in which it acquires place and status and in which power relations open up possibilities for the permanence of certain ideas as discourse.

Hook (2001) observes that a central concern in Foucault's notion of discourse is its connection to the material conditions and procedures that influence the production, selection, organization, and distribution of discourse. This materiality, Hook suggests, means that discourse needs to be located within political action and extra-textual fields. Discourse, he continues, is also that which "enables writing, speaking and thinking": the material conditions that, for example, determine access to the tools for the production and dissemination of discourse (p. 523). Thus, the focus of analysis needs to be centred on "discursive practices," which work "in both inhibiting and productive ways, implying a play of prescription that designate both exclusions and choices" (p. 523; see also Weedon, 1987).

For example, Aylwin's statement needs to be situated within the precarious and delicate political negotiations that made "peaceful" transition to democracy possible in Chile and that regulate how much the post-authoritarian nation can do about human rights violations without upsetting still-powerful military and conservative groups (see, for example, Garretón, 1999). This delicate balance of power, while not explicit in the statement, can be read in the manner in which Aylwin defines "individual responsibility" in opposition to the "the guilt, actions and responsibilities of everybody" and how both concepts are tied rhetorically to the imperative of "national cohabitation." It can also be traced in the forceful emphasis, the repetition and tone of voice with which he stresses who is to be included in the post-authoritarian nation: "compatriots, both civilian and military." By linking these concepts, Aylwin inscribes through avowal and disavowal an acceptable truth that carries a warning: individual responsibility can never become institutional responsibility or the responsibility of everyone if we are to achieve a national project of cohabitation and trust. In this simple statement, Aylwin enacts the power of his office, which vests his speech with the institutional force to determine what can and cannot be said—what truths can be produced—about Chile's history. Uttered at a pivotal moment in the history of the post-authoritarian nation, this statement is more than an idea; it becomes part of a regulating and normative discourse that carries force and power. It authorizes the Chilean military, for example, to maintain that they do not have information about the whereabouts of more than a thousand missing people, or that they did not order the torture or execution, or both, of tens of thousands. It also allows economic elites in the neoliberal order put in place by the dictatorship to argue that their social position of privilege is not sustained by violence.

Aylwin's speech does not stand alone, but is rather part of larger systems of meaning and discursive practices, within which what he says acquires meaning to those who listen. By itself, the statement is not discourse, but rather "a dense transfer point" of power loaded with the "instrumentality" of larger discourses that find expression, solidify, and crystallize in the statement (Foucault, 1990, p. 103). In other words, the statement is a discursive practice that is located within a longer history of ideas about, among other things, human rights, accountability, criminality, violence, and nationalism, which constitute the socially available repertoires that find expression and grant legitimacy to the speech (Fairclough, 2003). As a practice, the statement not only implicates the speaker, but also the listener who hears the statement and *makes perfect sense* of it. Speaker and listener are both caught in the larger discursive field within which the statement contributes to the production of truth and subject, and, through the enactment and adoption of the discourse for their own self-making, as well as for the regulation and discipline of others, speaker and listener reproduce the discourse and propel it forward (Macias, 2012).

## DISCOURSE AND BIO/POWER

As I have suggested, power is a critical consideration in FDA because certain statements acquire the status of truth through the work of power in discourse and through discourse. Foucault rejected the idea of power as solely acting from a top-down perspective, simply as repressive, or as only "carrying the force of prohibition" (Foucault, 1984b, p. 61). He identified also the productive aspects of power as enabling, promoting, and enticing. In his words:

> What makes power hold good, what makes it accepted, is simply the fact that it does not weigh on us as a force that says no, but that it traverses and produces things, it induces pleasure, forms knowledge, produces discourse. It needs to be considered as a productive network which runs through the whole social body, much more than a negative instance whose function is repression. (1984b, p. 61)

By taking power into consideration, Lois McNay (1994, p. 86) argues, we can explain how, out of an infinite number of possibilities and meanings, "there is a relative paucity or rarity of what is possible to think and say at any one time." Thus, the analysis of discourse needs to be concerned with the power struggles that determine meaning in discourse (Foucault, 1984b). Truth as a discursively constituted effect of power gives legitimacy to specific forms of knowledge, which in turn reinforce and reproduce power (Foucault, 1980, p. 93). Thus, power requires knowledge in the same way that knowledge is the effect of power (p. 102). As Foucault argued

(1995), "We should admit that power produces knowledge (and not simply by encouraging it because it serves power or by applying it because it is useful); that power and knowledge directly imply one another" (p. 27). The constant interrelation of power and knowledge and the recognition of the way in which they imply one another require that we concentrate not simply on the analysis of discourse, but also on analyzing the power-knowledge regimes that sustain and are sustained by discourse and within which discourse acquires meaning as truth.

Furthermore, power-knowledge regimes constitute the terrain within which subjects are produced and produce themselves. Subjects, as Foucault observes, are subjected in a dual sense: they are subjected to the complex, multiple, shifting relations of power at the same time as they are enabled to take up subjectivity in and through those relations (Allen, 2002; Foucault, 1982, 1989). In other words, power acts productively and repressively and is a condition for the possibility of individual subjectivity. To understand the full reach of power, we need to pay attention to how discourse constitutes subjects, regulates their desires, and implicitly and explicitly calculates their relationships with other subjects and with society. We also need to pay attention to how discourse defines and delimits the subject's freedom (Miller & Rose, 1995). In Foucault's (1989) view,

> it is already one of the prime effects of power that certain bodies, certain gestures, certain discourses, certain desires, come to be identified and constituted as individuals. The individual, that is, is not the vis-à-vis of power; it is, I believe, one of its prime effects. (p. 308)

Processes of subject formation can be revealed through the study of discourses such as sexuality and punishment, within which human conduct is minutely described, proscribed, and prescribed in ways that submit biological life to calculation, division, and management. Foucault (1990, 1995) identified how power-knowledge regimes target the body in ways that allow society to shape, manipulate, and train it to its most intimate and minute details. In his study of discourses of sexuality, for instance, Foucault (1990) uncovered how Victorian discourses actively produce and regulate the body of the masturbating child, the hysterical woman, the reproducing body, and the homosexual, transforming them into the field on which discourses of sexuality calculate and regulate sexual conduct. Through studying

processes of subject formation, Foucault finds an entry point into the inter-
connections among power, knowledge, and subjectivity that contribute to
the formulation of biopower, constituting one of Foucault's most critical
contributions. Biopower refers to the complex interrelation of techniques
of power and knowledge, and their effect in materializing a wide array of
conduct in public and political discourse (Foucault, 1990, p. 155).

FDA allowed me to delineate how human rights discourses in Chile
constitute a power-knowledge regime within which our understanding of
victims of human rights violations is shaped and we are able to understand
ourselves as post-authoritarian subjects/citizens. FDA made it possible,
then, to explore the biopolitical effects of discourse at two levels: the effect
of discourse on the regulation of subjects whose lives become captured in
discourse; and the subject-making practices that subjects enact through the
use of discourse. For example, FDA elucidates the biopolitical function
of Aylwin's statement and the ways in which it disciplines how authoritarian violence will be understood: as a product of relationships between
individuals who exist as delinked from each other and institutions. This
organizing effect is not to be taken lightly, for it carries the power of liberal
discourses of individualism, and the denial, in these discourses, of how
social structures, historical contexts, and state practices affect people's lives.
In a few words, Aylwin captures and disposes of the lives and claims of
victims and survivors, effectively telling *them* and *us* how we are to con-
ceptualize authoritarian violence, survivors' experiences of it, and what we
are to do about it. By capturing those bodies and acts, the speech becomes
an organic element of a power-knowledge regime that disposes of victims
and survivors, arranging them in relation to each other and to a larger
nation-building project. In the process, victims and survivors are rendered
specifically knowable and carefully regulated (for further discussion, see
Macias, 2013a, 2013b).

On the other hand, FDA allowed me to illuminate how the act of
describing victims and survivors, as well as the acceptance, articulation,
and reproduction of the official discourse, allows subjects to claim belonging and ideal subjectivity in the post-authoritarian nation (Razack, 2007).
Ideal subjects/citizens are those who voluntarily subject themselves to and
perform on themselves the work required to accept the official truth regarding the imperative of national cohabitation and personal accountability
and use that truth to discipline any desire or temptation for vengeance.
The acceptance of this official truth; its repetition in a multitude of speech

acts that precede, coexist, and branch out from Aylwin's speech; its dissemination in the media and in academic work; its distribution in public and private conversations; and its internalization in countless moments of intimate and personal reflection all work together to reproduce a discursive moral universe—what Sherene Razack (2004) calls a "coded national narrative"—within which the ideal Chilean subject can come to know him or herself as a truly post-authoritarian citizen. In other words, the official truth, the production of which is contributed to by Aylwin's statement, invites and seduces us to forge our own national subjectivity through mutual meaning-making and collective narration of the story that, by re/constructing the national narrative, produces an imagined national community (Anderson, 1983; Wilson, 2001).

## SOME NOTES ON METHOD: GENEALOGY, INTERTEXTUALITY, AND EVENTALIZATION

I have said little so far about methods, specifically methods of data collection and research design. I wish to remedy this silence by discussing three methods proposed by Foucault as tools for research: genealogy, intertextuality, and eventalization. Let's remember two conditions of FDA: its emphasis in studying how discourses *become* truth, and its premise that specific text and talk (or other expressions of discourse) are not, by themselves, discourse, but rather manifestations of discourse. Together, these conditions point to a genealogical approach to research in which intertextuality can be an analytical method and eventalization can be a design strategy.

At the centre of Foucault's genealogical approach is a skeptical attitude in relation to any statement that is presented as truth. This allows him to move away from a discussion of the veracity of specific statements in favour of a methodology that allows him to trace how a particular statement becomes truth. In the context of my study, this skeptical attitude opens up possibilities to challenge statements that are presented as truth while tracing their connection to other discourses that help to produce them as truth. Statements, or expressions such as "individual accountability" or "trust and cohabitation," can be questioned not through a struggle to prove that other statements are truer, but through an interrogation of those historical moments in which these statements acquire supremacy over others. We can also trace the process by which other statements become noise to discourse—that is, what is left out (Foucault, 1986).

Genealogy requires us to begin at a specific moment in the history of discourse (generally in the present, or even at that moment in which we may ask, "How have we come to know this as truth?") and then turn our gaze backwards toward the history of the discursive practices that have given rise to that moment. However, while traditional conceptions of genealogy rely on the notion of origin as the place where things begin, Foucault's genealogical approach is concerned not with the search for origin, but with challenging notions of origin as the "moment of birth" or as the "site of truth." This is Foucault's poststructural project: the search in history of the different, uneven, and multiple elements that influence what we know as truth in the present. The question that guides this genealogical inquiry concerns how we come to know what we know, and the answer is found in the past: a past that is not heritage, but rather "an unstable assemblage of faults, fissures and heterogeneous layers that threaten the fragile from within or from underneath" (Foucault, 1984a, p. 82). Genealogy allows the researcher to trace the many traits and events that work together to historically constitute a concept, disturbing that which is considered immobile (p. 82).

Aylwin's speech, while undeniably influential, does not constitute a point of origin for the national ideas it manifests and is not in itself completely original. In fact, as I have suggested, we find in the statement the manifestation of other discourses, some of which are quite old and whose history can be traced all the way to the European Enlightenment. Others, such as the notion of individual accountability, began to be articulated prior to the end of the dictatorship and in the context of political negotiations aimed at protecting the democratic transition and, by extension, the outgoing regime. The placing of Aylwin's speech in this historical context allows us, for instance, to appreciate how the statement becomes part of larger systems of meaning. Moreover, a genealogical approach also requires that we see Aylwin's speech in context with other forms of discourse in which his words are either quoted or evoked in ways that propel the discourse forward. At times, we may see moments of weakness and destabilization of the discourse, as, for example, in the discursive resistance of critical human rights activists. This analysis requires a sort of detective work, in which the researcher follows leads and clues in the history of discourse, collecting and analyzing specific forms of discourse while also paying attention to how specific discursive practices are linked and related to other discursive practices across time and space.

Genealogy also points to the intertextual character of analysis, for discourse cannot be studied simply by looking at the internal organization of specific discursive practices or speech acts. Rather, discursive practices, whether in public speeches, written texts, verbal communication, personal reflections, visual imagery, or another form, are, as Julia Kristeva (1980) observes, always connected to other discursive practices that together construct a discursive field or universe within which they make sense. As Foucault (1972) adds in the context of written texts, discourses are never autonomous, but are rather "caught up in a system of reference to other books, other texts, other sentences" (p. 23). A text, he continues, "is a node within a network." Therefore, in the genealogy of post-authoritarian human rights discourses I attempted in my work, I was required to always look at my data as "nodes" in a network of discursive relations that could be untangled, deconstructed, and studied by paying attention not only to the internal organization, content, and structure of specific forms of discourse (such as Aylwin's speech), but also at how discourses informed and were informed by other forms of discourse.

This attention to intertextuality within a genealogical design meant that my data expanded considerably, both across time and across a multiplicity of coexisting records. For instance, I collected speeches by public figures given at different times in the history of human rights debates, historical records of parliamentary debates, media reports, artistic expressions, and interviews. These records formed a network of discursive practices, the study of which allowed me to trace the formation, shifting, and change of discourses across time. Using a genealogical and intertextual research design meant that, while I began at a particular moment (albeit not necessarily a remarkable one) in the history of human rights debates in Chile, I also expanded my search to include contemporary as well as past records. Guided by the question of how specific discourses have become truth, I went into the archives and began collecting some of the records mentioned above. Archival research and initial analysis of the data was done simultaneously and very much evoked detective work; I searched for moments in which specific ideas or concepts re/emerged, changed, shifted, and experienced challenges. I paid attention to those instances in which human rights activists attempted to challenge the official story by putting forward alternative discourses. For example, human rights activists attempted at times to challenge the individual accountability discourse by insisting on the institutional character of authoritarian violence and on the limitations that individual accountability posed for justice. I understood these challenges as opportunities to see how power struggles determined and influenced discourse. Other instances of power struggles could be also observed in the internal organization of certain discursive practices. For instance, in the *Rettig Report* (1991) that resulted from the first Chilean truth and reconciliation commission, the official truth put forward in Aylwin's statement comes momentarily under scrutiny, but is then accepted as a national truth that will ensure national reconciliation. I could see in this report power struggles that left a trace in the internal organization of the text and could be observed in the very structure, semantic gestures, and rhetorical moves reflected therein.

When looking for the biopolitical effects of discourse, I began by paying attention to how experiences of authoritarian violence were captured and described in discourse. I asked, for example: What experiences of violence are described, and how? What experiences of violence receive less attention or are dismissed? What tools or technologies are used to organize a truth about violence? These questions allowed me to uncover, for instance, how human rights discourses produced specific images of victims of human rights violations—images that were discursively shaped in ways that determined the kinds of experiences of victimization that became publicly acknowledged and the notions of justice and retribution that became possible within the constrains of post-authoritarian politics (see Macias 2013a, 2013b).

I also traced the biopolitical effect of discourse in the manner in which subjects enacted human rights discourses and used them to produce themselves as national subjects/citizens and claim a place in the post-authoritarian nation. Farid Abdel-Nour (2003) argues that subjects become citizens with "every proud thought they have and every proud statement they make about the achievements of their nation" (p. 703), and when they can connect their personal subject-making stories to larger national narratives. With this argument in mind, I searched in interviews and archival data for those instances when subjects expressed pride over the perceived achievements of the post-authoritarian nation and when, for example, they wholeheartedly accepted the national truth. I saw these moments as subject-making moments not only in which the official discourse was reinforced and legitimized, but also in which subjects became subjects.

Genealogical and intertextual analysis can result in a daunting and rather challenging amount of data, made up of multiple genres and inter-relating across time in the long history of a discourse. Foucault (2003) argues that, when confronted with the impossibility of ascertaining pre-cise origins, eventalization constitutes a strategy that can prevent excessive data collection while pinning genealogical analysis to the political goals that guide social justice research (Chambers, 2001). *Eventalization* means to "make visible a singularity" or event in order to pinpoint it for analysis while still paying attention to the multiple processes that make the event possible, its continuities and discontinuities (Foucault, 2003, p. 249). In simple terms, eventalization allowed me to identify, out of a multiplicity of discursive practices with a long history, a set of historical conjunctures or events in which my analysis would be more specifically concentrated. While my research covered 15 years of human rights debates, I chose four historical moments in which to concentrate my data collection and analy-sis: the actual moment of the transfer of power to civilian rule in 1990 (of which the speech by Aylwin I have used here is a part); the creation of the Rettig Truth Justice and Reconciliation Commission and the release of its report in 1991; the creation of a Human Rights Discussion Commission in 1998; and the creation of the Torture Commission and the release of its report in 2004. I considered each of these historical moments an event around which discursive practices concentrated and dispersed in ways that critically informed the data analysis. Each event, in turn, was linked to the other events in ways that were identifiable in discourse and that offered both continuity and discontinuity to human rights discourses.

## THE POSSIBILITIES OF FOUCAULDIAN DISCOURSE ANALYSIS

My research emerged, as I have indicated, from a moment of disjuncture in which my own historical experience as a survivor of an authoritarian regime confronted normative discourses of truth, justice, and responsi-bility, such as those encapsulated in the quotation from Aylwin. At that moment of disjuncture, I felt not only a sense of injustice, but also what I can only call an enraged curiosity that prompted me to ask: How have we, Chileans, the Chilean nation, and even the international community arrived at this kind of understanding of human rights atrocities? And how have our experiences, the experiences of survivors and victims, been subverted by and subjugated to the normative power-knowledge regimes regulating politics of truth in Chile? These questions have political significance because they necessarily turn the gaze (admittedly an angry gaze) toward the state, prompting a process of interrogation of the work of power in social relations and historical narratives. This gaze is guided by a political commitment not only to make sense of the work of power, but also to uncover and illuminate those moments in which subversive discourses may have the most impact in shifting and changing the official story, as well as in calling attention to the repressive work of power. In assuming this political work, FDA can have socially and politically transformative possibilities when it aligns itself with the cause of subversive and resisting communities. These possibilities emerge from a central premise of FDA: by uncovering how truth and social conditions become, we have to accept that *they do not have to be the way they are.*

FDA allows us to interrogate and disentangle the complex historical processes that, by being presented as unquestionable truth, have become crystallized and immobile. The questioning itself has the potential to destabilize their apparently entrenched hold. This commitment to interrogation and disentanglement requires that we maintain a skeptical position "towards all those rationalities, explanations and statements that would validate themselves on the grounds of their proximity to a supposed truthfulness," paying attention to the conditions that make truth a product of discourse and power (Hook, 2001, p. 524). This skeptical attitude does not mean, Hook (2001) argues, that Foucauldian research accepts truth as a relative term; rather, it focuses on the power struggles to grant some statements more validity than others. Illuminating moments in which power struggles determine how discourse evolves normative discourses experience moments of weakness, uncertainty, and rearticulation present important transformative possibilities, because it is in these moments that we see that things do not have to be the way they are. As Hook (2001) continues, FDA allows us to uncover the "gaps and shortcomings" of discourse in order to "increase the *combative power* of potentially subversive forms of knowledge" (p. 536, italics in original). This skeptical attitude can allow us to "know how and to what extent it might be possible to think differently, instead of legitimating what is already known" (Foucault, 1985, p. 9). As Foucault (1997) observes, a critical understanding of how power works as an instrument of discourse can allow us to uncover how human life is captured in discourse and how, as a result, we are ruled and governed through discourse. By rendering problematic the triangular interrelation of power, discourse, and subjectivity, we can begin to articulate alternative ways of being regulated by discourse. Concrete and concerted efforts to find ways to privilege other forms of truth and subjectivity can lead us to ways of not being governed "quite so much."

All research is political, because research itself is a social activity located within social power relations, informed by social conditions and regulated by struggles to give meaning to the world out there. The politically and socially situated character of research means that decisions about methodology need to be critically informed by both personal and collective, politically aware reflection and alliances. Any decision about methodology needs to consider both its possibilities and its limitations: what it can and cannot accomplish. For instance, FDA is a good methodology to understand and map how power works to produce what we have come to accept as truth, and how these processes of truth formation have resulted in the marginalization of *other* truths and *other* subjects. But this methodology, as Strega (in this book) argues, is embedded in Eurocentric notions of knowledge, being, and research, and as a result, it might not be a good tool to account for *other* ways of being and knowing. For instance, FDA may be of use to Indigenous communities interested in understanding how power-knowledge regimes continue to sustain colonialism and White supremacy, and how Western knowledge has historically suppressed Indigenous knowledge. However, FDA might not be the best approach for exploring how Indigenous peoples experience or make sense of colonial domination, how Indigenous ways of knowing are preserved or defended by Indigenous communities, or how Indigenous communities organize activism and anti-colonial resistance. In my case, the objective of my research was precisely to speak to the power of the state and render knowable the power struggles that determine how and what we come to know as an official truth.

In deciding on the best methodology for social justice research, we must first understand what conception of social justice guides us, and how that conception informs ethical reflection about our role as researcher and our entitlement to engage in any research with any population. All research needs to begin with a critical and hard reflection on the goals that guide us and on our location as researchers within the research. Critical reflection on the kind of research we want to do may lead us to conclude there are some methodologies that should be avoided due to their history and potential for harm, and there are some research activities and communities we should stay clear of due to our social positioning and our historical entitlement. While I understand and agree with Strega's (in this book) hesitation to adhere to poststructural feminism and its Eurocentric roots, I also believe that all decisions about any research activity and methodology must be approached hesitantly.

In deciding what methodology to adopt for any research activity, we have to commit to an ethics of uncertainty and unsettlement, because these can keep us aware of the implications of the uneasy alliances into which we enter through our decisions. With these considerations in mind, I propose that Foucault offers some important methodological directions for research that can open up possibilities for critical and transformative research—directions that, like with any other methodology, are imperfect.

## REFERENCES

Abdel-Nour, F. (2003). National responsibility. *Political Theory*, *31*(5), 693–719.

Allen, A. (2002). "Power, subjectivity, and agency: Between Arendt and Foucault." *International Journal of Philosophical Studies 10*(2), 131–149.

Anderson, B. (1983). *Imagined communities: Reflections on the origin and spread of nationalism*. London, UK: Verso.

Aylwin Azocar, P. (1990). Discurso de S.E. el Presidente de la Republica, D. Patricio Aylwin Azocaren el Estadio Nacional, Santiago, 12 de Marzo de 1990. S. G. d. Gobierno, Gobiernode Chile. [Inaugural address by H. E. President Patricio Aylwin Azocar, National Stadium, Santiago Chile, 12 March 1990.] Retrieved April 20, 2015, from http://www.archivochile.com/Gobiernos/gob_paylwin/de/GOBdeaylwin0003.pdf

Chambers, S. (2001). Foucault's evasive maneuvers: Nietzsche, interpretation, critique. *Angelaki: Journal of Theoretical Humanities*, *6*(3), 101–123.

Comisión Nacional de Verdad y Reconciliación [National Truth and Reconciliation Commission]. (1991). *Informe Rettig: Informe de la Comisión Nacional de Verdad y Reconciliación* [*Retting Report: Report of the National Truth and Reconciliation Commission*]. Santiago, Chile: Gobierno de Chile [Government of Chile].

Fairclough, N. (2003). *Analyzing discourse: Textual analysis for social research*. London, UK: Routledge.

Foucault, M. (1972). *The archeology of knowledge*. London, UK: Tavistock.

Foucault, M. (1980). Two lectures. In C. Gordon (Ed.), *Power/knowledge: Selected interviews and other writings* (pp. 78–108). New York, NY: Pantheon Books.

Foucault, M. (1981). The order of discourse. In R. Young (Ed.), *Untying the text: A post-structural anthology* (pp. 3–14). Boston, MA: Routledge & Kegan Paul.

Foucault, M. (1982). The subject and power. In H. Dryefus & P. Rabinow (Eds.), *Michel Foucault: Beyond structuralism and hermeneutics* (pp. 208–226). Chicago, IL: University of Chicago Press.

Foucault, M. (1984a). Nietzsche, genealogy, history. In P. Rabinow (Ed.), *The Foucault reader* (pp. 76–100). New York, NY: Pantheon Books.

Foucault, M. (1984b). Truth and power. In P. Rabinow (Ed.), *The Foucault reader* (pp. 51–75). New York, NY: Pantheon Books.

Foucault, M. (1985). *The use of pleasure: Vol. 2 of the history of sexuality*. New York, NY: Pantheon Books.

Foucault, M. (1986). The discourse on language. In H. Adams & L. Searle (Eds.), *Critical theory since 1965* (pp. 148–162). Tallahassee, FL: Florida State University Press.

Foucault, M. (1988). The concern for truth. In L. D. Kritzman (Ed.), *Michel Foucault: Politics, philosophy, culture: Interviews and other writings* (pp. 255–267). New York, NY, and London, UK: Routledge.

Foucault, M. (1989). Power, sovereignty and discipline. In D. Held (Ed.), *States and societies* (pp. 306–313). Oxford, UK: Basil Blackwell.

Foucault, M. (1990). *The history of sexuality: An introduction*. New York, NY: Vintage Books.

Foucault, M. (1994). The ethics of the concern of the self as a practice of freedom. In P. Rabinow (Ed.), *Michel Foucault: Ethics, subjectivity and truth* (pp. 281–302). New York, NY: The New Press.

Foucault, M. (1995). *Discipline and punish: The birth of the prison*. New York, NY: Vintage Books.

Foucault, M. (1997). Subjectivity and truth. In S. Lotringer (Ed.), *The politics of truth* (pp. 147–168). Boston, MA: The MIT Press.

Foucault, M. (2003). Questions of method. In P. Rabinow & N. Rose (Eds.), *The essential Foucault: Selections from essential works of Foucault, 1954–1984* (pp. 246–258). New York, NY, and London, UK: The New Press.

Garretón, M. A. (1999). Chile 1997–1998: The revenge of incomplete democratization. *International Affairs, 75*(2), 259–267.

Heron, B. (2005). Self-reflection in critical social work practice: Subjectivity and the possibilities of resistance. *Reflective Practice, 6*(3), 341–351.

Hook, D. (2001). Discourse, knowledge, materiality, history: Foucault and discourse analysis. *Theory & Psychology, 11*(4), 521–547.

Kristeva, J. (1980). *Desire in language: A semiotic approach to literature and art.* New York, NY: Columbia University Press.

Macias, T. (2012). "In the world": Towards a Foucaultian ethics of reading in social work. *Intersectionalities: A Global Journal of Social Work Analysis, Research, Polity, and Practice, 1*(1), 1–19.

Macias, T. (2013a). "Tortured bodies": The biopolitics of torture and truth in Chile. *The International Journal of Human Rights, 17*(1), 113–132.

Macias, T. (2013b). "Tortured women and hungry widows": Patriarchal neoliberalism and the logic of compensational justice in Chile. *Affilia, 28*(2), 126–139.

McKenna, B. (2004). Critical discourse studies: Where to from here? *Critical Discourse Studies, 1*(1), 9–39.

McNay, L. (1994). *Foucault: A critical introduction.* Cambridge, UK: Polity Press.

Miller, P., & Rose, N. (1995). Production, identity and democracy. *Theory and Society, 24*, 427–467.

Moulian, T. (1997). *Chile actual: Anatomía de un mito* [Modern Chile: Anatomy of a myth]. Santiago, Chile: Arcis-LOM.

Razack, S. (2004). *Dark threats and white nights: The Somalia affair, peacekeeping and the new imperialism.* Toronto, ON: University of Toronto Press.

Razack, S. (2007). Stealing the pain of others: Reflections on Canadian humanitarian responses. *Review of Education, Pedagogy, and Cultural Studies, 29*(4), 375–394.

Richard, N. (1998). *Residuos y metáforas: Ensayos de crítica cultural sobre el Chile de la transición* [Vestiges and metaphors: Essays on cultural critique about Chile in transition]. Santiago, Chile: Editorial Cuarto Propio.

Sharp, L., & Richardson, T. (2001). Reflections on Foucauldian discourse analysis in planning and environmental policy research. *Journal of Environmental Policy and Planning, 3*(3), 193–209.

van Dijk, T. (1993). Principles of critical discourse analysis. *Discourse and Society, 4*(2), 249–283.

van Dijk, T. (2003). Knowledge in parliamentary debates. *Journal of Language and Politics, 2*(1), 93–129.

Weedon, C. (1987). *Feminist practice and post-structuralist theory.* Oxford, UK: Basil Blackwell.

Wilson, R. (2001). *The politics of truth and reconciliation in South Africa.* Cambridge, UK: Cambridge University Press.

# Chapter Ten

# Researching the Resurgence: Insurgent Research and Community-Engaged Methodologies in 21st-Century Academic Inquiry[1]

## Adam Gaudry

## INTRODUCTION

Undertaking community-informed Indigenous research is challenging, especially for university-based researchers. Universities have appropriated, dissected, and abused Indigenous knowledges; they have failed to appreciate the complexity and nuances of Indigenous worldviews; and they have even refused to acknowledge the validity of these knowledge systems (Tuhiwai Smith, 1999). As a result, Indigenous researchers often feel caught between the desire to be responsible to our communities and the necessity of navigating the institutional requirements of the academy. It is no surprise to those who have conducted community-engaged research that research in Indigenous communities involves a complex maze of ethical, social, and political considerations. In this chapter, I reflect on my experiences as a Métis researcher and scholar navigating this maze, and offer a particular approach to community-engaged academic research that I call *insurgent research.*

Insurgent research is motivated by grassroots-academic collaborations that resituate Indigenous interests and values in an otherwise alienating research process. The articulation of Indigenous research paradigms is part of a broader movement of Indigenous resurgence and decolonization, and therefore has motives beyond just the creation of interesting research (see Simpson, 2009a). Indigenous academics are tasked with challenging colonialism and dismantling its ideological underpinnings, working from within Indigenous frameworks to reimagine the world by putting Indigenous ideals into practice (Alfred, 2005). Many of us are, as Leanne Simpson (2009b) says, "the first generation of Indigenous scholars who have access to established Indigenous scholars to nurture, inspire, inform and support us" (p. 15). An Indigenous resurgence in universities also corresponds with a more broad-based, grassroots movement in Indigenous communities, which Waziyatawin Wilson (2005) describes as "challenging the academy from the outside" (p. 240). It is comprised of

> those who have lived their lives from a position of struggle, who have led resistance efforts in their own communities, [who] understand clearly how our traditional knowledge and language have been subjugated by the dominant society. As Indigenous communities become more forceful about exerting their own decolonizing agenda, new ways will be devised to regain control over our history and language. (Waziyatawin Wilson, 2005, p. 240)

In response to community critiques of research, engaged researchers make two conscious decisions: they place community concerns above all others in the research process, and they put forward an empowering and decolonized view of the people with whom they conduct research. An insurgent research program, then, requires the negotiation of four core ethical principles. First, it employs Indigenous worldviews as the starting point. Second, it engages in knowledge creation for use by Indigenous peoples and their communities. Third, researcher responsibility is invested in the Indigenous community and in maintaining the confidence of research participants. Fourth, it promotes community-based action that dismantles colonial structures in Indigenous communities. Before explaining the principles of insurgent research, I will first review the problems of dominant research approaches—what I call *extraction research*.

## EXTRACTION RESEARCH

Just as corporations aspire to extract natural resources from Indigenous lands, much research within Indigenous communities is an *extractive* process. In extractive research, something meaningful is removed: the *context, values,* and *on-the-ground struggles* of the people who provide data to the researcher. Researchers take Indigenous knowledge and worldviews and interpret them for third-party audiences, such as government or academia. In these cases, researchers and their audience have little staked on preserving the integrity of that extracted Indigenous knowledge (Tuhiwai Smith, 1999, p. 72). Those who participate in the research are rarely considered to be the primary audience for research dissemination, because few extractive researchers acknowledge their responsibilities to the communities they study (Tuhiwai Smith, 1999, p. 161). Rather, the impetus for the research comes from the researcher's interest in aspects of Indigenous lives that she finds interesting. When the "objects of research" are Indigenous peoples, and research is conducted *on* them rather than *with* them, familiar colonial narratives that justify occupation and oppression often result.

Extraction research tends to rehash stories of dependency, defeat, and alienation, which perpetuate outsider perceptions of Indigenous communities as fundamentally dysfunctional and in need of outside intervention. These discourses ultimately justify the entrenchment of colonial structures that disengage local decision-making processes and undermine traditional Indigenous governance at the community level, often disguising this intervention as the involvement of a benevolent, but unfailingly paternalistic, helper. It produces what Stephanie Irlbacher-Fox (2009) refers to as "the dysfunction theodicy," a situation where researchers reinterpret government-caused social suffering as self-imposed dysfunction brought on by individual choices. Through these narratives, policy-makers justify further colonial intervention in Native communities, although it is ironic that these sorts of interventions created this suffering in the first place (Irlbacher-Fox, 2009, p. 31). The solution to this supposed self-generated dysfunction is invariably a call for Indigenous peoples to modernize, to abandon traditional ways of being, and to assimilate into a Canadian existence (Irlbacher-Fox, 2009, p. 34). Whatever the intent of the researcher, the result of extractive research projects is the disempowerment of Indigenous communities and the marginalization of Indigenous voices.

Extraction researchers usually pursue their research without thinking of the devastating impact they can have on the community. In *The World We Used to Live In*, Vine Deloria (2006) recounts the death of the renowned 19th-century elder and medicine man Siya'ka, after being pressured by an ethnographer, Frances Densmore, to reveal an important vision he had received in his youth. When Siya'ka finally relented to Densmore's persistent requests, she records that

> Siya'ka was deeply affected by the narration of his dreams. Some men fear that such an act will cause their death, but Siya'ka did not speak of this. He took the writer's hand, saying that he had given her his most cherished possession. In little more than a year, Siya'ka was laid to rest in the prairie he loved. (quoted in Deloria, 2006, p. 213)

Densmore's reckless attempts to extract Siya'ka's most sacred vision were motivated primarily by the perceived need to record it for "posterity." So she recorded the vision, even though she knew that in revealing everything, Siya'ka was "bringing his life to a close, his life's work completed since the vision had become common property" (Deloria, 2006, p. 213). Even though Densmore sought to preserve Siya'ka's vision, she did so at both his expense and the expense of his community, for not only did this act likely lead to the closing of his life, it also robbed the community of the means of preserving Siya'ka's vision in their own way. When research like this is placed above and beyond the interests of the communities and individuals involved, thoughtless scholars cause great tragedies in Indigenous communities (Deloria, 2006, p. 213).

Even in more contemporary studies, research is often pursued at a community's expense, with extractive research practices justified through an appeal to an abstract sense of "the advancement of knowledge." Communities are pushing back in important ways, however. In 2010, marine biologists from the University of Windsor installed sonar beacons and sensors in Nunavut's Cumberland Sound as part of a multi-million dollar project to "track the movement of deep water marine life like turbot, Greenland sharks, and Arctic skate" (CBC, 2012). The sonar equipment proved to have adverse effects, with local Inuit hunters noticing drastic changes in whale and seal migration in the Sound. As a result, the community of Pangnirtung decided to pull its support for the project, resulting in the revocation of the territorial research license. So, in September 2012 the research equipment was pulled from the water. The researchers blamed the failure of the project on "a poor communication strategy," while the community saw it differently, noting that the project's stated benefits to the advancement of science did not outweigh the adverse impacts documented by traditional Inuit knowledge-holders (CBC, 2012). Because the researchers failed to live up to their ethical responsibilities of community-engaged research, the people exercised their prerogative to end the project. In today's Indigenous research environment, there is an emerging consensus that there is a need to transform academic research to meet the needs of local Indigenous communities.

A history of adverse effects from extractive research has led Indigenous communities and research funding bodies to institutionalized research protocols specifically designed to prevent further exploitation. The Government of Nunavut's Nunavut Research Institute (2013) requires all researchers first obtain a research license to conduct research in the territory. In a similar vein, the Métis Centre at the National Aboriginal Health Organization published a paper outlining "The Principles of Ethical Métis Research" (2010), providing researchers working in Métis communities with six basic protocols for conducting ethical and culturally informed research in Métis communities. In addition to these community initiatives, all researchers funded by one of Canada's three federal granting agencies are also governed by the *Tri-Council Policy Statement: Ethical Conduct for Research Involving Humans* (2010), which includes a chapter outlining specific requirements for working with Indigenous communities both within and outside of Canada. It requires that researchers obtain not only "free, informed, and ongoing consent" of individuals, but also that researchers seek collective approval from the community for any project that generates "research results that will refer to Aboriginal communities, peoples, language, history, or culture."

Even outside of institutional structures, a growing number of Indigenous and non-Indigenous researchers are challenging assumptions about how research should be conducted. The movement to Indigenize research articulates anti- and non-colonial worldviews, grounded in Indigenous knowledges, while producing challenging new research through meaningful community engagement. Corntassel, Chaw-win-is, and T'lakwadzi (2009), for example, argue that Indigenous stories "are critical to the resurgence of our communities ... and teaching our families and communities who we are and how to govern ourselves on this land" (p. 139). For Corntassel, Chaw-win-is, and Tlakwadzi, this knowledge sharing took the form of "restorying" residential school experiences in a way that supported Indigenous community needs, namely, the creation of community based histories of residential schooling on Vancouver Island, rather than official reconciliation narratives from the Truth and Reconciliation Commission that tended to reinforce Canadian jurisdiction over Indigenous nations (Corntassel et al., pp. 147–148). Indigenist research is an important way to share these stories in a community context, and to resist the ongoing struggle against the colonization of Indigenous knowledge.

Whatever institutional requirements we face, researchers still possess an ethical obligation to support the communities they are working in. Empowering research can, according to Leslie Brown and Susan Strega (2005), "make a contribution to individually and collectively changing the conditions of our lives and the lives of those on the margins." This process is powerful because "it challenges existing relations of dominance and subordination and offers a basis for political action" (p. 10). The focus of insurgent research is just that, insurgency—a collective challenge to the oppressive status quo so often experienced by Indigenous peoples in their relationship with settler societies. Insurgent research is all about relationships, so it directs its efforts at those who will most likely produce real and lasting change: Indigenous communities.

## INSURGENT RESEARCH PRINCIPLES

As a challenge to extractive research practices, insurgent research embodies four key principles:

1. Research is grounded in, respects, and validates Indigenous worldviews.
2. Research output is intended for use by Indigenous communities.
3. Researchers are responsible to Indigenous communities for the decisions that they make, and communities are the final judges of the validity and effectiveness of research projects.
4. Research is action oriented and inspires direct action in Indigenous communities.

In the following sections, I examine each of the four concepts of insurgent research, as well as the complications that insurgent researchers must navigate in transforming these theoretical principles into practice.

## INDIGENOUS WORLDVIEWS

In insurgent research, Indigenous knowledge is evaluated according to Indigenous standards, meaning the validity of knowledge and experience is judged from within its own worldview, not foreign standards. In Kaupapa Maori research, for example, Graham Hingangaroa Smith asserts that Indigenous research must "take for granted the validity and legitimacy" of Indigenous knowledges as a starting point (quoted in Tuhiwai Smith, 1999, p. 185). This means that Indigenous knowledges are not subjected to outside standards of scrutiny, nor do they require justification from within a Western knowledge system to be considered valid. Starting from the assumption that Indigenous knowledge is a self-validating system, insurgent researchers view oral traditions, creation stories, Indigenous cultural values, and cosmology as coherent, matter-of-fact truths. The stories of our peoples therefore "stand on their own" (Waziyatawin Wilson, 2005, p. 12).

I had to grapple with this first principle during my MA interviews in August 2008. During an interview with a Métis elder, I asked him what, in his opinion, makes a Métis person. I was expecting him to tell me what he thought a Métis person was in a legal or political sense, and get into a detailed explanation of identity to determine who was Métis and who was not. I thought he would make a clear distinction for me, a nicely compartmentalized definition that reflected the academic literature on Métis identity. Instead, the answer I got was, "A Métis person is honest, open, and proud." I realized that what this Elder understood as Métis-ness were the values and behaviours that made Métis people Métis, ideas that were based on kinship and relatedness that could not be simply boiled down into a bureaucratic group-belonging code. Something about the way I was thinking about identity was very different than the way the Elder saw it. I needed to rethink what I was doing. It was at this moment that I realized that my research project was based on a very different set of assumptions than those of the people I was working with. How was I supposed to communicate my research back to the community if we approached the fundamentals so differently? I was expecting the Elder's answers to conform to preconceived notions I had gathered from "the literature" and to be consistent with the theoretical approach I had pre-selected for my project. It was here that I understood that I privileged academic knowledge over lived experience.

Jennifer Nez Denetdale (2007), in her study of Diné history, provided me with many answers on how to re-adjust my understanding of Métis

identity. Responding to the common identity claims of American historians that Diné are "cultural borrowers" and "late arrivals in the Southwest"
(p. 7), Denetdale presents a thorough analysis of Diné identity according
to Diné people. She reaffirms the authority of Diné people to tell their own
stories, without the need to situate them within the disciplinary expectations of the academy. The claims made and remade by scores of outside
researchers have led many Americans to "see Navajo claims to land as less
valid than those of other tribal people in the region and somehow 'less
traditional' than other Natives" (Denetdale, 2007, p. 7). Rather than confronting these pre-existing historical narratives head on, Denetdale chose to
shift the debate. By refusing to confront outside historians on their terms
and thus validate their claims, she forces these historians to engage Diné
history on Diné terms, and from within a Diné worldview.

Denetdale begins her argument with the observation that, despite
persistent myths about being cultural borrowers and late arrivals, the
Diné "perceive their own past differently" (2007, p. 7). The oral tradition tells of how the Diné came into this world and their travels through
many other worlds, meaning that these stories contribute to the cultural
development of the Diné as a people. By focusing on what matters
to their identity—the Diné history of the Diné—Denetdale places the
Diné worldview at the centre of any discussion of Diné history. In this
context, Diné knowledge becomes much more valuable than non-Diné
knowledges. Rather than dignify the cultural borrower and late arrival
myths with a response, she instead chooses to discuss how Diné people
understand themselves, and what their knowledge system can teach us.
While many historians continue to write off oral history, Denetdale
instead points to its continuing relevance for both recounting the past
and teaching people to live as Diné. The purpose of her writing is to
restore the centrality of the Diné worldview in discussions about the
Diné people. She writes,

> For the Diné, evoking creation narratives, the events and the
> beings who act in them, provides lessons for life, allowing
> listeners to reflect on how hózhó [balance] can be regained.
> Events that took place during the creation and the journey to
> the present world still take place. We also learn from the stories
> what can happen when we do not follow directives set down
> during primordial times (Denetdale, 2007, p. 40).

What I learned was that self-conscious and community-connected research-ers use the knowledge of their peoples as the starting point of their research endeavours. When we operationalize the first principle of insurgent research, we create the opportunity to demonstrate the continuing relevance of the cultural knowledge of our own peoples. Indigenous knowledge is valid on its own terms and is capable of standing on its own. Insurgent researchers have the important task of reminding us all of this truth.

## RESEARCH BY AND FOR INDIGENOUS PEOPLES

Insurgent researchers direct their research output towards communities in a way that is both directed at, and accessible to, Indigenous people. In doing this, ethical research leans heavily on community involvement and participation from the project development stage to final dissemination. Ideally, community members always participate in the development of the research question, and community engagement is built into every step of the research process. The Indigenous Governance program at the University of Victoria, for example, structures its MA and Ph.D. research projects so that a community member is part of the student's supervisory committee. My dissertation committee included three academics and a Métis commu-nity member, whose specific role was to adjudicate the value of the research project to the community. The addition of a Métis community member was also instrumental in the pre-ethics review phase of project development, helping me to develop an engaging research program that was directly rel-evant to the needs of the Métis community in Victoria, as well as to the wider Métis Nation. My community committee member was instrumental in helping me (a newly arrived student) integrate myself into the Victoria Métis community. Possessing extensive Métis governance experience, she enabled me to navigate complex community dynamics, as well as to avoid the common pitfalls in entering a community as a researcher.

While many programs, especially Indigenous studies programs, can include community members on supervisory committees, other student researchers may lack a formal committee member-mentor that can provide advice on doing research in a specific community context. In those cases, researchers should take a little extra time to build the kind of respectful relationships that can lead to the involvement of an authoritative commu-nity member in the research project, and set aside the necessary resources such as honoraria, or a gift, or whatever else is appropriate to the situation and community. The committee member-mentor will provide information for the project, but her/his main role is to help the researcher become familiar with the community context in which s/he is conducting research. This person can also facilitate community input and involvement throughout the research project. The community member could be a family member, or a respected Elder or leader in the community—someone who not only supports the research and the researcher, but also someone who is able to critique research processes and tell you when you are off the mark.

Involving community can feel daunting, especially to student-researchers, given timeframes for program completion, deadlines for academic grant applications, and ethics review procedures. Some ethics review boards discourage community participation in any aspect of the research *prior* to it receiving institutional ethical approval, meaning that discussions in community settings are supposed to occur only after significant project development. Since research ethics review committees often require a comprehensive explanation of the proposed research before authorizing it to commence, researchers are paradoxically encouraged to bypass community engagement in the early stages of research. However, without community authorization and support, there is no guarantee that the proposed research will be accepted by, or be of any use to, the Indigenous community concerned. Therefore, from the beginning of the project, it is necessary to think about how the research program will be developed with meaningful community engagement.

Researchers are likely to find that community members are deeply interested in research projects relevant to their lives and their community. For example, as my dissertation developed, I was asked to make several presentations to the Victoria Métis community. I was able to share my work, and receive valuable feedback from these sessions. Researchers must be prepared to present their research to communities in an accessible format, at many different stages of its development, as a kind of ongoing dialogue with community. If a goal of insurgent research is to present our work to both Indigenous communities *and* to an academic audience, then we must be prepared to write and speak in a way that non-academics can understand. When we live our lives in academic circles, we can internalize academic jargon that unintentionally and inadvertently mystifies our audience. Since the community is the insurgent researcher's primary audience, how the research is communicated can mean the difference between a useful research project and yet another extractive research venture. This does not mean that researchers should "dumb down" their research, as Indigenous communities are intelligent and often quite critical of how their knowledge is interpreted. What it does mean is that we must avoid language that academics use as shorthand, which functions, intentionally or not, to exclude people. Sharing knowledge in this way allows Indigenous communities to reclaim their traditional methods of gathering and sharing knowledge, their traditional research methodologies, and to re-centre Indigenous communities in research projects. To this end, insurgent researchers benefit from utilizing the pre-existing traditional cultural practices in their communities to communicate in culturally appropriate ways.

These efforts may also assist in the resurgence of older protocols for Indigenous knowledge sharing. Qwul'sih'yah'maht (Robina Anne Thomas) used the Lyackson protocol of witnessing as the methodological basis for disseminating her research on her people's experiences in residential school. This methodology recreated a ceremonial process where "representatives from different communities are called upon to witness an event." Witnesses are given "a huge responsibility, because you are asked to pay attention to all the details" of the ceremony. The role of the witness, like the role of the researcher, was respected because "if there were concerns over what took place ... we could ask any of the witnesses. They will know this information because it was their responsibility to pay attention to all the details" (Qwul'sih'yah'maht, 2005, p. 244). This traditional approach allowed Qwul'sih'yah'maht to develop a culturally resurgent response to the violence and intergenerational trauma caused among her people by residential schooling:

> Certainly stories of residential school tell the other story—the story of colonization and genocide—but so do many other stories that First Nations have to tell: The stories of land dispossession; the stories of the sixties' scoop. These are all resistance stories because they validate the lives and times of our people. They tell stories that have been accurately documented in a new way. (Qwul'sih'yah'maht, 2005, p. 242)

This notion of witnessing is also representative of the responsibilities of researchers, because researchers are assuming the role of witnesses to a variety of human experiences—everything from historical traumas to traditional medicine knowledges to contemporary anticolonial Indigenous resurgence movements. Witnesses bear responsibilities similar to insurgent researchers: knowledge originates in the community, and the community calls upon the researchers to share the information with the community, and when needed with outside cultures. While research involves sharing knowledge, the community and its members hold the knowledge; it is just shared with, and by, the researcher. After all, there is often no better metaphor for describing a researcher than as a witness to everyday life.

## RESEARCH IS RESPONSIBLE TO INDIGENOUS COMMUNITIES

New researchers may be surprised that while they are doing research, their new role as a researcher will redefine their relationships with research participants, even those they've known their whole lives. A couple years ago, I interviewed my father about growing up Métis in Northwestern Ontario. Although we'd talked about this many times before in informal conversation, as soon as I started to record our conversation, my dad became more formal and more serious than I've ever seen him. My role had changed; I was now a historian documenting our family's history, a history that would soon be entered into the public records through my research. There was a lot at stake in the sharing of this knowledge, and the formality and seriousness of his tone told me just that. I was being entrusted with something special. If I was going to use this knowledge, I would have to be respectful of it, and I would have to be responsible with it. It was a subtle reminder that my responsibilities lay with my family, and whatever I did with this information, I must do it while maintaining my family responsibilities.

What does this say about the importance of community (or family) responsibility when using the insurgent research paradigm? Waziyatawin Angela Wilson (2005) presents us with a provocative standard for responsibility in research:

> Imagine a scholar sitting before a room full of elders from the culture he has been studying after his first book on them has just been published. Imagine him having to be accountable for his methodology, his translations, his editing, his terminology, his analysis, his interpretation, and his use of their stories. While a discussion like this between a scholar and his subjects

of study may never occur in this formal forum, the dialogue
will occur somewhere. (Wilson, 2005, p. 37)

We must divest ourselves of the idea that our primary responsibility is to
the academy, or our own personal success, and instead invest ourselves
in our responsibilities to the community. Both Indigenous communities
and Indigenous knowledges are, at their cores, relational. Shawn Wilson
notes that in an Indigenous worldview "reality is relationships" (Wilson,
2008, p. 73). He argues that that research responsibility is a type of "relational accountability." Relational accountability means that research is both
"based in a community context" and "demonstrate[s] respect, reciprocity, and responsibility ... as it is put into action" (Wilson, 2008, p. 99).
Because a central component of insurgent research is a community-focused
approach, many researchers are also community members, or at least allies,
and are in it for the long haul. For Indigenous researchers, our positions
within our communities means that we have a responsibility to listen to the
multitude of voices that speak there.

Insurgent researchers consider it our responsibility to work toward creating more harmonious relationships in our communities and to fight further
dysfunction, strife, and social suffering. This does not prevent researchers
from being critical or challenging the unjust systems that dominate Indigenous communities—far from it. In *Research as Ceremony*, Shawn Wilson
is adamant that research should focus on putting "point[s] of view forward
in a positive way" rather than leveling a predominantly negative critique
at other peoples' ideas (Wilson, 2008, p. 106). Although Wilson is skeptical about criticizing anyone, there is often a real necessity for leveling a
powerful and disabling critique at the colonial system. Powerfully negative
critiques can be eye opening. However, Wilson's point is that negative critique alone is not an effective means of unifying people, nor is it effective
at producing real action that may lead us to remedy the colonial situation.
There is a fine line between critical scholarship—in which strong criticism
can generate space for creative ideas to emerge—and overly negative criticism that is intended to dismiss, destroy, and dominate oppositional voices.
Focusing exclusively on negative criticism can, as Wilson says, "give more
power to disharmony" (2008, p. 106). But for many researchers, especially
many graduate students, negative critique becomes an overriding concern,
because we have read so many mistruths, misrepresentations, and flawed
narratives as we familiarize ourselves with the literature.

However, the desire to confront these works can potentially override the more pressing need for the construction of alternative Indigenous accounts: the reclamations of Indigenous histories, perspectives, and worldviews. By focusing primarily on what our cultures have to offer in terms of creative and anticolonial alternatives, we work toward something new and positive. While insurgent research possesses a powerful capacity to critique and undermine colonialism by deconstructing its misleading and disingenuous claims, it should nonetheless be a predominantly creative undertaking. Relational responsibility means that insurgent researchers must mind their relations; they must use the knowledge in the respectful way that it was shared with the researcher. Researchers already embedded in Indigenous communities and conducting research within their own communities have no other option, as their families and their fellow community members will inevitably hold them accountable for their actions as researchers. More peripheral researchers must take special care to build these relationships and be willing to invest themselves in these relationships, to adopt a responsible position within the community.

## RESEARCH IS ACTION ORIENTED

The fundamental goal of insurgent research is to create space for the self-determination and empowerment of Indigenous peoples. Whether the intent is to inspire direct action, to propose an alternative means of supporting people suffering the harmful effects of colonialism, or to reimagine traditional forms of governance in Indigenous communities, insurgent research yields practical results inside and outside of the academy. It is this fourth principle—action—that puts the insurgency in insurgent research. An action-oriented approach is the final defining feature of insurgent research; it is a component often overlooked by other research approaches. Research reports, even if inflammatory, damning, or enlightening, do not in and of themselves create action. Knowledge generation alone does not necessarily lead to social or political change. Insurgent research thus assists in renewing the connection between Indigenous knowledge creation and social action in the community. According to Margaret Kovach (2005), research and "the power politics of knowledge" are intricately connected to "the process of taking control of education, health, and social welfare" (p. 23). The primary goal of an insurgent research project is to produce a better life for community members, study participants, and Indigenous peoples in general.

The most obvious way of accomplishing this goal is to embrace multiple forms of research dissemination. While few Indigenous people read academic journals, and hardly anyone at all reads theses or dissertations, there is a large number of people who want to explore how to live a meaningful Indigenous life within an Indigenous worldview, how to practice an anticolonial existence, and how to engage in direct action to fight oppression. So researchers' projects will have a greater impact if they are available in an accessible format—blogs, zines, social media, community presentations, and local activism can all have tangible impacts. This is not to preclude academic publications as a place to publish insurgent research, as many researchers still use classic forms to articulate new approaches to decolonization and Indigenous empowerment. Many are cited in this chapter. Books, especially by smaller publication houses that target non-academic audiences, in addition to traditional academic markets, are reemerging even as the overall publishing market is in decline. An excellent example of such a work is Jim Silver's *In Their Own Voices* (2006), which reports on an action-oriented research project undertaken with the Indigenous community in the Broadway/Spence area of downtown Winnipeg, Manitoba. The writing of the book was coupled with the creation of an Indigenous community network to address local needs. One of the project's outcomes was the creation of an Indigenous-focused community group to combat the hostile and gentrifying force of a local homeowners' group, the Spence Neighbourhood Association (SNA). The research process was designed to get community members in a room discussing the issues affecting their lives, particularly the SNA's attempts to gentrify and displace their community. As a result of building relationships, discussing issues facing their individual lives, diagnosing the problem as lack of community connections, and realizing the commonality of their circumstances, community members and research participants decided to take action. The result was "a new and energetic Aboriginal neighbourhood residents' group, called I-CAN (Inner-City Aboriginal Neighbours)" (Silver, Hay, & Gorzen, 2006, pp. 68–69). While there are already many Indigenous organizations in Winnipeg, building relationships between Indigenous people in a marginalized neighbourhood is a big step in Indigenous mobilization and creates a new space for Indigenous empowerment.

Building lasting relationships through research is a central component of insurgent research methodologies. By focusing on community building and political radicalization, researchers can be indispensable partners in terms of developing the potential for grassroots community action. Scholars can act simultaneously as researchers, community organizers, and political leaders. Especially for Indigenous researchers, there is great promise in merging our family and community relationships with our research projects. Although many other academic research projects are, by necessity, engaging with Indigenous worldviews and including processes of some community engagement, action is central to insurgent research.

## IS INSURGENT RESEARCH FOR EVERYONE?

Perhaps the question I'm most often asked about insurgent research is, "Can non-Indigenous researchers also do insurgent research?" To explore this question, I enlisted the help of a couple of friends, Emma Battell Lowman and Corey Snelgrove, two non-Indigenous graduate students who are grappling with this very question in their own research. Emma is a settler Canadian with family ties to the United Kingdom. She is currently completing a PhD in the Department of Sociology at the University of Warwick and teaching on imperialism and colonialism in the School of History at the University of Leicester. Her research applies Indigenous research methods to settler histories, engaging the theoretical issues of relationships, reciprocity, and storytelling, through the study of the lives of two European missionaries to British Columbia in the late-19th and early-20th centuries. Corey is an MA candidate in Indigenous Governance at the University of Victoria. He is interested in the relationship between Indigenous nations and settler peoples. His research explores the relationship between settler mindsets and the ongoing processes of Indigenous dispossession and oppression. Both Emma and Corey suggest a research approach for non-Indigenous people doing community-based Indigenous research—an approach that we call "insurgent research for everyone." As they demonstrate, it is possible for non-Indigenous people to use insurgent research principles to engage with Indigenous and non-Indigenous knowledges in meaningful ways.

The first step in insurgent research for everyone requires non-Indigenous researchers to discard what Emma refers to as "researcher hubris," a condition that arises when researchers believe that their research is special or unique, and assume its unique character means that the researcher is the only person capable of carrying it out. Emma's antidote for this hubris is two interrelated ethical commitments that humble the researcher, and refocus their understanding of research away from a process overseen by a specially skilled individual towards a process grounded in a web of relationships (E. Lowman, personal communication, January 23, 2013). First, non-Indigenous researchers must take the primary responsibility for their own education in order to limit any burden that might be placed on the community or research participants. Second, researchers must accept that they will make mistakes during their research process, and own up to any shortcomings for which they are responsible.

Researchers should begin the self-education process some time before their research project begins. Emma notes that there is a well-developed body of research literature by Indigenous scholars, which makes self-guided learning easy and accessible:

> It's no one else's responsibility to teach you these things. I think you have to be actively and critically engaged, and that starts with educating yourself on your own positionality, who you are and how you came to occupy your place in settler-Indigenous relations. You shouldn't go into someone else's community and have a breakdown because you're still trying to figure out your place in the world, your own special self-ness. It's not about trying to change who you are, but to understand the political and power relationships that accompany the space you occupy. Self-education is the starting point for any research project. (E. Lowman, personal communication, January 23, 2013)

Even researchers with a strong commitment to self-education will make mistakes. Emma sees these as inevitable, and recommends researchers respond to mistakes with humility, understanding that they represent learning experiences, rather than a reason to abandon the project:

> *You will screw-up.* You will offend somebody. You will deviate from what was agreed to. It's going to be deeply embarrassing in that setting, you're going to cringe, and maybe you're going to cry. Someone is going to correct you, it may be forceful and

> that's okay, because that's part of it. It certainly means a lot to the
> community members involved when they see that you're trying,
> that you're accepting the criticism, and not arguing your way out
> of it, or fighting back. It is also important to realize that these
> relationships will continue after the criticism. Conflict is a part
> of building better relationships, but I think in Western societies,
> we're used to conflicts that are followed by a break, and that's
> not a great way of doing things ... building stronger relationships
> after a conflict is what good research is all about. (E. Lowman,
> personal communication, January 23, 2013)

When research is understood as an ongoing mutually beneficial relationship, mistakes and minor conflicts will not be catastrophic. It must remain
clear to the community that the researcher has made a long-term commitment to the community and that the research project will benefit the
people involved. If the project is valuable and the researcher sincere, minor
errors will usually only result in a correction, which if taken to heart is
likely to strengthen the relationship between community and researcher.

In a similar way, Corey argues that non-Indigenous settler researchers
can also engage in an "interdependent approach to research" that integrates
Indigenous and non-Indigenous struggles in the pursuit of social and
political justice. Non-Indigenous researchers hoping to carry out research
with Indigenous people or in Indigenous communities must be prepared
to navigate settler-Indigenous and colonizer-colonized relationships. Corey
outlined some of the specific actions required for non-Indigenous researchers to be insurgent researchers:

- Study and reflect on Indigenous worldviews in order to enable
  research grounded in respect for these worldviews.
- Think through and identify how you are implicated in colonial processes. All non-Indigenous people have benefited from dispossession
  —none are inherently innocent.
- Recognize oppression and colonization and consequently liberation
  and decolonization, as settler problems rather than "Indian problems."
- Embody specific and concrete commitments to social and political
  justice. (C. Snelgrove, personal communication, January 11, 2013)

Corey recommends that settler research emphasize settler responsibility to Indigenous communities that is,

> rooted in the conditions for settler existence on Indigenous lands—namely, non-interference in all aspects of nationhood. Because settler history has mainly been a history of interference, separation and domination of and over Indigenous peoples, settler responsibility entails not only preventing further colonial interference, but also working towards restitution and the reversal of such interference ... developing relationships with Indigenous communities is another fundamental aspect of settler responsibility. The importance of relationship building is that it provides a mechanism for accountability to Indigenous communities, prevents hegemony of one party over another, and supports the development of a relationship built on co-existence. (C. Snelgrove, personal communication, January 11, 2013)

When we look at Emma's research in particular, it embodies the key features of insurgent research for everyone. It engages with two missionaries working in Victorian British Columbia and their multifaceted motivations in both going to Indian country and in dealing with the people who live there. Emma deals with intimate Indigenous-settler relationships, but is primarily focused on settler stories, allowing her to explore settler colonialism in Canada while remaining cognizant of Indigenous peoples' resistance to this process. Emma's project utilizes what Corey calls an "independent approach," where outside-researchers can concern themselves with primarily settler responsibilities, without drawing extensively on Indigenous sources (C. Snelgrove, personal communication, January 11, 2013). For Emma, a significant amount of her research commitment is to begin to tell different stories—what she calls "a usable past"—that allow us to envision alternative relationships that displace the exploitative relationship that has been so prevalent in North America. By focusing on "dead white men" in "order to find out more of the story," her project allows contemporary Canadians to see themselves in the past—both as good people wanting to foster positive relationships, but also as those who have benefited immensely from exploitation and dispossession of Indigenous lands. These new narratives can better explain "how settlers became a people, positive ones from which we could draw good lessons, to the worst things that have happened so that we can confront the injustices perpetrated in the name of nation-building" (E. Lowman, personal communication, January 23, 2013). The result is a usable past that exemplifies positive settler-Indigenous relationship building, while recognizing negative repercussions that flow from the failure of settlers to honour their mutually agreed upon relationships with Indigenous nations:

> I think settler people need to research their own people. The term "settler" implies an understanding that we are always in a relationship with Indigenous people—as a political positioning, as an identity, because we relate through land, or we relate through colonialism. Research is about working that connection, and maintaining relationships between Indigenous and settler peoples, researchers and communities. And settlers need to take some responsibility focusing on the Settler problems, and I think some of that will happen by analytical comparison to Indigenous histories from the settler side of things, with the idea, especially in historical work, that creating a usable past for a future relationship, one that is much more balanced and just, can help us create the kind of future that we want. Right now, I don't think we, especially as settler peoples, have a usable past that supports the kind of deep change that is needed. (E. Lowman, personal communication, January 23, 2013)

Emma points out the need to revive much older understandings of Indigenous-settler relationships that highlight our common commitment to this land, as well as the still-binding treaty agreements that, were they enacted, would have created a much different present than the one we currently inhabit.

Engaging the socially conscious settler Canadian community, while still validating Indigenous historical experiences, embodies an insurgent research approach. By mobilizing critical settler knowledges, Emma and other researchers undermine dominant colonial narratives of Indigenous dispossession and Canadian sovereignty, replacing them with narratives that reflect Indigenous experiences and ongoing political independence. Researchers like Emma and Corey utilize the principles of *insurgent research for everyone* to transform settler-Indigenous relations in Canada, and help us all envision new ways to coexist on this land.

## CONCLUSION

Whether they are Indigenous or non-Indigenous, engaging with both the academy and Indigenous community forces insurgent researchers to engage with two distinct ways of knowing. While there are certain constraints placed on researchers by the academy, like ethics review processes and publication requirements, we cannot be distracted from our ultimate responsibility to Indigenous communities. Being grounded in community relations is what remains important to our communities. But there is also a risk to writing off the academic world entirely, as it can be a powerful tool for articulating Indigenous worldviews and struggles. Insurgent research projects can push the boundaries of what is acceptable in the academy and challenge what counts as legitimate knowledge and research dissemination activities.

Insurgent research is grounded in an Indigenous worldview, is responsible to the community where research is undertaken and to the participants in it, is intended to be read by Indigenous community members, and, most importantly, is used to further the possibility of community action. In contrast to extraction research, the entire insurgent research process revolves around the community, with most of the actual research steps (framing the research question; collecting data; and presenting that data) taking place there. Given the emancipatory potential of this type of research, insurgent researchers can enliven the struggle for decolonization. Increased understanding of researcher responsibilities and more knowledge of how to conduct research from within an Indigenous worldview mean that new and exciting research projects are possible.

## NOTE

1. Some of the ideas presented in this chapter were first discussed in an article in *Wicazo Sa Review 26*(1) (2011). I thank editor James Riding In and the anonymous peer reviewers that provided excellent feedback for the development of the original article. I also acknowledge the Social Sciences and Humanities Research Council (Canada), which funded my original research through a Canada Graduate Scholarship, and thank the Ethnicity, Race and Migration Program at Yale University, who hosted me as the Henry Roe Cloud Fellow and gave me the time and space to write this chapter.

# REFERENCES

Alfred, T. (2005). *Wasase: Indigenous pathways of action and freedom.* Peterborough, ON: Broadview Press.

Brown, L., & Strega, S. (2005). Transgressive possibilites. In L. Brown & S. Strega (Eds.), *Research as Resistance: Critical, Indigenous, and anti-oppressive approaches* (pp. 1–17). Toronto, ON: Canadian Scholars' Press.

Canadian Institutes for Health Research, Natural Sciences and Engineering Research Council of Canada, & Social Sciences and Humanities Research Council of Canada. (2010). Research Involving the First Nations, Inuit and Metis Peoples of Canada. *The Tri-Council Policy Statement: Ethical Conduct for Research Involving Humans.* Retrieved from http://www.ethics.gc.ca/pdf/eng/tcps2/TCPS_2_FINAL_Web.pdf

CBC. (2012, December 5). Part of multi-million-dollar Nunavut fish project axed. *CBC News.* Retrieved from http://www.cbc.ca/news/canada/north/story/2012/12/05/wdr-university-windsor-turbot-shark-project.html

Corntassel, J., Chaw-win-is, & T'lakwadzi. (2009). Indigenous storytelling, truth-telling, and community approaches to reconciliation. *English Studies in Canada, 35*(1), 137–159.

Deloria, V. (2006). *The world we used to live in: Remembering the powers of the medicine men.* Golden, CO: Fulcrum Pub.

Denetdale, J. (2007). *Reclaiming Diné history: The legacies of Navajo Chief Manuelito and Juanita.* Tucson: University of Arizona Press.

Gaudry, A. (2011). Insurgent research. *Wicazo Sa Review, 26*(1), 113–136.

Irlbacher-Fox, S. (2009). *Finding Dahshaa: Self-government, social suffering and Aboriginal policy in Canada.* Vancouver: University of British Columbia Press.

Kovach, M. (2005). Emerging from the margins: Indigenous methodologies. In L. Brown & S. Strega (Eds.), *Research as resistance: Critical, Indigenous, and anti-oppressive approaches* (pp. 19–36). Toronto, ON: Canadian Scholar's Press.

Métis Centre at National Aboriginal Health Organization. (2010). *Principles of ethical Métis research.* Retrieved from http://www.naho.ca/documents/metiscentre/english/PrinciplesofEthicalMetisResearch-descriptive_001.pdf

Nunavut Research Institute. (2013). *Licensing process.* Retrieved from http://www.nri.nu.ca/apps/authoring/dspPage.aspx?page=process

Qwul'sih'yah'maht. (2005). Honouring the oral traditions of my ancestors through storytelling. In L. Brown & S. Strega (Eds.), *Research as resistance: Critical, Indigenous, and anti-oppressive approaches* (pp. 237–254). Toronto, ON: Canadian Scholars' Press.

Silver, J. (2006) *In their own voices: Building Aboriginal communities*. Halifax, NS: Fernwood Publishing.

Silver, J., Hay, J., and Gorzen, P. (2006). In but not of: Aboriginal People in an inner city neighbourhood. In J. Silver (Ed.), *In their own voices: Building Aboriginal communities,* (pp. 40-69). Halifax, NS: Fernwood Publishing.

Simpson, L. (Ed.). (2009a). *Lighting the eighth fire: The liberation, resurgence, and protection of Indigenous nations*. Winnipeg, MB: Arbeiter Ring Publishing.

Simpson, L. (2009b). Oshkimaadiziig, the new people. In L. Simpson (Ed.), *Lighting the eighth fire: The liberation, resurgence, and protection of Indigenous nations* (pp. 13–21). Winnipeg, MB: Arbeiter Ring Publishing.

Tuhiwai Smith, L. (1999). *Decolonizing methodologies: Research and Indigenous peoples*. New York, NY: Zed Books.

Waziyatawin Wilson, A. (2005). *Remember this! Dakota decolonization and the Eli Taylor narratives*. Lincoln, NB: University of Nebraska Press.

Wilson, S. (2008). *Research is ceremony: Indigenous research methods*. Winnipeg, MB: Fernwood Publishing.

# Contributor Biographies

**Leslie Brown** is a researcher, grandmother, motorcyclist, and currently the director of the Institute for Studies and Innovation in Community University Engagement at the University of Victoria. She is the co-chair of the Pacific Housing Research Network and principal investigator of Siem Smun'eem, the Indigenous Child Well-being Research and Training Network. Her research and practice interests include community-engaged research and learning.

**Heather Fraser** has been a social work educator for 25 years and identifies as a critical social worker and feminist. Heather teaches courses related to human rights, diversity, and addictions. Having published on women's relationships of love and abuse and narrative analysis, she is now pursuing her interests in human-animal studies and their potential import into Australian social work.

**Adam Gaudry** is Métis and an Assistant Professor in the Department of Indigenous Studies at the University of Saskatchewan. His research focuses on the historical development of Métis governance and contemporary Métis identity politics.

**Jenny Holder** has been a community-based social worker for the past 15 years and is currently the director of programs at Bridges for Women Society in Victoria, BC. She completed her MSW at the University of Victoria. Her practice areas include gender-based violence, complex trauma, sexualized violence, and the interconnection between intimate partner violence and women's experiences of poverty. She is an advocate for social justice and has a special interest in training professionals in the area of feminist anti-oppressive social work practice ethics.

**Michele Jarldorn** is from Adelaide, in South Australia. She is currently a PhD candidate in the School of Social and Policy Studies at Flinders University, researching the post-release experiences of ex-prisoners using the participatory method photovoice.

**Margaret Kovach** is of Plains Cree and Saulteaux ancestry. She is an associate professor in the College of Education, University of Saskatchewan. Maggie is an active teacher, researcher, and scholar with a focus in the area of Indigenous methodologies and Indigenous knowledges within post-secondary learning contexts.

**Teresa Macias** was born in Santiago, Chile, and grew up there during the Pinochet dictatorship. She has degrees from Ryerson University and OISE/University of Toronto. Her PhD thesis, entitled *"On the Pawprints of Terror": The Human Rights Regime and the Production of Truth and Subjectivity in Post-Authoritarian Chile*, traces 20 years of history in the development of state policy to deal with human rights abuses. Teresa teaches in social work at York University.

**Elizabeth (Eli) Manning** is a PhD candidate in the Gender, Sexuality, and Women's Studies program at Simon Fraser University and holds an MSW from the University of Victoria. Her research interests include critical HIV studies, public health policy, sex and sexuality, critical race theory, and feminist poststructuralist thought.

**Mehmoona Moosa-Mitha** is an associate professor in the University of Victoria's School of Social Work. She has undertaken extensive community action research on poverty around the globe. Mehmoona has published in the area of citizenship studies, particularly the citizenship rights of children and Muslim citizens living in the West. She has also undertaken research in social work ethics and published in the area of critical, anti-oppressive theories and social work practice.

**Karen L. Potts**, originally from Saskatchewan, is a PhD candidate at the University of Victoria and has been teaching community development, research, and evaluation as a sessional instructor for 15 years. Karen's academic degrees are in economics and social work, which support her personal and professional interests in social justice, citizen participation, local food security, community libraries, precarious labour, and sustaining public goods, services, and spaces.

**Susan Strega** teaches in social work at the University of Victoria. Her past research includes work with young mothers in care, fathers whose children are involved with child protection, "failure to protect" in child welfare, and sex workers and their families. Susan's current project looks at male customers of street sex workers.

**Qwul'sih'yah'maht (Robina Anne Thomas)** is a member of Lyackson First Nation. Robina is an associate professor in social work and the director of Indigenous Academic and Community Engagement at the University of Victoria. Robina has written extensively in the field of Indigenous studies, including a master's thesis focused on Kuper Island Residential School and her doctoral dissertation on Indigenous women and leadership. Her research interests include Indigenous women and children, residential schools, storytelling, community engagement, and anti-colonial/anti-racist practices as a way of life.